MT. PLEASANT ✓ LIBRARY
PLEASANTVILLE, NY

THE EDGE OF REASON

The Edge of Reason

A RATIONAL SKEPTIC IN AN IRRATIONAL WORLD

Julian Baggini

YALE UNIVERSITY PRESS

NEW HAVEN AND LONDON

Copyright © 2016 Julian Baggini

All rights reserved. This book may not be reproduced in whole or in part, in any form (beyond that copying permitted by Sections 107 and 108 of the U.S. Copyright Law and except by reviewers for the public press) without written permission from the publishers.

For information about this and other Yale University Press publications, please contact:
U.S. Office: sales.press@yale.edu   yalebooks.com
Europe Office: sales@yaleup.co.uk   yalebooks.co.uk

Typeset in Minion Pro by IDSUK (DataConnection) Ltd
Printed in the United States of America

Library of Congress Cataloging-in-Publication Data

Names: Baggini, Julian, author.
Title: The edge of reason : a rational skeptic in an irrational world / Julian Baggini.
Description: New Haven : Yale University Press, 2016.
Identifiers: LCCN 2016009433 | ISBN 9780300208238 (hardback)
Subjects: LCSH: Reason. | Rationalism. | BISAC: PHILOSOPHY / Movements / Rationalism. | PHILOSOPHY / Ethics & Moral Philosophy. | PHILOSOPHY / Criticism.
Classification: LCC BC177 .B18925 2016 | DDC 128/.33–dc23
LC record available at http://lccn.loc.gov/2016009433

A catalogue record for this book is available from the British Library.

10 9 8 7 6 5 4 3 2 1

In memory of my father, Lino Baggini. This was the book he most wanted me to write.

Contents

Acknowledgements

This books brings together and develops ideas that I first explored in various journal articles, conference papers and book chapters. I am grateful to all those who have given me the opportunity to develop my thinking, and I apologise if the following list leaves anyone out: Russell Blackford, Havi Carel, Catherine Fieschi, David Gamez, Alastair Hannay, Volker Kaul, Chad Meister, J.P. Moreland, Rachel O'Brien, Anthony O'Hear, Udo Shüklenk, J.B. Stump, A. Sweis.

Richard Newhauser's enthusiasm for an earlier iteration of this project was critical to its eventual completion and I am only sorry we could not work on it together. At Yale University Press, I am indebted to Melissa Bond, Rachael Lonsdale and Heather McCallum. I am also grateful for Lizzy Kremer's solid and consistent support. The rock at the base of it all is, as ever, Antonia.

Introduction

We have lost our reason, and our loss is no accident. Gradually, the contemporary West has become more and more dismissive of the power of reason. Caring for it less, we often find we have carelessly left it behind. When we do try to use it, we're not quite sure how to do so. We have become suspicious of its claims, unwilling to believe that it can lead us to anything worthy of the name 'truth'.

Once outré dismissals of reason have become the new common sense. Once radical claims like 'People who lean on logic and philosophy and rational exposition end by starving the best part of the mind' now feature in many collections of inspirational quotes (attributed to W.B. Yeats). Our image of the typical human being is now like Dr Nathan in J.G. Ballard's *The Atrocity Exhibition*, for whom 'reason rationalizes reality for him as it does for the rest of us, in the Freudian sense of providing a more palatable or convenient explanation.'[1]

In the popular imagination, reason has ceased to be a universally admired faculty and is portrayed as the enemy of mystery and ambiguity, a cold tool of desiccating logic. It is seen as standing in opposition to emotion, denying the role of feeling and sentiment in daily life. Rationality is dismissed as a tool of hegemonic oppression, a patriarchal construct, a Western imposition or a mistaken privileging of one hemisphere of the brain over the other. The Enlightenment is no longer almost universally revered but often condemned as the birth of the age of dehumanising industrial capitalism, the start of the road that led to Auschwitz. Popular culture has absorbed bastardised versions of many of these ideas, and it is now widely believed that we are guided more by genes, manipulative corporations and unconscious psychological biases than we could ever be by reason.

It was not always thus. For millennia, rationality was held up as the highest human achievement. We once followed Aristotle in maintaining that the capacity to reason is what sets us apart from the other animals. Reason was not the cold hard enemy of warm-blooded virtues like love, faith or aesthetic appreciation. St Augustine, for instance, said 'we could not even believe if we did not have rational souls'.[2]

We have always recognised that irrational impulses can take a grip on us, but it was believed that, with effort and application, our better, rational selves could reign sovereign over the soul. Plato, for instance, said that 'It's not at all uncommon to find a person's desires compelling him to go against his reason, and to see him cursing himself and venting his passion on the source of the compulsion within him.' Yet he insisted, 'I'm sure you won't claim that you had ever, in yourself or in anyone else, met a case of passion siding with his desires against the rational mind, when the rational mind prohibits resistance.'[3] Aristotle also accepted that there is 'some element in the soul besides reason, opposing and running counter to it'. But he too believed that this element, 'in the soul of the self-controlled person, at least, obeys reason and presumably in the temperate and the brave person it is still more ready to listen, since in their case it is in total harmony with reason'.[4]

It is true that we have in the past often placed too much trust in our capacity to think rationally and that a greater recognition of the limits of reason is necessary and welcome. But it is not for nothing that 'losing your reason' means to go mad. Reason needs to be put in its place, and if that place is not close to the centre of human life then our minds are left rudderless to float this way and that on the waters of whim, emotion and the influences of others.

The book is an attempt to help us recover our reason. To do this we have to understand what reason really is. This is a curiously neglected question. There is a great deal written about particular forms of reason, such as deductive logic and inductive inference, but much less on what reason, in the most general sense of the word, involves. This lacuna is reflected in the fact that we have two words – reason and rationality – which lack agreed, precise philosophical definitions and are in practice synonyms. (I will use the two interchangeably.)

The rehabilitation of reason is urgent because it is only through the proper use of reason that we can find our way out of the quagmires in which many big issues of our time have become stuck. Without a clear sense of what it means for one point of view to be more reasonable than another, it seems that the position one adopts is ultimately based on nothing more than personal opinion or preference. People take sides in debates not on the basis of evidence or argument but on the basis of the side where they feel more at home. What is best for the economy? Either what Wall Street wants or what it doesn't, depending on which faction you belong to. Are human beings responsible for global warming? Just see what big business or progressives are saying and back your horse accordingly. If science appears to challenge your faith, then either reassure yourself that science has nothing to do with religion or take solace from the sizeable minority of scientists who are religious. In all these debates people offer reasons for their positions but, whatever they say, dissenters can tell themselves 'they would say that' and ignore them.

Most worryingly, a lack of faith in the power of reason makes good international relations seemingly impossible. When we give up on reason, the only tool we have left is coercion. For instance, 'The brutality of terrorists in Syria and Iraq forces us to look into the heart of darkness,' said one senior American politician. 'The only language understood by killers like this is the language of force.' That politician was not a notorious hawk but President Barack Obama, often criticised for not being forceful enough in exerting American power in the world. Obama saw a role for reasoned diplomacy in the Middle East and even in Afghanistan, but that did not make him popular.

Since reason has become a debased currency, it is no surprise that fewer and fewer believe it has any value when dealing with threatening foreign powers.

Obama made his remarks in a speech to the 69th assembly of world leaders at the UN headquarters in 2014. It is telling that the headlines focused on the suggestion of Manichean conflict beyond the scope of reason. 'In UN Speech, Obama Vows to Fight ISIS "Network of Death"' proclaimed the *New York Times*. 'Obama Addresses Islamic State Threat in United Nations Speech', said the *Wall Street Journal*. And yet the bulk of his address was actually about the necessity for world powers to work together peacefully. 'The ideology of ISIL or al Qaeda or Boko Haram will wilt and die if it is consistently exposed and confronted and refuted in the light of day,' he said.[5] This message of the potential of reason to defeat terrorism was lost, in part at least because fewer and fewer of us believe it.

Plato, Aristotle and their heirs may well have taken an overly optimistic view of the power of reason. But they were right to think that our capacity to resolve our differences and arrive at conclusions in the shared space of public reason is one of our most precious human capabilities. To restore proper esteem for this, we need to understand how the embrace of rationality does not require a retreat into a heartless, sterile, scientistic world-view, but simply involves the application of critical thinking wherever thinking is needed.

Reason as a concept comes in a variety of thinner and thicker forms. At its thinnest it is merely an appeal to the use of the intellect to think through issues. At its thickest it specifies the precise methods by which such thinking should be conducted. Such thick conceptions of reason may demand variously that it is deductive, scientific, dialectical. Reason, thinly conceived, has the virtue that most people find themselves able to endorse its value, but this agreement comes at the cost of defining 'reason' so vaguely that it does not provide us with any real information on what it practically means to use it. Thicker conceptions get over this problem but at the price of consensus. People simply do not agree on which thick conception of reason we should employ.

What we therefore need is a conception of reason which is thin enough for there to be mutually comprehensible reasoning between individuals and cultures in a shared discursive space, without it being so thin as to enable anything to count as reasoning, from nuanced step-by-step argument to thumping the table and insisting on the correctness of your position. The project of this book is to develop a notion of reason which is both sufficiently thin and sufficiently substantive to enable this kind of public dialogue, one which allows for a wide variety of opinions on what is in fact reasonable but is not so permissive as to allow any sincerely held opinion. It is thus an attempt to try to bring as many people as possible together into a single 'community of reason' in order to protect and strengthen the domain of public reason.

This thin conception sees rational argument not as a formal, mechanistic, rigid method but simply as the process of giving and assessing objective reasons for belief. These reasons are those which are assessable and comprehensible by any competent thinker, which stand or fall irrespective of our personal values and are compelling yet open to revision if the evidence changes.

This form of rationality takes us to the edge of reason, where it can be hard to keep our balance. First of all, from a psychological perspective it is easy to tip over and end up simply defending prejudices, blinded by unconscious internal biases and externally created distortions of information and argument. Second, away from its solid core of rigorous logic, reason can be thinner ice than optimistic rationalists of the past have believed. Those of us who want to champion reason must be merciless in pointing out its limitations and frailties. Reason is powerful but to use any power to its fullest potential you need to understand its weaknesses even better than your enemy does. When we do this it can induce a sense of trepidation as we realise that the edges of reason on which we are walking are not as solid as we believed. But we have no choice. If we resort to wishful thinking, trusting in faith or instinct, then we allow our feet to leave the ground and we take off into flights of intellectual fantasy. If, on the other hand, we seek to debunk reason, then we are taking a pick to the ice beneath our feet and are left floundering in the freezing waters of irrationality.

Only our most intimate friends know our deepest flaws, and in the same way the greatest skeptics about reason should be those who seek to defend it. If we do not debunk the grandiose myths of reason then its enemies will do so far more destructively. My positive case for rationality therefore requires taking us through four key myths of rationality, all of which can be traced back to Plato. These myths are: that reason is purely objective and requires no subjective judgement; that it can and should take the role of our chief guide, the charioteer of the soul; that it can furnish us with the fundamental reasons for action; and that we can build society on perfectly rational principles.

Behind all four myths is a false principle espoused in some form by almost all reason's defenders. John Stuart Mill put it most clearly when he wrote, 'No one can be a great thinker who does not recognise, that as a thinker it is his first duty to follow his intellect to whatever conclusions it may lead.'[6] This idea goes back to Plato, who has Socrates say in the *Republic*, 'we must let our destination be decided by the winds of the discussion',[7] and in the *Euthyphro*, 'the lover of inquiry must follow his beloved wherever it may lead him'.[8]

The metaphor of *following* reason is a powerful one which contains an important truth, namely that we should always try to see things as they are, not as we want them to be. But it fundamentally misunderstands how reason actually works. We do not follow it, but nor does it simply follow us. Rather, we take reason with us to help us find the way, as neither its slaves nor its masters.

At this point it is worth saying a little about how these ideas have developed. After completing my PhD in philosophy I pursued a career outside academe, editing a philosophy magazine and writing books and articles. I have at the same time kept one foot in the academic world, writing textbooks, journal articles and book chapters as well as commissioning and editing pieces by academics. One of the greatest benefits of this was that over the years I have had the opportunity to interview many of the world's leading philosophers. Several of those conversations are directly quoted in this book.

This idiosyncratic career has turned me both by necessity and choice into something of a generalist. I would like to think that this has given me an unusual perspective, one that I think helps me to see the whole forest, which is unfortunately populated mostly by specialists who are transfixed only by certain trees, or even leaves. It has also made me keen to focus my writing on philosophy about what I take to be of enduring interest. This means I am not as eager as some to add a reference to at least one item in the literature for every single point made, as though every footnote adds legitimacy to the argument. I am encouraged in this by the example of a wonderful philosopher, Philippa Foot, who modestly said, 'I really am terribly ignorant about much philosophy. I have a terrible memory and I don't do it in quite the way clever people who have very good memories and are splendid scholars do.'[9]

I hope my writing contrasts with the standard academic style, which 'seeks precision by total mind control, through issuing continuous and rigid interpretative directions', as Bernard Williams put it. I have tried to avoid this and instead to fulfil his 'hope that the objections and possible misunderstandings could be considered and no doubt influence the text, and then, except for the most significant, they could be removed, like the scaffolding that shapes a building but does not require you after the building is finished to climb through it in order to gain access.'[10] My hope is that my academic training combined with my broad perspective has enabled me to appreciate facets and virtues of reason that are less evident from other viewpoints.

Reason has only been knocked off its pedestal because it was raised up too high. Paradoxically, a more modest version of rationality will prove to be more powerful and valuable than the almost omnipotent mythological version which preceded it. Reason is, as Michael P. Lynch puts it, 'marked with frailty, fed by our sentiments and passions, whose pale promethean flame must be cultivated lest it gutter and dim'.[11]

PART I: THE JUDGE

One of the central myths of rationality is that if we use it properly, we can do away with the need for personal, subjective judgement. It is always rebarbative to the philosopher to reach a point in an argument where it is necessary to admit that others may be presented with the same chain of inferences yet justifiably reach a different conclusion. The intolerability of this is implicit in Plato's idea of 'following the argument' and has been most explicit in the rationalist tradition, where Descartes talked of following the 'natural light' of reason, and Spinoza set out the argument of his *Ethics* as a set of quasi mathematical deductions. It also emerges in twentieth-century analytic philosophy – the dominant tradition in Britain and North America – which put the learning of symbolic logic at the heart of the undergraduate curriculum. Students were encouraged to believe that if they could translate their arguments into the language of logic they could neatly divide those that could be decreed objectively sound and those that were fallacious.

The dream that many philosophers have had is of a form of reason in which subjective judgement is banished and everything that matters can be demonstrated with the rigour of an algorithm. Reason leads to one correct conclusion and one only. Given this high benchmark, it is perhaps not surprising that many have taken the fact that it hasn't been reached as evidence that rationality has been seriously overrated. For instance, it has been creditably argued that in science the observed facts always, or at least almost always, fit more than one possible theoretical explanation. Ideas like these have led some to more extreme positions in which scientific knowledge is dismissed as having no special status and as just another human construct or narrative.

If we are to save a realistic yet robust notion of what it means to be rational, we need to debunk the myth that reason requires no judgement without leaving ourselves reliant on subjective opinions that cannot be rationally criticised or examined by others. This is the purpose of the first part of this book, which will focus on the use of reason in religion and science. In these and in other domains of reasoning, there is an ineliminable role of judgement, but that does not entail a debilitating skepticism about reason and rationality.

CHAPTER ONE

The Eternal God argument

The big issues of God and religion are among the most weighty and important that each of us has to confront. Does God exist? Is science compatible with religion? Can there be morality without God? Although I have given each of these considerable thought, when I am invited to debate one of them in public I have become less and less inclined to accept. Having seen what such events involve, the whole exercise increasingly looks like a charade. One side presents its arguments, followed by the other. Reasons are stacked up to support both cases. But at the end, almost everyone believes exactly what they believed at the beginning. Only a few genuinely uncertain or confused members of the audience might be swayed one way or another. Such debates are framed as battles of intellect, philosophical trials where arguments are presented and assessed. In reality, they are like sporting contests when everyone comes out to cheer their own team and leaves convinced it was the best, whatever the result. It seems to me that the only constructive effect of such events is that they remind the audience that civil disagreement is possible and that those they oppose might be good, intelligent people too.

This sense of futility is not confined to set-piece debates. It is evoked even more by the academic world of philosophy of religion. Here we find very smart people, all committed to being as rational as possible about their beliefs. They write books and journal papers full of incredibly arcane, subtle and complex arguments. These are clearly people who take reason very seriously indeed. But how often do you find any of them changing their minds on any of the major issues?

Hardly ever. The academic traffic between theism and atheism is virtually non-existent. On the rare occasions when someone switches allegiance, it's big news; so much so that even a vague wavering counts as exciting. When the famous atheist Antony Flew, for instance, appeared in very old age to endorse a kind of deism, headlines like 'Famous Atheist Now Believes in God' appeared around the world.

If these philosophers of religion were simply following the arguments wherever they led, you might expect considerably more movement as they were led first one way, then another. The truth, however, is that such arguments appear to lead only to the next counter-argument. When, for instance, an atheist comes across a clever new version of an argument for the existence of God which she cannot refute, she does not say 'Ah! So now I must believe in God!' Rather, she says, 'That's clever. There must be something wrong with it. Give me time and I'll find out what that is.' Similarly, a theist will not lose her belief just because she cannot refute an argument for atheism. Rather, that argument will simply become a challenge to be met in due course.

All this might appear to be scandalous. The currency of philosophy of religion is supposed to be rational argument, but it can't buy an opposing position at any price. However, to despair at this would be to misunderstand the nature of rational argument and its importance for big life commitments such as whether to believe in God or not. Reason does have an important role to play here, but it is not that of the independent, objective judge. The final judge is not reason, but the reasoner, for whom rationality is a tool, not some kind of authority.[1]

1. Big pictures, broad brushes

One reason why the latest, subtlest arguments don't make one jot of difference to people's fundamental religious convictions is that when it comes to the big issues, it's the big arguments that carry weight. Philosophers and theologians love to work with fine details, but it's the broad brush that generally carries the day. You could call this the 'end of the day' test. Ask someone what, at the end of day, makes them convinced of their general position and I would bet you that virtually no one (there's always the odd eccentric) would say 'a journal paper'. And if they did, it would be because that paper managed to pin down a big point, not a little one.

Intellectuals do not like to admit this because it brings them down the same level as much simpler folk, like Homer Simpson. One of my favourite episodes of *The Simpsons* sees Homer stop going to church. He doesn't stop believing in God, he just can't see the point in worshipping him. His reasons for this are hardly sophisticated, but I find it hard to better them:

> What's the big deal about going to some building every Sunday, I mean isn't God everywhere?
>
> Don't you think the almighty has better things to worry about than where one little guy spends one measly hour of his week?
>
> And what if we've picked the wrong religion? Every week we're just making God madder and madder?[2]

Of course, there might be any number of good reasons to go to church, whether God exists or not. Homer's points merely show why he is not doing anything wrong by not going to church. All his arguments really point to the same general one: isn't it bizarre to think that an omnibenevolent God would really think it important that people went to a particular place each week to worship him? Indeed, if God were like that, then we are likely to pick the wrong place of worship and annoy him even more. This is all mad anthropomorphism, in which God is imagined to be an egotistical despot who demands that his subjects prostrate themselves before him.

As I've said, I can imagine reasonable arguments for why it it would be good to go to church, if God exists, and even that God has reasons for wanting us to do so. But the idea that he would look unkindly on people who don't seems so obviously absurd that considering clever counter-arguments would appear to be a bad use of limited intellectual resources.

That 'obviously' is significant. Because what really convinces are big, broad points and not small, intricate arguments; often the right general answer does seem obvious. Take an example from my personal experience. When I was a teenager, I voluntarily went to a Methodist church that no one else in my family attended. I was a believer, but my doubts grew. I did not have a de-conversion moment, but one incident did cement my loss of faith. It was at the London weekend of the Methodist Association of Youth Clubs. I had been throwing up from the moment we arrived, so when the worship came round on Sunday morning in the awe-inspiring setting of the Royal Albert Hall, I was sat in the first aid area, which was – ironically, it would turn out – somewhere up in the gods. So there I was, not feeling 100%, observing more than participating in the worship: detached, not involved.

It was a revelation. Suddenly, the central fact about the worship became blindingly, transparently obvious. My road back from Damascus moment came when I saw that the Holy Spirit was not at work at all: this was all people's doing. You could see how the emotion was built up, reaching a crescendo at the key point where people were asked to make or renew their commitment to Christ. To call it mass hysteria may be a little over the top, but not by much.

Although I'm sure that some evangelists are con artists, this is certainly not how I saw the MAYC. I believe that the organisers genuinely thought that all they were doing was creating the right environment for the Holy Spirit to do its work. (In the same way, some 'psychics' use cold-reading techniques to dupe their hapless victims, while others sincerely use what are essentially the same techniques and are so impressed by the results that they really believe they have special powers.)

My close study of John's Gospel at school had already made it pretty clear to me that the Bible was the work of men, not God. The

London weekend helped convince me that the same was true of every other aspect of my religion too. A mental switch had been flipped: God was man-made, more fully than Christianity understood.

What I think is of more than just autobiographical interest is that once this cognitive corner is turned, it doesn't take long before the human-made nature of religion becomes not just something one believes to be true, but something that seems obviously true. At the same time, however, for many believers, the reality of God is just as obvious and evident.

A very clear example of this is something the Christian and physicist Russell Stannard once said in an interview with my colleague Jeremy Stangroom. He was being asked about how one could ever get evidence that prayer established contact with God. 'I think that what you have to realise,' said Stannard, 'is that when you are talking to a religious person, they feel that they have such strong internal evidence. It's like Jung said, I don't have to believe in God, I know that God exists – that is how I feel.'[3]

Up until that point, Stannard had been talking quite dispassionately about evidence for belief in God, as though He were a hypothesis to be confirmed by a scientific method. This comment, however, revealed that this was in a way a façade, because the believer needs no third-party verifiable evidence at all: inner conviction suffices.

I think this is typical of this kind of obviousness of belief. It is obvious because it feels or seems obvious, and no one other than the believer is required to verify its obviousness. Another example I have sometimes quoted is the last man on the moon, Eugene Cernan, who said, 'No one in their right mind can look in the stars and the eternal blackness everywhere and deny the spirituality of the experience, nor the existence of a Supreme Being.' It is an appeal to the obvious, but without any evidential back-up. It is like saying, 'if you felt what I felt you'd find it obvious too'.

That is not to say there can be no rational argument at all between people for whom what seems obvious is very different. I would argue for the superior obviousness of belief that religion is a human construct. This obviousness does not rely on subjective feeling alone, but on the mass of evidence which is available to all. The sociology, history and psychology of religions all point to their human rather than divine origin. What makes this obvious is the overwhelming weight of evidence that points to this interpretation, rather than one which ascribes a divine cause. The same is true of other obvious tenets of atheism. That we are biological organisms whose being and consciousness depend on a functioning body and brain is obvious because the evidence is clear and overwhelming, not because we feel it must be true.

Hence we can see that there are at least two kinds of obviousness. But there is another level of obviousness here too. To the naturalist it seems obvious which type of obviousness carries most weight: that which rests on the kind of empirical evidence available to all and not that which rests on subjective experience. But as we shall shortly see, this is not at all obvious to everyone. If someone judges the experience of the presence of God to be more clearly real than scientific observations, it is difficult to show conclusively that this cannot be 'properly basic'.

Intelligent believers and non-believers alike do not generally say things like 'it's obvious' except to people who share their basic commitments. It is as though we understand that this is an intellectually disrespectful and disreputable way of talking, like referring to common sense. Yet there is a kind of dishonesty in this, because many people do indeed find core elements of their faith, or lack of it, obvious. I'd go further and suggest that the obvious is usually what is most powerful in determining which fundamental beliefs people have about God and spirituality. Academics in particular maintain the illusion that, on the contrary, things like the complex details of the latest revision of the ontological argument might actually matter when it comes determining whether or not God exists. But if they did, we might see more regular changes of mind. As it is, philosophers of religion seem to be at least as constant in their fundamental commitments as anyone else.

This might provoke a cynical response, but I would argue that this is just as it should be. We use reason well when, as Hume said, we proportion belief to the evidence and arguments. In this proportioning, it is entirely proper to give more weight to arguments that rest on general observations and points of logic where the truth is clear, rather than on smaller observations and arcane logical technicalities. After all, the more nuanced the argument, the more scope for sophistry. It's like a criminal trial: the major, indisputable evidence carries more weight than that which rests on just one testimony or uncertain scientific tests. If the victim has a bullet in his heart, we assume he was shot dead unless we have very good reason indeed to think otherwise.

When it comes to religion, although it makes sense to hear all the evidence, it is clear that the verdict is going to hinge on the facts that neither prosecutor nor defender can dispute, such as the facts that people have a strong sense of God's presence, there is no good scientific evidence that anything other than the stuff of physics exists and that holy books were written by fallible humans. The difference between this and a criminal trial, however, is that there is more room for people to disagree about which piece of such evidence provides the bedrock of the case. Why should this be so?

2. Choose your bedrock

In my experience, believers and non-believers do not usually differ significantly in their declared belief in the importance and value of reason. Naturalists – people who believe that the natural world is all there is and so do not believe in a theistic God – and theists alike can number among their bedrock beliefs the demands of consistency, non-contradiction and rational coherence. In that sense, both may be equally committed to rationality. (I say *may* be because there are some who argue that faith defies reason.) But in a sense this is not a particularly extensive piece of common ground. It concerns only the procedures of reasoning and not the premises on which the reasoning is based. Logical reasoning is often compared colloquially to a sausage machine: what you get out crucially depends on what you put in. Start with correct premises, reason well, and you will end up with correct conclusions. Start with false premises and although you might by chance end up with a true conclusion, much more often even impeccable reasoning will lead you to the wrong conclusion.

The difference between naturalists and theists is often that they take different central premises as the bedrocks of their belief systems. For naturalists, these premises derive from evidence of the hard, objective kind that anyone can examine and assess for themselves. For the religious, however, it's quite different. 'Maybe a few people accept religious beliefs strictly on the basis of what they take the evidence to be,' writes Alvin Plantinga. 'But for most of us, our religious beliefs are not like scientific hypotheses' and 'we are none the worse [for that]'.

Plantinga is here referring to his enduring contribution to the theory of knowledge, his idea that belief in God is 'properly basic'. Plantinga argues that most philosophers accept that the justification of beliefs has to stop somewhere and so some beliefs are 'basic'. Basic beliefs are ones we 'accept but don't accept on the basis of any other beliefs'. Plantinga offers as examples, 'I believe that 2 + 1 = 3, for example, and don't believe it on the basis of other propositions. I also believe that I am seated at my desk, and that there is a mild pain in my right knee.' We also have beliefs, some justified, some not, which are not basic. These 'are rationally accepted only on the basis of evidence, where the evidence must trace back, ultimately, to what is properly basic'.[4]

Belief in God is often thought to be non-basic. It must be justified on the basis of arguments and evidence that in turn depend on nothing more than basic beliefs we can all accept. Plantinga argues that this is false. 'Belief in God need not be based on argument or evidence from other propositions at all. [. . .] the believer is entirely within his intellectual rights in believing as he does even if he doesn't know of any good theistic argument (deductive or inductive), even if he doesn't believe that there is any such argument, and even if in fact no such argument exists.'[5]

How can this be so? Given that Plantinga has devoted much of his career to defending this claim, any short answer is bound to be somewhat simplistic. But the nub of the answer is straightforward enough. Plantinga's argument is that everyone has to accept that some beliefs are basic in order to believe anything at all. However, not just any belief can be considered basic, or there would be no way of distinguishing sense from nonsense. I cannot just assert, for example, that I take the existence of Santa Claus to be basic. So which beliefs can be accepted as *properly* basic?

Plantinga says that beliefs are usually accepted as properly basic if they are incorrigible or self-evident.[6] This, however, he argues is too strict a test. Apply the criterion to itself, for example, and it fails: it is neither incorrigible nor self-evident that beliefs are properly basic if they are incorrigible or self-evident. Furthermore, although these might seem like objective criteria, they in fact depend on personal judgement. What does it mean to say that $1 + 2 = 3$ is incorrigible or self-evident, for example? That it is impossible for it not to be true? But in fact, the most we can honestly say is that we *cannot imagine* how it could possibly be false. To assume that our lack of ability to imagine otherwise is proof that it really can't be otherwise is to trust too much to our judgement.

Accepting this lets in the thin edge of the wedge of subjectivity, but let it in we must. If we are honest, we need to accept that we cannot provide a strict test which distinguishes between what is genuinely incorrigible or self-evident and what merely *seems* incorrigible or self-evident to us. That does not mean we should rashly rely on our own first subjective judgements, of course. We can seek out the views of others and examine the evidence thoroughly in order to test our conviction. But ultimately, we will be left to make the final judgement by ourselves. Truth is not a democracy, so even if we find that others do not believe a proposition is incorrigible or self-evident, if they cannot persuade us, we should not follow them.

Once we allow this, we can see how it can be that, for some, belief in God is properly basic. They have a sense of his reality and presence which is as strong as, or perhaps even stronger than, their belief in their own existence or that of the external world. If we don't feel the same, then we may be baffled, but, Plantinga argues, we cannot assert that their belief is not properly basic. To do so would simply be to assert on the basis of no evidence whatsoever that they are not telling the truth about the strength with which the reality of God imposes itself upon them.

If you do grant that certain religious beliefs are properly basic, you effectively provide a 'get out of jail free' card for almost all apparent cases of conflict between religious beliefs and empirical truths about the world asserted by naturalists. For example, for the naturalist, certain religious claims become untenable on the scientific evidence base, such as the idea that life was created by God rather than emerging from random mutation and natural selection. If only empirical observations and principles of logic were admitted as properly basic, this would be decisive. But many religious people would say that their evidence base includes facts other than scientific ones, such as the existence of a loving creator. If you add that to the scientific evidence for evolution, you will think that the most likely explanation for the emergence of life is that God works through random mutation to ensure creatures like us evolve. And, as Plantinga argues, nothing in evolutionary theory denies that possibility. The idea that the process is entirely unguided is a 'metaphysical or theological add-on'. For all the theory of evolution says, 'God could have achieved the results he wanted by causing the right mutations to arise at the right times, letting natural selection do the rest.'[7]

This room for variety in our properly basic beliefs is what explains the vanishing unlikelihood, if not actual impossibility, of any philosophical dispute about religious belief leading to a decisive victory for one side. Where the conflict really lies is right down at the very bases of why people believe what they do, yet the war is fought over the beliefs that flow from them. It's like trying to get rid of

Japanese knotweed by hacking at the stems when the root system is too deep, capable of regenerating itself even when viciously cut. Philosophers have pretty sharp scythes in the form of arguments and generally speaking they wield them well. But all they do is provide space for new weeds to grow again before they too are cut down to size and the whole cycle starts again.

The idea of 'properly basic beliefs' allows us to see more clearly why it is that people's positions on big issues rest more on big, broad arguments and hence why ever finer reasoning cannot end the dispute between the religious and the non-religious. More and more careful reasoning is impotent unless it leads us to something that very clearly undermines something that disputants take to be properly basic. If it does not, then they will quite reasonably reach their conclusions on the basis of the broader arguments rather than the more nuanced ones, because it is rational to place more weight on what seems clear and evident than that which we have reason to suspect might merely demonstrate cleverness and ingenuity in reasoning.

3. The holism of reason

The notion of 'basic' beliefs is, however, somewhat misleading, in that it lends itself most easily to metaphors of reason that see it as a bottom-up process, one in which arguments are constructed on solid foundations. This is the *foundationalist* approach, historically most associated with Descartes, who believed it was necessary to 'demolish everything completely and start again right from the foundations if I wanted to establish anything at all in the sciences that was stable and likely to last'.[8] Foundationalism seeks to find a firm foundation for knowledge, some kind of rock-sure certainty upon which all other beliefs can stand.

This 'foundationalist' understanding of reason has a long history, but is fundamentally misguided. To see why, it is useful to return to the metaphor of 'following the argument wherever it leads'. The use of the singular here is profoundly *mis*leading. To follow *the* argument would be deeply irrational, since there is always more than one argument and the rational inquirer has to take all the good ones into account.

Health provides clearer and less contentious examples of this general principle than religion. Take the link between high saturated fat consumption and heart disease. This link has been made on the basis of numerous studies, many of them very large, supplemented by some understanding of the biological mechanisms by which eating a lot of saturated fat results in damage to the heart.

What then happens if you read an article in a reputable newspaper with the headline 'No link found between saturated fat and heart disease'?[9] First of all, of course, you try to find out if the newspaper has accurately reported the findings of the study. In this case, you would see the conclusion is indeed that 'Current evidence does not clearly support cardiovascular guidelines that encourage high consumption of polyunsaturated fatty acids and low consumption of total saturated fats.'[10] Having established this, the one thing you should not do is simply follow the argument of that study and conclude that toasted cheese and beef dripping sandwiches should become a daily staple. Rather, you have to consider how this new study fits in with the existing evidence. What could explain the apparent contradiction?

There are several possible answers to this. One is that the old theory is just wrong, because it mistook correlation for causation. So, perhaps increased heart disease is a consequence of eating certain foods such as processed meats and dairy produce, which happen to be high in saturated fats but which are bad for you for other reasons. Because it is hard to divide people up into those who eat largely unprocessed fats and those who eat processed ones, researchers might have missed the crucial difference.

Another possible explanation is that the new study has stumbled upon a misleading correlation. There is good evidence that many, perhaps most, people in the West who reduce their fat consumption end up eating more refined carbohydrates, including sugars. So it could be that any benefit that they gain from reducing saturated fat intake is offset. Any large study which didn't look at exactly what people were eating instead of saturated fat would be unable to tell whether or not reducing consumption was good or bad for you. It would be a bit like concluding that cutting down on alcohol is bad for your health because it turns out those who did so in your study ended up smoking more instead.

There are of course many other possible explanations for the surprising new result. The key point, however, is simply that you don't find it by looking at the new study in isolation. The research brings more evidence to the table which the rational inquirer needs to consider in the context of all the other evidence that is already there. A better injunction is to follow the *arguments* wherever *they* lead, recognising that they do not individually all lead the same way.

It is particularly important to note here that you do not need to have any idea about how the new study might be flawed in order to reserve judgement on it. Our reasons for suspending judgement can be internal or external. They are internal when we can see which premises in the argument or which steps taken are dubious. They are external when we have good reasons to believe that the conclusion of the argument contradicts things which we have very good reasons to believe to be true. This means that if you believe the current evidence overwhelmingly supports the link between saturated fat and heart disease, then you have very good reasons not *immediately* to change your mind on the basis on one new study, *even if the logic of that study appears to be flawless.*

The analogy with arguments for or against the existence of God should be clear. Philosophers of religion are generally persuaded of several arguments that support their position. Some of these they might believe to be so powerful that they cannot even imagine how they might turn out to be wrong. So when a new argument comes along that appears to support a contradictory claim, it is rational for them to reserve judgement on it and proceed on the assumption it will turn out to be wrong. Of course, it would be irrational to assume that it definitely is wrong, and to refuse to be open to the possibility that the argument is sound. But such extreme dogmatism and intransigence is not rationally required to refuse to rush to follow this *one* argument in isolation from all others.

One further external rational justification for withholding assent to an apparently rational argument is that experience might have shown us that, time and again, similar apparently strong arguments or evidence have proven to be weak. This is why we are justified in dismissing uncanny stories of the supernatural. You might be told, for instance, of a clairvoyant who made a prediction so accurate that it seems inconceivable it could have been correct just by luck. But we know from experience that every such case to date has turned out to be far less compelling than it seemed at first sight. Hence we have good reasons to distrust similar new claims when they crop up.

When you have become well versed in an intellectual dispute, a similar 'meta-inductive' skepticism is justified. If you have seen dozens of attempts to prove God's existence by pure logic, for example, and all have failed, you would be justified in believing that there is probably a good reason why they have all failed. So when you see a new twist on the old approach, it is perfectly rational to assume that this will probably go the same way as its predecessors.

So to understand why arguments rarely lead people to change their minds in many intellectual disputes we have to understand the holistic nature of reasoning. We believe what we do because of a number of overlapping and mutually reinforcing reasons and arguments, rarely because one settles the issue either way.

4. Between a rock and hard node

However, there is a difference between, say, the case of health advice and that of religious belief. With the example of saturated fat, we would expect that in time the holistic case would clearly support one side of the debate and so expert opinions would converge. With religious belief, however, this would appear to be a forlorn hope.

Experts continue to disagree and the idea that we are awaiting some killer argument or decisive piece of evidence that would settle the dispute looks hopelessly optimistic. Why is it then that reason does not over time lead to agreement?

To answer that question we need to combine the idea that reason works holistically with the insight that certain beliefs are nonetheless 'properly basic' bedrocks. For people on all sides of the religion debate, some beliefs in their holistic networks are so unshakeable that everything else simply has to arrange itself around them to fit. If you believe that, by definition, God surpasses all understanding, then you don't even need to comprehend how these rearranged beliefs fit together. So if there is a conflict between, say, the evident existence of all sorts of terrible suffering in the world and the belief that God is all-loving, all-powerful and all-knowing, it is logically quite easy to conclude that God has reasons for allowing all this pain that we just can't understand.

To understand the nature and limits of reason, it is important to understand clearly how it is that the holism of belief exists alongside the bedrock nature of certain beliefs, since this might appear to be contradictory. To use the current standard terminology, there appears to be a clear difference between foundationalism and coherentism, which argues that our beliefs must fit together and fit with the evidence in such a way as to add up to the most overall coherent picture of reality. For example, Nicholas Rescher writes:

[Foundationalism] has its diametric contrast in a coherentism that dispenses with any appeal to basic, foundational truths of fact, categorically rejecting the view that knowledge of the actual, and even of the probable, requires a foundation of certainty. For the coherentist, knowledge is not a Baconian brick wall, with block supporting block upon a solid foundation; but rather a spider's web in which each item of knowledge is a node linked to others by thin strands of evidential connection, each alone weak, but together collectively adequate to create a strong structure.[11]

In this debate, I side with the coherentists. However, I also believe that the distinction is not quite as neat as the textbooks pretend, and that the central truth in coherentism that I want to appeal to can be and usually is accepted by the foundationalist. Even the most rigorous rationalist philosophers who have pursued the pure foundationalist approach have needed their foundations to be mutually supporting to some degree. Descartes, for example, notoriously needed to count among his foundations both the principle that 'whatever I perceive very clearly and distinctly is true' and a belief that a good God exists. But the two principles could not be independently verified: he could only establish God's existence by means of clear and distinct perception of the proof for his existence; but he could only trust his clear and distinct perception on the assumption that God existed. For many critics this 'Cartesian circle' is vicious and undermines his argument. A more charitable explanation is that no foundationalism is pure and that a degree of coherence is required even here.

Perhaps even more significantly, coherentists do not necessarily dispute that some beliefs are more foundational than others. Most notably, Susan Haack has argued for a position she gives the ungainly name 'foundherentism', which acknowledges that although beliefs hang and fall together, like words in a crossword puzzle, there is a sense in which experience provides the foundations for the whole interlacing edifice.[12]

Credible versions of coherentism have to make, I argue, some such concession to foundationalism. That is to say, they have to accept that some principles in the 'web of belief' serve as first principles. This is not inconsistent. Wittgenstein captured this in his idea that when we arrive at the rock bottom of our convictions we 'might almost say that these foundation-walls are carried by the whole house'.[13]

That coherentism needs some kind of first principles is clearly shown by Bertrand Russell, with the example of the principle of non-contradiction:

'[C]oherence' presupposes the truth of the laws of logic. Two propositions are coherent when both may be true and are incoherent when one at least must be false. Now in order to know whether two propositions can both be true, we must know such truths as the law of contradiction. But if the law of contradiction itself were subjected to the test of coherence, we should find that, if we choose to suppose it false, nothing will any longer be incoherent with anything else. Thus the laws of logic supply the skeleton or framework within which the test of coherence applies, and they themselves cannot be established by this test.[14]

Russell himself thought this a counter-argument to coherentism. But there is in fact no reason why a coherentist can't allow for the existence of some such first principles. We can see why first by considering coherentism through the metaphor of the 'web of belief', using, with Rescher, the term 'node' to denote where the strands of the web connect. If one considers how a web-like structure works, it is easy to imagine webs in which certain nodes are essential for the whole web to hang together. In a spider's web, for example, the web is usually anchored by just one or two key threads. Cut these and the web collapses. Cut a few links on the web itself, however, and the web as a whole remains standing.

Metaphors can mislead, but in this case the key features carry over. In arguing that beliefs fit together in a mutually sustaining 'web' rather than sit upon one or two key foundations, the coherentist does not need to claim that all points in this web are of equal importance. It is just obvious, for example, that the principle of non-contradiction is vital for any coherent web of beliefs to stay intact, while for most of us little or nothing hinges upon the truth about the temperature in New York on 7 May 2002.

So the coherentist should accept that certain points in the web of belief are more important than others in keeping the network of justified beliefs intact. They are vital because they are what I call 'critical nodes' – beliefs to which many other beliefs in the network are connected and which are required to hold the network together. Such is their importance that they are essentially the coherentist's first principles. Unlike the first principles of traditional foundationalists, however, these 'critical nodes' are not immediately and securely known, typically by sense experience or self-evidence. For instance, Descartes appealed to 'clear and distinct ideas',[15] while Locke talked of 'that evident lustre and full assurance that always accompany that which I call intuitive'.[16] In contrast, 'critical nodes' are only justified by their place in the wider 'web of beliefs'. As Wittgenstein wrote, 'It is not single axioms that strike me as obvious, it is a system in which consequences and premises give each other mutual support.'[17] The principle of non-contradiction, for example, is not upheld because we can know it to be self-evidently true in isolation, but because we can see that without it, no web of belief can hold together. They are indispensable rather than indisputable.

The coherentist/foundationalist distinction is therefore not as sharp as is often assumed. Whatever your theory about how rational beliefs are justified, there will always be certain beliefs which occupy a special foundational or quasi-foundational status. Every edifice of belief stands or falls on certain rocks or nodes. And crucially, because these support rather than are supported, our justifications for believing them have in a sense to stand on their own feet. But that does not mean there is nothing at all we can say to justify them. Michael P. Lynch notes that although there are some principles and beliefs we must take for granted, 'this doesn't mean that we can't provide reasons for what we take for granted. It just means that the reasons we can provide must be of a different kind.'[18]

There is also common ground in how both positions judge the extent to which beliefs are 'defeasible', meaning open to revision or rejection on the basis of any new information or arguments that are forthcoming. It is often thought that while the foundationalist establishes certain beliefs as indefeasible, the coherentist is committed to the defeasibility of all truth-claims, since coherentism has to be open to the possibility that the web of justified beliefs may develop in the future in such a way as to make what once seemed obvious or self-evident problematic.

However, the issue of defeasibility can be seen as independent of a foundationalist or coherentist approach. There is a sense in which all honest inquirers ought to accept the defeasibility of all their beliefs: even good foundationalists should accept that they could be wrong. So the real issue is not whether any beliefs are defeasible as such, it is rather the extent to which certain beliefs are taken to be so well established that they are not in practice doubted. Here, the coherentist and the foundationalist can be in pretty much the same place. The coherentist who accepts that certain critical nodes are essential to stop the whole web of rationality from collapsing might believe these are as rock-solid as the foundationalist's first principles. The law of non-contradiction, for example, could be as unseverable a critical node as it is an unshakeable foundation.

5. Reason as apologetics

One final reason why rational argument does not lead people to change their minds as much or as often as might be thought is that much of it is essentially *apologetics*. This term is most closely associated with religious theology. Christian apologetics, for instance, is the attempt to rebut arguments against the rationality of theism and to show that faith is compatible with reason. Apologetics is therefore essentially *defensive* rather than *constructive*. The goal is not to use reason to build the rational basis of faith: faith's foundations lie elsewhere. It is rather to use reason to show that religion's foundations are not logically flawed or fatally undermined by scientific, historical or any other empirical evidence.

Theodicies provide the clearest examples of apologetics in action. A theodicy is an attempt to explain how it can be that an all-loving, all-knowing and all-powerful God nonetheless permits all sorts of evil, from wicked human actions to natural disasters. This 'problem of evil' appears to be a rationally decisive argument against the existence of God, since it would seem that if God allows, for example, people to die of the horrible Ebola virus, then He either can't stop it (He isn't all-powerful), doesn't know about it (He isn't all-knowing) or doesn't want to stop it (He is not all-loving). Theodicies attempt to get out of this trilemma by showing that, for example, God must allow these sorts of things to happen for our own good, and so it is more loving to permit the short-term evil than deny us the long-term blessing.

Another example concerns the doctrine of the Trinity, in which God is comprised of the Father, the Son and the Holy Spirit. As the medieval Scutum Fidei represents visually, this is a somewhat paradoxical doctrine, since it asserts that each of the Father, the Son and the Holy Spirit is God, but the Father is neither the Son nor the Holy Spirit, the Son is neither the Father nor the Holy Spirit, and the Holy Spirit is neither the Father nor the Son.

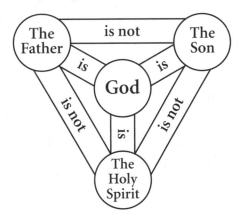

This would appear to defy the most basic principles of logic. According to standard logic, if (A = B) and (B = C) then (A = C). So, for example, if Bill Clinton is the 42nd President of the United States of America and the 42nd President of the United States of America is the father of Chelsea Clinton, then Bill Clinton must be the father of Chelsea. The doctrine of the Trinity defies this apparently inexorable logic. The Father is God and God is the Son but the Father is not the Son. The work of apologetics is therefore to show how this circle can be squared.

In the cases of both theodicies and the Trinity, the position being defended is not one which arises out of rational argument. It is rather an article of faith, the basis of which lies in tradition, revelation, scripture or some mixture of the three. Reason's role is therefore simply to keep standing that which has been erected using other tools.

When reason is used in this way, it should be very clear why it does not lead people to change sides very often. If the foundations of the position are not built on reason, then showing that reason cannot support the position is hardly going to shake them. It may not even matter that the apologetics fail. There are many believers, for instance, who accept that none of the existing theodicies is entirely satisfactory. Nonetheless, given that they have innumerable other grounds for their faith, they do not take this as decisive. The existence of evil in God's universe is simply accepted as an unsolved mystery.

To many naturalists, this only goes to show how unreasonable religious faith is. However, there are at least two reasons why we should take the lessons of religious apologetics to have a wider significance.

First of all, there is nothing intellectually scandalous about accepting unsolved mysteries, such as the numerous philosophical paradoxes which defied solution for centuries. Science is also well stocked with unsolved conundrums. For nearly a century now, scientists and philosophers have struggled to understand quantum physics in such a way as not to contravene fundamental laws of logic or common sense. These scientists are not obliged to jettison all their theories because of the existence of these problems, as the rest of their science is extremely well grounded. This does not, of course, mean giving up the hope that one day these mysteries and contradictions can be cleared up. But if we do not yet have any idea how we might do that, living with the mystery in the meantime can be a reasonable choice.

This ties back with the ideas of holism, coherentism and properly basic beliefs. Both the quantum physicist and the theologian accept the logically paradoxical corollaries of their beliefs because they take those beliefs to be better founded than any alternatives. The key difference between them is simply that the theologian accepts non-scientific as well as scientific grounds for belief. Much as naturalists may dislike this, there is no easy way of showing this to be in principle irrational. It is not a scientific claim to say that science is the only basis for justified belief. This is rather *scientism*. Scientism, however, is a philosophical position that needs to be argued for. Science cannot discover that only science leads to truth.

Indeed, we should go further and see that a great many scientists – probably the majority – are not scientistic. They do not, for example, base their moral beliefs on laboratory findings, and nor do they devise experiments with which to test the veracity of their partners' love. When judging the aesthetic merit of a poem or a piece of music, they use criteria which are not remotely scientific.

So there is nothing inherently irrational about accepting that your position has paradoxical implications, nor of having grounds other than scientific ones for belief. Apologetics is therefore not unique in embracing these, nor is it fatally undermined by them.

But second, and perhaps more important, much more reasoning is a form of apologetics than first appearances suggest. In domains other than theology, people will rarely say explicitly that they are using reason only to defend positions they already hold for other reasons, some rational, some not. But in practice this is precisely what they often do.

Take pretty much any debate in philosophy and you will find people who take a certain stance on it. Look then at their writings and you will not be surprised to find that their work adds up to a systematic attempt to defend that stance against critics, by developing the position to make it stronger and more nuanced. This seems so natural that we can overlook how easily it could have been otherwise. One can imagine, for example, a world in which philosophers write a variety of papers around a topic, some for a particular stance and others against it. If they were completely dispassionate observers, this is precisely what we would expect of them. Exceptions only prove the rule here. Hilary Putnam, for example, became famous for changing his position on a number of key issues over his career. 'I've never thought it a virtue to adopt a position and try to get famous as a person who defends that position,' Putnam once said, 'like a purveyor of a brand name, or someone selling corn flakes.'[19] But that is precisely what most of his peers have done. Perhaps in an ideal philosophical world, the people who stood out would be those who *didn't* change their minds.

It might be argued that the difference between the apologist and the philosopher is that although both use *reason as a defence*, what they are defending is, in the case of the philosopher, ultimately *based on reason* too. There might be some truth in this, although, as I hope to show throughout this book, it cannot be as straightforward as this. But even if it were, it still needs to be accepted that reason is used more often as a tool for a kind of apologetics than it is as a means of objectively establishing which position is actually correct.

6. The dim light of reason

We might appear to have arrived at a dim place for reason. Once we accept that reason works holistically, that beliefs cohere rather than have unshakeable foundations, and that our most basic beliefs do not necessarily themselves rest on reason, then it becomes clear why reason is so often powerless to end important intellectual debates, such as those surrounding the existence and nature of God. If we add to that the empirical fact that reason is used at least as much to defend positions as it is to establish them, then we might be forgiven for thinking that when we reason, we merely rationalise: we make rational to ourselves and others what we believe for non-rational reasons.

But we should not despair too quickly. When we see that something we believed to be all-powerful is actually much weaker than we thought, we can either abandon it or make best use of the strengths it has. And reason has plenty of genuine strengths, whatever its limitations.

First of all, the idea of properly basic beliefs cannot be an excuse to take just any belief as a legitimate bedrock, as Plantinga himself clearly accepts. We can use our reason to question just how legitimate certain basic beliefs are. This involves asking two key questions: are these beliefs *indispensable* and are they *reliable*?

The first question asks if we need a belief we take to be basic. Some beliefs clearly do pass this test. We cannot say anything sensible at all if we do not accept that we are not mad, that the basic laws of logic such as the law of non-contradiction are sound, that our perceptions are not systematically mistaken, that other minds are real, that physical events are the result of physical causes, and so on. Radical skepticism about all of these is possible in the armchair of hypothetical speculation, but impossible if we are to go on to live and think in the world. Such beliefs are then properly basic because they are indispensable.

The second question is whether this basic belief is reliable. Even some of the beliefs I have identified as indispensable may not be entirely reliable but they are certainly more trustworthy than the alternatives. If we act on the belief that physical events have physical causes, for example, we find this to be reliable: it allows us to manipulate things and make predictions far more accurately than if we did not have the belief.

If we ask these two questions of religious beliefs, however, we find that the answers are negative. Quite clearly people do not need to believe in God in order to make sense of the world. The reliability issue is even more important. Many people take their experience of God as admissible evidence that His existence is real, in the same way that our experience of the physical world is taken as admissible evidence that its existence is real. But these two experiences are of very different kinds. The experience of the external world is universal as well as indispensable and it leads people to navigate through the world reliably. However, the experience of God is not at all universal and does not lead to any improved reliability in being able to move around the world. Indeed, people who see God's hand in too many things are made less reliable, since they see purpose where there is only physical action and reaction.

Most damningly, purported experience of the divine is a demonstrably unreliable kind of evidence. Many people claim to have such experiences and yet what they believe this shows varies enormously from person to person and culture to culture. If religious experience can reveal both a personal God and an impersonal godhead, the religious experience cannot be reliable since both cannot be right, and so at least one must be wrong. We can therefore use reason to raise serious objections to the claim that certain kinds of religious belief should be considered properly basic.

A further role for reason is that since some nodes in the web of belief are more important than others, and some of these nodes do rest in one way or another on evidence, it is possible to weaken severely a coherentist position by problematising these nodes.[20] Of course, religious beliefs come in many forms, but many are vulnerable in this way. Take, for example, those varieties of dualist religion which assert the existence of an immaterial soul as a substance distinct from physical matter. The critical nodes in the counter-argument are: first, that we are a biological species, human beings; and, second, that all the sound evidence we have suggests that a properly functioning brain is necessary and sufficient for consciousness. These are rock-solid, and, if true, incompatible with the dualist view. Similarly, there are varieties of Christianity which maintain the infallibility of the Bible. Here there is a great deal of hard evidence that this position is untenable, given how the Bible was written and its internal contradictions.

This shows how we can avoid the pessimistic conclusion that the role of basic beliefs and the coherentist structure of argument mean there is so much room for people to choose their fundamental premises that there is simply no way to show which view is more rationally grounded. That's too pessimistic. The point is rather that there is no shortcut. Very few nodes in a net of belief are so critical that destroying them brings the whole belief system down. And very few nodes can be critiqued wholly independently of everything else in the net. Rather, the net has to be unstitched piece by piece.

In practice, this is probably little different from the pessimistic conclusion. When you have strong desires to believe something, it is always possible to convince yourself that a decisive argument against one node wasn't decisive after all, or that you have found a reply to it. Mending and making do can enable one to think a web of belief still holds together, even after a good critic has ripped it to shreds. But the fact that we know reason will not convince everyone is beside the point. Whether an argument is sound or whether it is persuasive are two different questions. It should come as no surprise that good rational arguments often fail to persuade people. The case for reason is not that it is always psychologically efficacious but that it genuinely helps us towards the truth. However, just as you can lead a horse to water but you cannot make it drink, so you can lead a mind to reason but you cannot make it think.

CHAPTER TWO

Science for humans

At a major international conference on quantum physics in 1999, 90 of the world's leading physicists were polled on which interpretation of quantum theory they endorsed. They did not concur with each other: four voted for what is known as the Copenhagen interpretation, 30 backed the 'Many Worlds' view, while 50 selected 'none of the above or undecided'.[1] Such disagreement is not unusual in quantum mechanics, even when it comes to the foundations of the field: in another survey of 33 conference participants, opinion was more or less evenly divided on the question of whether 'physical objects have their properties well-defined prior to and independent of measurement'.[2]

The existence of such stark disagreements clashes with the image of a scientific method which merely follows the evidence and leaves no room for differences in opinion. Perhaps we can reassure ourselves that quantum physics is unusual, and that when science is at the cutting edge, different theories do coexist and compete. So it is not unreasonable to hope that, in time, as the evidence becomes clearer, physicists will all converge on the same view.

It is true that the current state of physics does not contradict the view that science in time converges on truth. But if we look at how the process of convergence occurs in scientific disputes, we can see something very important not just about how science works, but about how all good reasoning works. What we see is that scientific reason is and can never be free of disorderly, imprecise and hard to justify personal judgement.

This is not the same as claiming that science simply provides 'narratives' each of which has no greater legitimacy than any other competing one. If there is a disagreement between scientific and scriptural accounts of the origins of the universe, for example, then the scientific ought to prevail. My central point is not to belittle science or downgrade its findings, but to promote a realistic understanding of how it works.

This is important because science is often held up as both the pinnacle and paradigm of human reason: if we want to know how to think, we should try to emulate how scientists think. This simplistic view is misguided in part because not all problems are scientific problems, and so to try to fix them with the methods of science is as useless as trying to use a dentist's drill to dig for oil. (I'll say more about this in chapter eight.)

The other big problem with singling out scientific reason for special praise is that it often assumes there is a particularly scientific form of reasoning which dispenses with all the messy, unsatisfactory elements of personal judgement that infect most of our other reasoning. I think most scientists know that this is not true. There is, however, an unwillingness to admit it too openly for fear of encouraging the pernicious fools who wish to deny that scientific theses have any special claim over any others. My aim is to show how accepting the role of judgement in science in no way undermines it, but it does require us to rethink how we assume reason works.

1. Fitting the facts

The common-sense version of science maintains that theories are determined by the evidence. If there are two competing theses, then the one that wins out will be the one that best fits the facts. There are, however, specific historical examples which suggest that this is at very least something of a simplification.

Take, for instance, Copernicus's model of the orbit of the planets around the sun. We now take it to be clearly superior to Ptolemy's geocentric system, but until Kepler discovered the elliptical orbits of planets, it was not more accurate. In other words, the observed facts fitted the Ptolemaic and Copernican theories equally well. That does not mean, however, that until Kepler there was nothing to choose between the two competing theories. It simply means that the superiority of Copernicus's theory was not due to its better fitting with observed data. It was preferable for other reasons, mainly those of simplicity and economy of explanation (which we will return to shortly). Evidence in itself was not the conclusive factor. Both theories were *underdetermined* by the evidence, meaning that the evidence was not sufficient to establish the truth of either.

A more recent example might be the competing theories of Schrödinger and Heisenberg in quantum physics. As the science writer Manjit Kumar puts it, these theories 'appeared to be so different in form and content, one employing wave equations and the other matrix algebra, one describing waves and the other particles'. And yet not only were they equally compatible with the data, they were 'mathematically equivalent'.[3] In other words, they were underdetermined both by evidence and mathematics.

Over-confidence that a theory flows inexorably from the observed data can lead scientists to ignore alternative possibilities. For example, when the physicist John Bell came across David Bohm's version of pilot wave theory in 1952, he saw a viable alternative to the then dominant Copenhagen interpretation, which was being presented as though its theoretical conclusions flowed inexorably from the observed facts. The reality was, thought Bell, that the interpretation's 'vagueness, subjectivity, and indeterminism, are not forced on us by experimental facts, but by deliberate theoretical choice'.[4]

These might be assumed to be historical exceptions to the general rule, but according to the thesis of 'the underdetermination of theory by evidence', evidence is *never* by itself the conclusive factor in determining the truth of a scientific explanation. This idea is today most closely associated with the Duhem–Quine thesis. Pierre Duhem was a French physicist and philosopher of science who formulated various problems of underdetermination in science in his 1914 book *The Aim and Structure of Physical Theory*. W. V. O. Quine developed and extended these ideas in the second half of the twentieth century, arguing that the problem of underdetermination applied to all forms of human knowledge, not just in science.

However, the general idea of underdetermination predates the formulations of Quine and Duhem. John Stuart Mill, for instance, wrote in *A System of Logic* that a hypothesis 'is not to be received as probably true because it accounts for all the known phenomena, since this is a condition sometimes fulfilled tolerably well by two conflicting hypotheses'. This he thought all 'thinkers of any degree of sobriety' believed. While this is only obvious in some cases, it seems clear that Mill believed it would always be true and that only a lack of imagination of alternative possibilities prevents us from seeing this. 'There are probably a thousand more [hypotheses] which are equally possible,' he wrote, 'but which, for want of anything analogous in our experience, our minds are unfitted to conceive.'[5]

We are, however, perfectly able to conceive of various outlandish theories which are entirely compatible with even the simplest observed facts. Descartes did this when he admitted that nothing in his experience was incompatible with the possibility that he was being systematically deceived by an evil demon. Nick Bostrom has more recently proposed that not only could we be living in a computer simulation, but that this is highly probable.[6]

Scientists are usually very dismissive of the Duhem–Quine thesis and its associates. In practice, they claim that – Copernicus, Ptolemy, Schrödinger and Heisenberg notwithstanding – there is often only one credible theory that fits the data and that the logically possible alternatives dreamed up by philosophers are irrelevant. But this misses the point. The value of the underdetermination thesis is not to make us seriously consider all alternatives to the most powerful and tested scientific explanations. Its value is that it makes it clear that even when the evidence appears overwhelmingly to support one theory rather than another, there is always a gap, however small, between what the evidence *requires* we conclude and what we *actually* conclude.

In ordinary speech we sometimes appeal to what is 'reasonable' to fill this gap, and scientists sometime do the same. For example, in his ongoing debate with Einstein, Niels Bohr demonstrated that it was impossible to measure both the energy of a photon and the time of its escape in a hypothetical device known as a light box. For reasons which few non-physicists could ever pretend to understand, this was a critical victory for Bohr. Einstein, however, was unconvinced. When he lectured on this thought experiment in Leiden in 1930, he said 'I know, this business is free of contradictions, yet in my view it contains a certain unreasonableness.'[7] The word is well chosen, for we do indeed use our reason in such cases. But this part of reason is a form of judgement, something which is not purely demanded by reason or evidence alone. Something didn't sit right for Einstein but he could not fault the data or Bohr's deductions from them.

In this case, it might simply be that Einstein was being too stubborn and that there was nothing unreasonable in Bohr's argument at all. Nonetheless, there are plenty of other cases where we legitimately reject a theory on the basis of its unreasonableness rather than on demonstrable flaws. For example, it is indeed unreasonable to believe that the Earth is the centre of the universe, but not because the observational data make such a hypothesis impossible. This is why there are still very intelligent people who are young Earth creationists. They are able to make their beliefs compatible with the data because they are prepared to accept some convoluted but consistent arguments that make this possible. In arguing against such people, it is normal to start by trying to show that they are in denial of the facts. But when the creationists are sufficiently smart, rebuttals usually end up appealing to terms like 'unreasonable', 'outlandish', 'implausible' and 'convoluted'.

Take, for instance, the debate between Bill Nye 'the science guy' and creationist Ken Ham. Nye described Ham's explanation of how Noah's Ark could have held 14,000 people as 'frankly . . . extraordinary' and his assertion that all the animals were vegetarians before they got on the Ark 'really remarkable'. Objecting to the idea that radiometric testing of the age of objects is unreliable, he said 'it's just not reasonable to me that everything changed just four thousand years ago'. As for the claim that Noah could have built his ark with seven family members, again he said, 'to me it's just not reasonable'. Overall, he finds the evolutionary account 'much more reasonable'.[8]

When people like Nye use terms like these it is not evidence that they have had to give up on reason and have resorted to name-calling. Rather, it illustrates how reason relies not just on logic and evidence, but on forms of judgement that can only be described in these and other frustratingly vague terms. Nye was right: Ham's claims are unreasonable, but there is no strict rule that would allow us to distinguish such arguments from ones which are reasonable. We have to use our judgement.

We will be looking more closely at what this kind of judgement is in the coming chapters (in particular three and six). For the moment it is sufficient to point out that it exists, and that scientific reasoning depends upon it.

2. Scientific method

The biologist Lewis Wolpert once wrote that it is 'doubtful that there is a scientific method except in very broad and general terms.'[9] Wolpert is particularly vociferous in his denunciations of philosophy of science, saying that the subject is 'not relevant to anything'.[10] Wolpert may be unusually forthright but many, perhaps most, of his more temperate colleagues would agree with his basic claim that no one has 'discovered a scientific method that provides a formula or prescriptions for how to make discoveries'. That is not to say scientists can't say anything at all about how to do science well. Among the advice given by various famous scientists, Wolpert lists:

> [T]ry many things; do what makes your heart leap; think big; dare to explore where there is no light; challenge expectation; *cherchez le paradox*; be sloppy so that something unexpected happens, but not so sloppy that you can't tell what happened;

turn it on its head; never try to solve a problem until you can guess the answer; precision encourages the imagination; seek simplicity; seek beauty.

Nonetheless, it is important to recognise that 'No one method, no paradigm, will capture the process of science. There is no such thing as *the* scientific method'.[11] Although the most famous philosophers of science tried to codify the scientific method, plenty of others share Wolpert's skepticism about whether this can be done. For instance, Tim Lewens says that although there are 'plenty of scientific *methods* . . . when we try to pinpoint some recipe for inquiry that all successful sciences have in common, we run into trouble'.[12]

It would be wrong, however, to blame a handful of philosophers alone for perpetuating the myth of the scientific method. Scientists themselves help create the false impression of a regular, orderly method by writing up their findings in ways which gloss over the real messiness of discovery. The biologist Peter Medawar spoke about this in a BBC talk in 1964, saying that 'the scientific paper in its orthodox form does embody a totally mistaken conception, even a travesty, of the nature of scientific thought'.[13] Papers suggest that scientists work by an orderly method of induction, observing facts and drawing general conclusions from them. The reality is much messier. 'Hypotheses arise by guesswork' and 'inspirations', said Medawar, 'by processes that form the subject matter of psychology, and certainly not of logic. [. . .] Scientists should not be ashamed to admit, as many of them *are* apparently ashamed to admit, that hypotheses appear in their minds along uncharted by-ways of thought; that they are imaginative and inspirational in character; that they are indeed adventures of the mind.'

This goes much deeper than the widely acknowledged fact that progress in science is influenced by its sociology, in ways that descriptions of method alone do not capture. We all know that progress in science is affected by all sorts of contingencies such as where funding is allocated or who is appointed to a certain position, and the latter is not always settled entirely by competence. For instance, even after he had published some of the most important papers in the history of physics, Einstein had several job applications rejected simply because he did not have a PhD.[14] The ideas of Thomas Young were resisted too firmly, too long simply because they contradicted those of the then untouchable Newton, leading Young to say of the giant that 'his authority has, perhaps, sometimes retarded the progress of science.'[15] Resistance to ideas is arguably more rooted in prejudice and habit than in any deference to scientific fact. As Max Planck famously said, 'A new scientific truth does not triumph by convincing its opponents and making them see the light, but rather because its opponents eventually die, and a new generation grows up that is familiar with it.'[16]

One could sanguinely acknowledge the ways in which personal and social factors *interfere* with the scientific method, yet maintain that the method itself is still purely objective and explicable in formal, logical terms. The fact that people often don't follow the method is not in itself an argument that the method isn't real. But this defence of method is inadequate for two reasons.

First, if the scientific method only really exists in the idealised abstract but is never actually followed by scientists, its value as a paradigm of human rationality is vastly diminished. Indeed, it would become instead a paradigm of inhuman rationality, something scientists aspire to but never achieve.

Second, if we look at how science proceeds, then it seems that it does not follow a clear method with a few imperfections resulting from culture and psychology. Rather, the quirks and deviations from the official version of pure experiment and deduction are deeply embedded in the way science works. That is the really challenging idea that Medawar presented.

Judgement – usually referred to in such cases as intuition – is central to the way scientists work. This is most evident at certain moments of insight. Poincaré's description of how he came to realise that quadratic forms were identical with those of non-Euclidean geometry provides a vivid example. 'I turned my attention to the study of some arithmetical questions apparently without much success and without a suspicion of any connection with my preceding researches,' he wrote:

> Disgusted with my failure, I went to spend a few days at the seaside and thought of something else. One morning, walking on the bluff, the idea came to me, with just the same characteristics of brevity, suddenness and immediate certainty, that the transformations I had used to define the Fuchsian functions were identical with those of non-Euclidian geometry.[17]

There is nothing mystical about such 'eureka' moments. 'In every case where scientific illumination occurs suddenly, it is preceded by a long period of intensive conscious study,' says Wolpert, adding, 'as Einstein pointed out, a scientist's intuition rests on a technical understanding of what can be regarded as reliable and important'.[18] Also, of course, after the flash come the careful checking, the mathematical calculations, the experimental tests and so on. As Medawar pointed out, discovery and proof are two different things. The problem is that attempts to describe the scientific method confuse them.[19] So we distort the real nature of scientific reasoning when we do not acknowledge the fact that before the formal processes of calculation and verification come moments of clarity which can arise all of a sudden, without being immediately preceded by conscious thought. Reason has aspects which are systematic and conscious but also aspects which are unknown and unconscious. To pretend it only involves the former is to fail to conform theory to observation.

The relationship between theory and observation is itself a good example of how the scientific method defies formalisation. It is not that one always precedes the other. Rather, sometimes scientists are led by theory, sometimes by observation, and there appears to be no general rule as to which ought to be given more weight.

Wolpert assembles various stories of scientists who did not allow the absence of evidence to diminish faith in their theories.

Copernicus' heliocentric theory, for example, was not only no better at predicting the movements of the planets than Ptolemy's, it had problems in accounting for the phases of Venus. It took half a century for Galileo to resolve these, thanks to his telescope, but Galileo believed that Copernicus was a 'sublime intellect' precisely because he held his line without having the conclusive data that would prove it. 'With reason as his guide,' wrote Galileo, 'he resolutely continued to affirm what sensible experience seemed to contradict.'[20]

Boyle was similarly persistent in holding to his theory when observation refused to confirm it. On 49 occasions he tested his hypothesis that smooth bodies that stuck together in air would come apart in a vacuum, without success, yet succeeded on the 50th attempt.[21] Einstein said 'the general theory of relativity will be untenable if the prediction it made about the gravitational shift of spectral lines were not observed', but he was convinced his theory was correct even though the prediction was only confirmed after his death.[22]

Robert Millikan was another scientist who often rejected data that did not fit his ideas. Wolpert suggests that he often did so on the basis that the apparently disconfirming experiment wasn't rigorous enough. There is an obvious danger of self-serving bias in interpretation here: it would be very convenient for a scientist to dismiss experiments that produce contradictory data as flawed while welcoming those that produce confirming data as sound. Bad scientists will make these distinctions purely on grounds of convenience. Nonetheless, the distinction is a real one and being able to make the judgement well, and not merely for self-serving reasons, is for Wolpert 'a crucial feature in distinguishing the good, even great, scientist from the less so'.[23]

Several scientists have not only refused to allow conflicting data to invalidate their theories, but have even explicitly said that theory, at least sometimes, should take precedence over observation. Arthur Eddington, whose observations during the solar eclipse of 1919 confirmed the gravitational bending of light, said, 'It is a good rule not to put overmuch confidence in the observational results that are put forward until they have been confirmed by theory.'[24] Planck said,

'A conflict between observation and theory can only be confirmed as valid beyond all doubt if the figures of various observers substantially agree with each other', suggesting that evidence has to be overwhelming before it should be seen as falsifying a theory.[25]

The complexities of the relationship between theory and observation are made especially clear by two very different remarks made by Einstein. In 1971 Heisenberg recalled meeting Einstein for the first time in 1926. It did not take long for Einstein to put him straight. 'It is quite wrong to try founding a theory on observable magnitudes alone', he said. 'In reality the very opposite happens. It is the theory which decides what we can observe.' This had a very specific relevance for Heisenberg's ideas about matrix mechanics. 'Your claim that you are introducing none but observable magnitudes is therefore an assumption about a property of the theory that you are trying to formulate', Einstein told him. Heisenberg later admitted, 'I found his arguments convincing.'[26]

On the other hand, Einstein also complained at the Solvay conference in 1930 that 'Almost all the other fellows do not look from the facts to the theory but from the theory to the facts; they cannot extricate themselves from a once accepted conceptual net, but only flop about in it in a grotesque way.'[27] So on some occasions, Einstein believed theory actually determined what was observed, while on others he believed a too-rigid commitment to theory blinded people to conflicting evidence.

There is no formal contradiction here. It is, rather, another vivid example of how the scientific method cannot be reduced to a formula but must always require the use of good judgement. This judgement is a kind of skill developed by years of practice, what the Greeks called *phronēsis* or practical wisdom. Scientists all agree that, ultimately, data are sovereign. The problem is that often the data are not of such a clear, unambiguous and theory-independent kind that they can be used to resolve a dispute definitively. Indeed, the question of whether an experiment or observation counts as critical – sufficient to settle a dispute – is itself a judgement.

The fact that not even the relationship between theory and observation can be described in a precise, prescriptive form is perhaps the most striking piece of evidence showing that although science has its methods, and they are very successful, there is no single, homogeneous scientific method. Rather there are numerous techniques that have proven their worth, which skilled scientists must use their judgement to employ. What is true of scientific reasoning is true of reason as a whole. Although there are certain defined methods of reasoning, such as deduction and induction, and these are very successful, there is no single, homogeneous rational method. Rather, there are numerous techniques and good reasoners must use their judgement to decide which they select and how they use them.

3. The feeling of truth

Why do scientists make different judgement calls when faced with the same facts? Distasteful though it may be to those who would like reason to be cool and detached, part of the answer has to be the varying temperaments and emotional characters of scientists. Many of those who know science intimately accept this. The physicist Alain Aspect, writing in *Nature* about the different competing interpretations of quantum physics, concluded that the philosophical 'conclusion one draws is more a question of taste than logic'.[28]

There are numerous examples in the history of physics that attest to the importance of fundamental dispositions and 'tastes'. Comparing Wolfgang Pauli and Max Born, for example, Kumar says, 'Pauli trusted his sense of physical intuition in pursuit of a logically flawless argument when tackling any physics problem. Born, however, turned much more readily to mathematics and allowed it to lead his search for a solution.'[29] Similarly, 'While Heisenberg's first port of call was always the mathematics, Bohr weighed anchor and sought to understand the physics behind the mathematics.'[30]

This should not surprise us. There are many different grounds for theories and there is no algorithm that tells us which one is most likely to be decisive. That means that different scientists will tend to be drawn to different kinds of grounds first, and this will depend at least in part on which they are most comfortable with. Those with mathematical minds will be drawn more to the numbers, those of a more philosophical bent to the interpretation of the theories, experimentalists to empirical results, and so on.

What's more, no matter how powerful their brains, scientists tend also to listen very closely to what their guts tell them. Schrödinger for one did not think scientists should fight their instincts, saying that physicists did not need to 'suppress intuitions and operate only with abstract concepts'.[31] He himself said, 'I can't imagine that an electron hops about like a flea', and thought that was a good reason to disbelieve that they did.[32]

Sometimes these gut reactions are emotionally very strong indeed. For instance, Kumar says that Bohr 'abhorred the quantum theory of light'.[33] We might suspect that this extreme emotion is merely a product of the biographer's imaginative licence, were it not for the fact that such reactions are not unusual. Heisenberg used even stronger language, saying, 'The more I think about the physical portion of the Schrödinger theory, the more repulsive I find it.'[34]

Often the language is less visceral but still points to feeling rather than reason. Einstein's problems with the Copenhagen interpretation of quantum physics, for example, were often justified purely on the basis that they offended his intuitive feeling for what must be right. Prefacing his famous statement that 'I, at any rate, am convinced that He [God] does not throw dice,' Einstein wrote, 'Quantum mechanics is certainly imposing. But an inner voice tells me that it is not yet the real thing.'[35] It is telling that this comment was made in a letter to Bohr. Much of what I have quoted here has come from discussion and letters, where people are more likely to be candid about how they really make their decisions. No scientist would defend in a paper a claim on the basis that an 'inner voice' says it is correct, and yet as a matter of fact such inner voices are at work, helping to form conclusions. That they are never formally recognised does not mean that they are not real and important.

Another of Einstein's remarks is extremely revealing. He once said, 'I find the idea quite intolerable that an electron exposed to radiation should choose *of its own free will*, not only its moment to jump off, but also its direction. In that case, I would rather be a cobbler, or even an employee in a gaming-house, than a physicist.'[36] The basis for his objection is not that he finds the idea incoherent, inconsistent or insufficiently grounded in evidence but that it is simply 'intolerable'. His remarks are also interesting because they suggest his commitment to physics is not primarily a commitment to the truth. It is as though his love of physics is deeply connected to the fact that he believes it brings regularity and harmony to our understanding of the world, and that at bottom it makes good orderly sense. If it did not, it would be better to be a shoemaker.

Einstein is not alone in this. Poincaré wrote a remarkable passage, worth quoting almost in full, in which he explains why the beauty of science, rather than its truth, is its main attraction:

> The scientist does not study nature because it is useful; he studies it because he delights in it, and he delights in it because it is beautiful. If nature were not beautiful, it would not be worth knowing, and if nature were not worth knowing, life would not be worth living. [. . .] It is, therefore, the quest of this especial beauty, the sense of the harmony of the cosmos, which makes us choose the facts most fitting to contribute to this harmony, just as the artist chooses from among the features of his model those which perfect the picture and give it character and life. . . . And it is because simplicity, because grandeur, is beautiful, that we preferably seek simple facts, sublime facts, that we delight now to follow the majestic course of the stars, now to examine with the microscope that prodigious littleness which is also a grandeur, now to seek in geologic time the traces of a past which attracts because it is far away.[37]

Time and again in the history of science we see how the primary positive reaction to a new theory is marvel at its beauty. Einstein employed aesthetic language on several occasions. He described Bohr's 1922 paper on the structure of atoms as 'the highest form of musicality in the sphere of thought.'[38] When he saw how his own theory of relativity predicted Mercury's orbit he was moved to say that 'the theory is beautiful beyond comparison.'[39] He also said, 'the only physical theories that we are willing to accept are the beautiful ones.'[40] Such is the importance placed on beauty that Nobel laureate physicist Frank Wilczek wrote, 'In beauty we trust, when making our theories', in a book he titled *A Beautiful Question: Finding Nature's Deep Design*.

Non-scientists sometimes find themselves puzzled by this talk of beauty. In general terms, theories are described as beautiful when they have a combination of simplicity and great explanatory power. For instance, molecular scientist Ashutosh Jogalekar calls the Dirac equation beautiful because 'it can be written on a napkin and can explain an untold number of phenomena in a spare, lucid line of symbols.'[41] But 'simplicity' is of course, a relative term. To a non-scientist like myself, there is nothing simple about the equation at all:

$$\left(\beta mc^2 + \sum_{k=1}^{3} \alpha_k p_k c\right)\psi(x,t) = i\hbar\frac{\partial\psi(x,t)}{\partial t}$$

And yet even we who are unable to begin to decode the equation can appreciate how it is a remarkably concise way to bring quantum mechanics and relativity together to explain spin.

However, although some sensible things can be said about what makes scientific theories beautiful, as with art, there are no universally agreed standards and ultimately beauty does appear to be in the eye of the beholder. Paul Dirac claimed that 'it is more important to have beauty in one's equations than to have them fit experiment,'[42] but admitted that mathematical beauty 'is a quality which cannot be defined, any more than beauty in art can be defined, but which people who study mathematics usually have no difficulty in appreciating.'[43] This makes beauty somewhat useless as an arbiter of value since different judges will have different views of what is beautiful and there are no criteria to decide the matter. Jogalekar goes on to note 'how simple equations in chemistry can look beautiful and yet be approximate and limited' and 'how complicated equations can look ugly and yet be universal, giving answers precise to six decimal places. Which equation do you then define as being the more "beautiful" one?'

What's more, even though there are plenty of examples of beautiful scientific theories, many scientists appear to privilege beautiful theories more than can be justified. As George Ellis and Joe Silk point out, 'Experiments have proved many beautiful and simple theories wrong, from the steady-state theory of cosmology to the SU(5) Grand Unified Theory of particle physics, which aimed to unify the electroweak force and the strong force.'[44] Science writer Philip Ball points to other examples of true inelegance, such as Andrew Wiles's proof of Fermat's Last Theorem. 'The basic theorem is wonderfully simple and elegant,' says Ball, yet 'the proof anything but: 100 pages long and more complex than the Pompidou Centre.'[45]

This casts doubt on the idea that the preference for beautiful theories can be justified in scientific terms, on the basis that such theories have been shown to be more likely to be true. Were beauty simply a criterion to decide between two theories when all else is equal, we might accept this. But many go further and believe that all true theories are beautiful and that ugliness is indicative of a deep flaw.

As we have seen, one element of scientific beauty is supposed to be the way in which a single, simple law holds universally. But Nancy Cartwright calls 'fundamentalist' the idea that if a law is true then it is 'universal' and 'holds everywhere and governs in all domains'. She argues that we have no good reason to suppose this to be true. Instead, she proposes 'metaphysical nomological pluralism', which maintains that 'nature is governed in different domains by different systems of laws not necessarily related to each other in a systematic or uniform way'.[46] The appeal of the idea that laws must hold universally would appear to be an aesthetic preference for the simple and powerful, a preference which at root is based on nothing more than temperament.

We should not be surprised to discover that scientists, like all intellectuals, are influenced by their temperaments and personal preferences. As we will see in chapter four, philosophers are no different in this regard. Human psychology is extremely complicated and excellence often comes along with idiosyncratic, in some ways even deviant, character types. One study of Apollo moon scientists, for example, found that higher levels of creativity were correlated with more resistance to change. This might seem surprising, since creativity is a form of openness while resistance to change is a kind of closure. In science, however, it seems it helps to have a mixture of the two: the openness to see new possibilities but the narrow-mindedness to then pursue these when others would have become disheartened or doubtful. Whatever the full explanation, it should by now not surprise us that all the scientists in the Apollo study 'agreed that the notion of the objective, emotionally disinterested scientist is naive.'[47] And because scientists are not disinterested, they are clearly often motivated by what they want to be true, as well as by what the evidence suggests is true.

4. The impurity of science

Although I have quoted Lewis Wolpert approvingly for his skepticism about the scientific method, I think he misses something when he dismisses the importance of philosophy to science. 'Nothing in Popper or in any other philosophy of science has anything relevant to say about science,' he once said. 'I don't know of any scientist who takes the slightest interest in the philosophy of science. [. . .] Science has done very well without any philosophy whatsoever.'[48]

And yet his very rejection of a definitive scientific method, far from keeping science pure from philosophy, actually points to its contamination by it. Science, it turns out, is not something that can be done only using equipment and algorithms. It requires judgement and with that also interpretation. Nowhere is this clearer than when it comes to the nature of the scientific enterprise itself. Is science an accurate description of the physical world or is it just instrumental, a tool for helping us to make sense of it?

Scientists have disagreed about this. Max Planck said, 'I had always regarded the search for the absolute as the loftiest goal of all scientific activity.'[49] So, for example, when he came up with an improvement on Wien's law, he thought it would have no more 'than a formal significance' unless he fulfilled 'the task of investing it with true physical meaning.'[50] Einstein was of a similar bent, saying that 'What we call science has the sole purpose of determining what is.'[51]

Bohr, on the other hand, completely rejected this scientific realism. 'There is no quantum world. There is only an abstract quantum mechanical description,' he said. 'It is wrong to think that the task of physics is to find out how nature is. Physics concerns what we can say about nature.'[52] Wolpert might like to think that these philosophical differences are unimportant but in fact they deeply affected all great physicists' scientific work. Disagreements like these underpinned the huge disagreements about quantum physics that continue to this day.

To say that science is 'impure' is not to denigrate it. Nor should we underestimate how powerful data and experiments are in the long run for determining scientific truth. But mathematics and the physical sciences are fortunate in this regard. In almost every other field of human inquiry, it is just not possible to be certain or precise enough about the data to come up with an account which all informed, intelligent observers must agree is correct. The success of science should not lead us to believe that it provides the model for all reasoning; rather that the domain of science is one which is especially conducive to the use of reason.

While we should not diminish the success of science, it is important to counter the unrealistic and misleading image of science that some have projected in which there is no role for judgement, disposition, preferences and personalities. This is also an unrealistic image of reason in general. This misconception has the consequence that when people point to the non-algorithmic aspects of reason, it is usually seen to be an attack on reason. Instead it should be a defence. We need a more expansive notion of what it means to be rational, one which includes all the elements that are left out when we focus only on the strictly formal and empirical ones. At the heart of this notion we need to place judgement. So far we have seen *why* we need to do this, and in the chapters that follow we'll see more about *how* exactly we should do it.

If it seems shocking to some that scientists are not cold computers but human beings with different preferences, dispositions, skills and temperaments then they must have a very strange idea of how people think. Science is indeed a rational pursuit par excellence. But it does violence to the notion of rationality if we pretend that it is not a complicated, somewhat messy capacity.

CHAPTER THREE

Rationality and judgement

Our discussions so far of the role of rationality in religious and scientific inquiry have begun to explain why it is that reason cannot act as a neutral, objective, decisive judge, adjudicating between arguments. Reason by itself does not have this power. Ultimately, reasoners have to do some of the judging for themselves, answering questions like: Are these beliefs properly basic? Does this set of beliefs cohere better than these others? Is this paradoxical corollary something that undermines that which gives rise to it, or must it simply be accepted for now as an unsolved mystery? Reason gives us tools that help us to decide the answers to questions like these, but it does not provide anything like an algorithm for taking that decision away from us.

We have already seen some of the reasons why this must be so. In this chapter, I want to explain the most fundamental reason why individuals' judgements can never even in principle be purged from reason. Before I do that, however, I want to say something about why it is that the role of judgement has not been more widely acknowledged already.[1]

1. Philosophy's dirty secret

Anglo-American analytic philosophy – the tradition I was trained in – prides itself on its adherence to logic and rigour in argument. However, most philosophers know there is a difference between a merely smart – even merely *very* smart indeed – and a truly good philosopher. The merely smart can instantly formalise arguments into symbolic logic, spot an invalid deduction at 100 yards, and exploit any weakness in a colleague's paper, ripping it to shreds in front of their peers. Such a thinker is often swiftly hired and promoted, and touted as one of the bright young hopes. Yet by the time they retire these philosophers have left no mark on their subject. They have produced only intellectual pyrotechnics and have failed to get to the heart of a truly important debate or say anything substantial and enduring about it.

Really good philosophising requires something more than a razor-sharp brain, something that is sometimes called subtlety of mind, a philosophical sensibility or insight. I call it judgement, which I define somewhat cumbersomely as as *a cognitive faculty required to reach conclusions or form theories, the truth or falsity of which cannot be determined by an appeal to facts and/or logic alone.* There are numerous examples of this, but perhaps the clearest comes from moral philosophy.

Utilitarian ethics requires that we do whatever has the best overall consequences for the greatest number of people. There are innumerable versions of utilitarianism, but in the majority we are required to do whatever most reduces overall suffering. It is often argued that this places a very strong demand on those in wealthy countries to give away much more than they do. For Peter Singer, the demand is particularly onerous: 'we ought to give until we reach the level of marginal utility – that is, the level at which, by giving more, I would cause as much suffering to myself or my dependents as I would relieve by my gift.'[2] The logic behind this apparently extreme claim is simple: if you have enough to eat and can afford a decent home, then every further dollar you spend on 'luxuries' – meaning anything non-essential – would better serve the cause of reducing suffering if it were spent on the very poor instead. So we are in effect obliged to live as meagrely as possible in order that our wealth is used to improve as many lives as possible.

What is significant here is that most proponents *and* critics of utilitarianism accept the logic of the argument. But how can the very same argument be used to advocate a position and argue against it? Because when a valid argument has a strongly counter-intuitive conclusion we always have two choices. We can say that the argument reveals common sense or received opinion to be very wrong; or we can say that the argument shows there must be something wrong with the premises that lead us to this conclusion. In this case, the choice is between saying that utilitarianism is a profound challenge to conventional morality or that since accepting utilitarianism leads logically to impossible demands on us, utilitarianism must be false.

This latter form of argument is known as a *reductio ad absurdum*. The logic of a *reductio* follows from the fact that if you construct a valid argument – one where each step follows logically from the one before – on the basis of true premises, then the conclusion of the argument must be true. So, if you have a valid argument and the conclusion is false, you know there must be something wrong with the premises. This is all well and good when the conclusion is demonstrably false, but as the name suggests, in many cases the conclusion is merely 'absurd'. As we know from crime dramas where the accused says the detective is being absurd, what seems absurd often turns out to be true. Absurdity is often only in the mind of the beholder.

So in the case of utilitarianism, and many others, we are faced with a choice of either accepting that the argument is a *reductio* or biting the bullet of its implausible conclusion. The problem is, as David Chalmers describes it, that we are often 'frustrated to find opponents biting the bullet ... without this serving as any sign of defeat'. This might require taking on surprising commitments, 'but these commitments are rarely untenable to maintain'. The result is that 'philosophical arguments typically lead not to agreement but to sophisticated disagreement'.[3]

Whether we bite the bullet or take the hit, it is clear that our choice goes beyond what is demanded by logic or the facts. Indeed, what one is often doing in such an argument is judging whether the logic of the argument has a greater claim on us than the facts its conclusion seems to deny. In that sense one is going beyond what the facts and/or logic demand because they appear to be demanding different things.

Philosophy is replete with similar choices between accepting an argument as sound or using it as a *reductio*. Bertrand Russell's biographer Ray Monk has described another:

> Russell developed a causal theory of meaning and he was challenged by Braithwaite, who asked, 'Why, if the causal theory is true, am I not caused to utter the word "cow" whenever I see a cow?' Russell's reply to this was that, 'I don't know about you, but whenever I see a cow, I feel an involuntary movement in my larynx.' It is a feature of Russell's style that he is willing to accept absurdities because the argument seems to be leading there, and he thinks that's a virtue – the rejection of common sense.

But of course if Russell had been different, he could have jumped the other way. 'Whether it's a sound argument or a *reductio* will depend on how obviously unacceptable the conclusion is,' says Monk, and 'certainly people vary with regard to what they're prepared to swallow on the basis of an argument.'[4]

The need to choose between judging an argument to be sound or a *reductio* is an example of the kind of judgement good thinking needs when the algorithms of logic alone cannot establish the best answer. Of course, the judgement is informed by other arguments and other facts. But one would have to be an extremely optimistic kind of rationalist to suppose that these other arguments and facts settle the matter and that there is no role left for judgement as I have defined it.

Judgement is therefore not some additional 'factor X' that allied to sound logic yields good philosophy: it is an inherent part of the philosophical process. The problem is that although this fact is sometimes recognised, little is said about it, and its consequences for how we view the project of philosophy are rarely drawn out, at least not in the formal literature. In the context of an interview or discussion, however, I have often found that philosophers are happy to acknowledge that 'insight' or 'judgement' that cannot be reduced to mechanical logical calculations is needed in order to produce good, interesting philosophy. Michael Martin, for example, was a leading analytic philosopher who fully endorsed the need to present clear, valid arguments. 'But for that to be illuminating, you've got to get the right assumptions, ones which seem intuitively appealing, or correctly represent how we take the world to be in some aspect, and that is where the real work goes and that's where it gets hard,' he said. 'I can't describe for you a Turing machine which enables you to sort the good pieces of philosophy from the bad ones.'[5] Martin is surely right, but 'intuitively appealing' is rarely if ever listed among the important attributes of good arguments in textbooks and lectures about philosophical reasoning.

Ray Monk says something very similar. 'The great philosophers are those with insight, insight into something important,' he says:

Who reads Nietzsche, who reads Wittgenstein, who reads Kierkegaard, laying it out as if it were a piece of propositional calculus and says this argument goes through or it doesn't? It would be impossibly boring and would miss the point. A problem with training students in the way that we do is that we encourage them to be concerned with whether an argument is valid or not, and we don't encourage them very much to consider the question of whether the argument is interesting or not.[6]

And of course there is certainly no algorithm for determining whether something is 'interesting'.

Hilary Putnam goes so far as to argue that we need to exercise judgement even to understand what is being said: 'What we say a word means or what we mean by a sentence on a given occasion, that's very often a judgement as to what it's most reasonably taken to mean.'[7]

'Intuitively appealing', 'interesting', 'reasonable': these words are rarely uttered in the same breath as 'valid', 'sound' or 'demonstrable', and yet these elements of good judgement are at least equally important if you want to do philosophy well. While philosophy has made progress with systematising and developing criteria for good arguments and reasoning, it has had less to say about what constitutes this kind of 'good judgement' and acknowledging its indispensability.

I think there are at least three reasons why judgement has been sidelined by philosophers. The first is that the logical side of philosophy can be schematised and formalised in a way that judgement obviously cannot. Therefore it is just easier to come up with something to say about formal logic and the structure of arguments than it is to come up with some real insight into the nature of judgement.

The second reason concerns the academicisation of philosophy. For better or for worse, the work of academic philosophy increasingly takes place at the level of fine detail. Professional philosophers need to publish, and by applying the formal, analytic skills of their discipline to problems which have already been explored in some depth, it is possible to come up with something that satisfies the requirements of an academic paper to be 'original', to produce a 'result' and to display high professional standards. There is therefore a premium on the analytic, logical side of philosophy because this gets results faster, even if the results are uninteresting.

The third reason is perhaps more significant. Judgement represents the ineliminable limits of rational argument, and because philosophy always aims to pursue rationality as far as it can go, it is an unrelenting quest to reduce the role of judgement as far as it can, since it cannot entirely eliminate it. We want as little as possible in philosophy to depend on judgement while at the same time we know that we cannot do without it. Because our arguments become more rationally compelling the less they depend on judgement, we can make our arguments appear more rational by disguising or concealing the place of judgement in them. Judgement is therefore philosophy's dirty secret.

2. Logic and judgement

From what I have argued so far, it might be thought that judgement is only necessary in reasoning if and when logic and evidence alone are unable to bring us to an uncontroversial conclusion. Judgement takes us the extra yard between where reason leaves us and where the answer lies. But the role of judgement goes deeper than this. It is an inherent part of the process of reasoning itself, not merely an adjunct required when it cannot solve a problem.

The most obvious reason why this is so is that most reasoning is not deductive, and only deductive reasoning can make an even *prima facie* claim of not depending on judgement. Deductive reasoning is the kind that can be expressed in terms of formal logic. The elegance and purity of deduction is that, given certain premises, certain conclusions must follow with the same inexorable necessity as a mathematical proof. The oldest system of deductive logic is the syllogism, which can be traced back to Aristotle. Syllogistic logic identifies the general form of specific arguments. So, for example, one syllogism could be:

No humans have wings.
George is a human.
Therefore George has no wings.

This fits the very precise form of the syllogism in which the first line is a general proposition (the major premise), the second is a specific proposition (the minor premise) and the third is a conclusion drawn from them. Each proposition can be universal ('all' or 'none') or particular ('some'). Logicians have studied all the various forms syllogisms can take and have identified the 24 varieties that are valid, meaning that the conclusion logically follows from the premises. In such valid arguments, if the premises are true, then the conclusion must also be true.

The example above takes the following valid form:

No A is B.
All Cs are A.
Therefore no Cs are B.

It might require a double-take to see that this indeed the form of the argument. When a syllogism involves a singular entity – such as 'George', 'Paris' or 'the Mona Lisa' – it still fits the form of a universal proposition. So 'George' is in effect 'all Georges', meaning not all people called George but the entirety of the class of which this George is the only member. The other potentially confusing thing is that our argument uses the verb 'to have' whereas the syllogistic form uses 'to be'. This isn't a problem: from a logical point of view 'no humans have wings' is the same as 'no humans are winged', it's just that the former is a more natural way to put it.

The syllogism is the most primitive example of a formal deductive argument. These days, logicians use more complex forms of symbolic logic, which are not confined to three lines and a very limited variety of propositions. These allow for much more complex lines of argument to be set out and tested for validity. The basic principle is, however, the same. Arguments are analysed in terms of their general form; symbols and letters are used to represent the relations between terms; and rules are established to determine which inferences are valid and which are not. The resulting logic is closer to mathematics than it is to argumentation in natural language. In maths, once we define what numbers and terms like '+', '–', '√' and 'θ' mean and understand the axioms of mathematics (which have all been proven), whether or not a calculation is correct is a matter of objective fact. In the same way, once we know how logical operators such as '¬', '∃', '⇒' and "∀" are defined, and have understood the axioms of logic, whether an argument is valid or not becomes a matter of objective fact.

The goal of rendering an argument in a formal, logical form could therefore be said to eliminate the role of judgement and to make it objectively determinable whether an argument is sound. But this is impossible. The role of judgement can and should be minimised by such a process, but judgement is involved at virtually every stage of the process.

First of all, we need to decide which axioms are correct. This is clearly something that cannot be determined by the logical system itself since that would be circular: you cannot use the very system, the legitimacy of which you are trying to establish, as the criterion for whether the system is legitimately constructed. If logic were the sole judge of its own soundness then it would at best be only *internally* consistent but would have no *external* legitimacy. This means that at some point we have to have some external affirmation of the soundness of the axioms of logic, and this requires a judgement, since that affirmation is providing something the logical system itself cannot provide.

That validation of the system could come from a kind of intuition which states that we can just *see* when an axiom holds, as we can see that $1 + 1 = 2$, so long as we understand what those terms mean. Alternatively, this external judgement could be purely pragmatic: we should follow this rule because it results in arguments which we find reliable. There is a strong tradition in philosophy of accepting this kind of reliability argument as the ultimate justification for rules of logical and argumentation, most notably in American pragmatism. This is clearly a form of judgement since it goes beyond what logic and evidence can demonstrate. What works is what works for us and this is a matter of judgement, not fact, since people can disagree about 'what works' means. So, for example, accepting certain religious texts as authoritative can work for some believers, whereas refusing to accept any texts on authority can be deemed to work for others.

Let us imagine, however, that you could somehow define the axioms objectively, without any role for judgement. This would still only deliver results of mathematical precision if you only used logic with numbers and letters. But philosophy would not be very interesting to anyone other than logicians if the best it could do was to show how if no A is B; and all Cs are A; therefore no Cs are B. It's only of any use if we can apply this to real As, Bs and Cs. Doing this requires at least some judgement, even in the most simple cases.

Take the argument I used as an example earlier: No humans have wings; George is a human; Therefore George has no wings. The major premise 'No humans have wings' might seem obviously true, but the category 'human' is one that we have created to divide up the animal kingdom and it is not uncontroversial. It has been argued that if we were to be consistent in our taxonomies, the genus *Homo* would include three species: *Homo troglodytes* (common chimpanzee), *Homo paniscus* (pygmy chimpanzee) and *Homo sapiens* (us). This would not affect this argument since chimps don't have wings either, but it illustrates the complexity and judgement that sits disguised behind an apparently simple premise.

We need also to remember that the whole point of offering examples like these is that they demonstrate arguments so clear and obvious that their basic structure and validity become transparent. In practice, no philosopher – or zoologist, for that matter – would ever construct an argument to show that a particular human being has no wings. Philosophical arguments only get interesting when the premises are somewhat meatier, but this of course means that they are also less self-evident.

Take, for instance, a canonical philosophical text like Descartes's *Meditations*. Descartes, like virtually all the great philosophers, doesn't present his arguments in neat premise/conclusion form, but it is a reasonably straightforward task to identify his key premises and the conclusions he draws from them. Paraphrased into single propositions, the kinds of premises Descartes invoked include:

If God were good, he wouldn't allow me to be deceived. (First Meditation)

If I can conceive of myself without a property, then that property is not a part of my essential nature. (Second Meditation)

There must be at least as much reality in the efficient and total cause as in the effect of that cause. (Third Meditation)

Everything that is clearly and distinctly perceived to belong to a thing really does belong to it. (Fifth Meditation)

The faculty of sense perception is passive: one cannot control the nature of what it is one perceives. (Sixth Meditation)

Each one of these premises requires both justification and interpretation. None is a simple, logical axiom, and nor is any a straightforward empirical observation. Hence determining whether they are true requires our judgement, just as Descartes had to use his own judgement when formulating them.

One further complication is that logical languages are not natural languages. That means if you want to use ordinary propositions as the basis for arguments in formal logic you first have to translate them, and that is not always straightforward. Even in our simple example, for instance, we had to do some awkward translation, so 'no humans have wings' was rendered 'no humans are winged', and 'George is a human' became 'All members of the class "George" are human'. This was easy enough to do but, as we have already seen, it was a particularly simple, even banal argument.

In theory, one reason why modern logical languages can deal with very complex arguments is that whole clauses can be replaced with single letters. For instance, take Descartes's premise 'If I can conceive of myself without a property, then that property is not a part of my essential nature'. To express this logically we need to divide the premise into the antecedent (the clause covered by the hypothetical 'if') and the consequent (what 'then' follows from it). So we can label the antecedent 'I can conceive of myself without a property' X, and the consequent 'that property is a part of my essential nature' Y. We then use the symbol '⊃' to represent the 'if/then' relation and '¬' to negate the consequent and thus have the neat formula 'X ⊃ ¬Y' to work with.

There is of course a role for translating an argument into logic and seeing if the deduction works through. If Descartes has not got the relation between his Xs, Ys and Zs correct, then his argument doesn't work. But it is worth remembering that people identified the flaws in Descartes's reasoning before modern logics allowed them to be expressed formally. Also, more often than not the real nub of an argument has already been effaced when a premise is reduced to a letter. What makes Descartes's argument interesting is not that its premise is of the form 'X ⊃ ¬Y' but that it has the specific content 'If I can conceive of myself without a property, then that property is not a part of my essential nature'.

There are therefore two different problems with translating ordinary language premises into logical symbols, both of which point to ways in which judgement is indispensable. First there is the danger of mistranslation, and whether a translation is good will always require judgement. But even when the translation is accurate, it is the nature of such translations that they strip premises of all their meaning. So to know whether an argument is sound you can never rely on what the logical structure of the argument shows by itself: you always have to make a judgement about the truth of the premises.

3. The constraints of logic

It might still at least be claimed that rationality is *constrained* by the fundamental laws of logic. Even if logic itself has no rock-solid external foundation, we seem to need to accept it, and once we do, we need to ensure that our thinking conforms to its fundamental demand of consistency. This could be maintained even allowing for what I have said about times when we need to park a paradox. In such cases, we accept that something is wrong but we also accept that we can see no way to fix it that would not make things even worse. It is a version of the argument that the best should not be the enemy of the good: if only two options are available and both are inconsistent, go with the least inconsistent for now. But make no mistake: neither way is ultimately satisfactory.

The basic principle here is expressed in a variety of forms, such as the law of excluded middle, the principle of bivalence or the law of non-contradiction. The fundamental idea behind all of these is that any proposition must be true or false, and can't be both or neither. It is often claimed that this is not a universal law of good reasoning but something particular to Western logic. Eastern philosophies embrace a 'both/and' logic rather than an 'either/or' one. But this seems to me to misunderstand both Western and Eastern philosophy. In Eastern philosophies, when contradictions are embraced it is almost always in order to show the limitations of the contradictory concepts, not to show a genuine coexistence of real contraries. In a deep sense then, both traditions uphold the law of excluded middle, in that it takes the existence of a genuine, rather than apparent, contradiction to be evidence that something is not right. The difference is that Western philosophers try to dissolve the contradictions by refining their use of language whereas Eastern philosophers often dissolve them by appealing to a reality beyond language where such contradictions do not exist.

Taoism, for example, stresses that language is an imperfect tool for dealing with reality and does not provide an adequate representation of it. So rather than trying to resolve all the contradictions that language gives rise to, we should often instead try to leave words behind. 'Words are for meaning,' wrote Zhuangzi. 'When you've got the meaning, you can forget the words. Where can I find someone who's forgotten words so I can have a word with him?'[8]

It is not therefore chauvinistic to take the law of excluded middle to be a central demand of good reasoning. But does this grant too much to the demands of logic? Although it certainly seems to be a sound principle of reasoning that it should usually be constrained by logic, I see no *a priori* grounds for saying that it is necessarily *always* so constrained. Let me give one example to illustrate what I mean. Imagine that scientific inquiry leads to a logically paradoxical finding. For instance, theoretical physicists come to agree that the only way to understand the indeterminacy of the position of a given particle is that it is neither true nor false that a given particle p is at location a or b. (I am certainly *not* claiming that this conclusion is what is currently demanded by quantum theory.) Put formally, they agree that we must in this case accept the statement 'P & not P', in defiance of the law of non-contradiction. There are many ways to respond to such a finding, which I would summarise under three broad headings: Denial, Revision and Rejection.

Denial is the position that this cannot possibly be true, since it entails a breach of the logical principle of bivalence, or the excluded middle, which states that any proposition has to be true or false and there is no third alternative.

Revision is the position that this may be true *and* that the principle of bivalence is true, because logic is a self-contained system and the world itself may or may not conform to logical principles. We assume that it does, because working on this assumption has proven to be a fruitful way of conducting empirical inquiry. But there is no *a priori* reason why the assumption must be true, and if the evidence for this strange finding about the position of particles is overwhelming, we have merely discovered one of the limits of applying logic to the real world.

Rejection is the more radical position that the finding destroys the very basis of logic and shows that its founding principles are false.

For my present purposes we do not need to decide which of these responses would be correct. After all, we cannot know which is better in the absence of information about the strange hypothetical findings of this thought experiment. My point is simply that in such a situation we would be able to sensibly ask which response is *more rational*. The very fact that such a question makes sense shows that our conception of rationality does not seem to be necessarily constrained by or coextensive with our conception of logic, for what is precisely at issue is how far, if at all, it is rational in such a case to accept, revise or reject what logic appears to demand. In other words, whether or not it is rational to accept an illogical finding is an open question. The apparent illogicality of the finding is not sufficient reason to reject it on rational grounds unless one has some other good reason to believe that rationality's sovereign is logic. If logic is on at least one occasion neither necessary nor sufficient for settling a rational argument, then rationality cannot be necessarily constrained by the demand to follow the basic laws of logic. Logic becomes one tool rationality uses, not the essence of rationality itself.

4. Scarce deductions

There is one final reason why judgement is an inherent part of reasoning and not merely a fallback when logic fails. The truth is that the deductive mode of argument, formalised in logic, just isn't the main way we reason at all. 'Who thinks deduction gets you around the planet,' as the philosopher Patricia Churchland put it. 'Really? I mean like maybe I do a deduction about twice a week. I'm being ironic: I don't know how many times I do a deduction but it's not very often.' Most of our reasoning is quite different. 'You can call it abduction, and call it inference to the best decision or inference to the best explanation,' says Churchland, but whatever the name, 'We don't know how that's done.'[9] I take that last claim to mean not that such reasoning is completely mysterious, but that we don't know how the human brain makes such inferences and nor do we have clear rules or algorithms to tell us when we're making them correctly. We look at the evidence and we create hypotheses about what best explains it. Logic comes in to the extent that we test for consistency and see if our explanation has any absurd consequences (although, as we have seen, these need not always be fatal). At the end of the day, however, whether or not such an argument is good cannot be objectively demonstrated. Once again, we use our judgement.

The claim that rationality is not coextensive with deductive logic should be uncontroversial, since there are many forms of rational argument, such as induction and abduction, which are by definition not themselves deductive in character. There should be nothing surprising or objectionable here to anyone who accepts something like Hume's distinction between reasoning concerning matters of fact and matters of logic.[10] Hume's goal was not to show that non-deductive reasoning concerning matters of fact is irrational but that rationality does not just consist of deductive logic. If he had thought it did, then he would have thought that his own arguments against miracles, for example, were non-rational or irrational, since they were based wholly on inductive principles.

Nonetheless, despite the esteemed status of Hume in the history of Western philosophy, it seems his core message has not been taken sufficiently to heart. Students being introduced to the ways of philosophy focus much more on the formal reasoning structures of deduction than on the more informal ones. And it is very rare indeed for a philosopher to acknowledge too loudly or clearly that all this non-deductive reasoning requires the use of judgement.

If the idea that philosophy doesn't actually depend that much on deduction seems heretical, the fuller truth is even more surprising: it often doesn't rely on arguments at all. Time and again in the history of philosophy, the key moves made by philosophers turn out on careful examination to be more like observations than arguments. What the philosophers have done is noticed something extremely important and directed our attention to it. Once we do the same, we find ourselves agreeing with them about what it is we can see. Arguments don't come into it.

There are innumerable examples. Let me give just some of the most notable. First of all, there is Descartes's *cogito* (I think), popularly expressed in the formula 'I think therefore I am' (*cogito ergo sum*). This is the formulation Descartes used in the *Discourse on Method* and it has at least the superficial form of an argument. In the *Meditations*, however, he says something quite different. 'I am, I exist, is necessarily true whenever it is put forward by me, or conceived in my mind.'[11] This is more of an observation than an argument. What Descartes is really doing here is directing our attention to the fact that at the moment of thinking we cannot at the same time have any doubt that we exist. To think 'I do not exist' would be a self-contradiction. This is not a purely logical point, which is why it is possible to dispute Descartes's claim. Nor is it an argument, since it has neither premises nor conclusions. Rather, it is an observation, a fact about the world we are invited to attend to and then interpret as best we can.

Similarly, David Hume did not use an argument to rebut the Cartesian idea that we all have an indivisible self. Rather, he simply invited us to attend more carefully to what is going on when we think. 'For my part,' he wrote, 'when I enter most intimately into what I call *myself*, I always stumble on some particular perception or other, of heat or cold, light or shade, love or hatred, pain or pleasure, colour or sound, etc. I never catch my self, distinct from some such perception.'[12] Again, this is no more than an invitation to attend and draw the right conclusions. So here we can see, in one of the biggest philosophical debates in history on the fundamental issue of the nature of the self, there is an exchange not of arguments but of observations.

These are not unusual exceptions. In moral philosophy, observations are even more evidently bedrock. Consider, for example, what the highest good for humankind is. Many have claimed it is happiness, but they do not really argue for this position. Rather, they ask us to consider the kinds of choices we would make, the different societies we would select between, and attempt to persuade us that in each case the only reason why one is preferable to the other is that one results in more happiness. Those who disagree simply ask us to attend to different things. So, for instance, Robert Nozick's famous experience machine thought experiment invites us to consider whether we would prefer uninterrupted happiness in a virtual reality designed only to make us happy, or a more up and down life in the real world.[13] Most people choose the latter, which is said to show that we do not consider happiness to be the highest good. But this is not an argument. It is merely a clever way of making us notice that we do not always prefer what makes us happier.

Attending is often more useful than argument. As Wittgenstein put it, the best way to respond to a skeptic who says, 'I don't know if there is a hand here' is to say, 'look closer'.[14] Attending is a crucial element in good reasoning and provides the clearest example of the ways in which philosophising inevitably requires the use of judgement and cannot rely solely on what logic and evidence dictate. But as we have seen, judgement is required in *every* kind of philosophical argument, from constructing the very axioms of logic, through the use of deduction, to the making of the key observations on which many philosophical positions rest. I have called this philosophy's dirty secret, but any filth is merely imagined by unrealistic souls who believe that reasoning can and must have an other-worldly purity. For more grounded thinkers, there is nothing dirty about it.

A proper appreciation of the indispensable role of judgement in reasoning helps us to understand how there can be radical disagreement in philosophy without it being possible to definitively pinpoint an error which shows one side is wrong. Such is the case with the debate over whether abstract objects have a real, independent existence. An extensive survey of academic philosophers and graduate students found that 39% believed they did, 38% believed they did not, and the remainder either didn't know or endorsed an alternative position.[15] If philosophy required no judgements, the existence of these kinds of radical disagreements would be puzzling. I would suggest that it is precisely because rational argument ultimately depends on judgements rather than logical algorithms that the existence of such disagreements is not only comprehensible but probably inevitable.

Many will worry that if we place too much emphasis on judgement we will end up with an unacceptable degree of subjectivism where we have no grounds to arbitrate between two people whose judgements lead them to different conclusions. This is too pessimistic. As we have already seen in the examples of science and religion, accepting the role of judgement is not the same as saying anything goes and that no reasoned arguments can have any force in a debate. The coming chapters will develop this further. For now, however, we must simply accept what is too evident to be ignored. If the maxim 'follow the argument wherever it leads' has any truth in it at all, it is that we should not shy away from the truth just because we fear it has unpalatable consequences.

PART II: THE GUIDE

Like the first myth of reason as the faculty that does away with the need for personal judgement, the second can also be traced back to Plato's dialogues. In the *Phaedrus*, the soul is likened to a chariot pulled by two horses, one unruly and one of noble breeding. Intellect or reason is the charioteer, keeping troublesome emotion in line with the more obedient rational part of the self.

The metaphor reflects a historically common idea that although emotion can take charge if we let it, it is both desirable and possible to be guided by reason. It also reflects the related error of believing reason and emotion to be two autonomous drives. When these errors come face to face with the facts, they threaten to leave reason looking like an illusion. If we investigate how philosophers actually work, we find that they do not sit solely on Plato's steeds of noble breeding but ride a more mongrel beast. And if we look at what psychology tells us about how the mind works, the idea of the rationalist thoroughbred seems as fanciful as the mythical unicorn.

By giving due consideration to the so-called irrational elements of thinking, we can revise our understanding of reason to show that while it does have an important role in guiding us through life, it does not and cannot do its work independently from the emotions and other psychological drives. To push the equine metaphor to breaking point, reason is no ass, but is more of a hard-working mule than a pedigree racer, and none the worse for that.

CHAPTER FOUR

Lives of the mind

Earlier I described the inescapability of judgement in reasoning as 'philosophy's dirty secret'. But perhaps the discipline has an even darker skeleton in its closet: how people philosophise is largely determined by their personalities. Most outside the discipline would consider this an obvious truth, since it has become a truism that our beliefs and values are shaped by a combination of congenital inclinations, upbringing and culture. But while the wider world may have no problem accepting this, it poses a threat to philosophy's image as reason-led, not reasoner-led.

There is a reassuringly simple way to acknowledge the evident truth that character influences the way we think without letting it threaten the detached objectivity of philosophy. It's the same way that scientists reassure themselves that their methods do not fundamentally depend on individual quirks and foibles. This is to accept that of course personality and values shape the way scientists go about their work. Some are more experimental, creative, conservative, thorough or patient than others. Which particular area scientists are drawn to will also depend on their dispositions. And people's values may incline them to seek a particular result, one which accords with their own wider world-views. None of this, however, threatens the pure objectivity of scientific findings themselves. Character may cause people to discover what they do, but evidence and reason alone determine whether what they find is indeed a true discovery or a mistake. Science as a pursuit is coloured by the personalities of scientists but science as a set of results is as true for an introvert as for an extrovert, for a conservative and for a radical, a theist or an atheist.

As we saw in chapter two, things aren't quite as simple as this, even in science. But even if this defence of the objectivity of science is broadly correct, can we really accept that philosophy works in the same way? I don't think we can. The influence of personality in philosophy runs far deeper than it does in science, which undermines the claim that philosophy is as impersonally objective as science. This has significance beyond philosophy, since it reflects a broader truth: that reason can never completely escape the personal and the human.

To make this case, I want to look at an often justifiably neglected literary genre, the philosophical autobiography. Most such works are frankly dull reads. People who lead the life of the mind often have much more interesting minds than lives. These books do, however, cast clear light on the relationship between character and reason in numerous ways.[1]

1. The thinker and the thought

Having read various philosophers' autobiographies, I am struck by how often what is revealed of their personalities sheds light on how they thought as philosophers. Sometimes the connections between life and thought are drawn explicitly. For instance, in the most famous chapter of his autobiography, John Stuart Mill discusses his mental breakdown, which, borrowing words from Coleridge's 'Dejection', he describes as 'A grief without a pang, void, dark and drear, / A drowsy, stifled, unimpassioned grief, / Which finds no natural outlet or relief / In word, or sigh, or tear.' Mill is clear that this experience had 'very marked effects on my opinions and character', ones which altered his philosophical views. First, although he remained convinced that happiness was the highest good, he came to think that 'Those only are happy ... who have their minds fixed on some object other than their own happiness; on the happiness of others, on the improvement of mankind, even on some art or pursuit, followed not as a means, but as itself an ideal end.' The second change was a shift of emphasis from the political to the personal: 'I, for the first time, gave its proper place, among the prime necessities of human well-being, to the internal culture of the individual.'[2]

Rousseau, in his *Confessions*, frequently identifies events in his life as causes of his intellectual development. For example, recounting an incident when he was a child and was punished for something he did not do, he asks us to imagine the effect this had on his younger self: 'What an upset of ideas! What a disturbance of feelings! What revolution in his heart, in his brain, in the whole of his intellectual and moral being.'[3]

But it is not just events in life and their influence on thought which are of interest in a philosophical autobiography. It is also the connection between character and thought, especially those aspects of character which are formed at a young age. Take, for example, W. V. O. Quine's autobiography. The book is a relentless catalogue of travels and events, in which he keeps a count of how many states he has visited and talks of making diversions merely to tick off another his list, wanting to complete the set. 'After five weeks in Howland Street, our border-crossing propensity impelled us to hitchhike into Rhode Island and Connecticut,' is how one typically gripping paragraph opens. 'Subsequent outings of the kind netted New Hampshire, Maine and Vermont.'[4] This reveals a thinker who has a deep-rooted longing to bring mental order and tidiness to as much of his world as possible, one who as a toddler sought the unfamiliar way home, which he interprets as reflecting 'the thrill of discovery in theoretical science: the reduction of the unfamiliar to the familiar.'[5]

In contrast, Paul Feyerabend recalls how, not yet ten, he was enchanted by magic and mystery and was comfortable with ambiguity and paradox. For instance, he writes of the first time he realised that the Saint Nicholas who came into his bedroom at Christmas with presents was actually his father in a costume. 'It was my father; clearly it was my father,' he wrote, 'yet equally it was not my father but the saint.'[6] Quine and Feyerabend, of course, went on to write very different kinds of philosophy: Quine's in a formal, logical, systematising tradition (though typically on the limits of such formalisations); Feyerabend's anti-reductive and anti-systematising.

When we read these mature works, it is natural to ask which is right, the anti-method of Feyerabend or the drier logic of Quine. But as soon as one is confronted in their autobiographies by the seemingly obvious fact that these different philosophical theories reflect deep-seated differences in personality, it becomes hard to accept that impersonal reason and truth alone are the adjudicators here. It would take a great deal of faith in the objectivity of philosophy and philosophers to think that Feyerabend and Quine arrived at their respective philosophical positions simply by following the arguments where they led, when their inclinations so obviously seem to be in tune with their settled conclusions. And if that is true of them, it is at least as true for the rest of us who cannot claim to have such fine philosophical minds.

Perhaps even more important than how they *arrived* at their positions is what explains why they *remained* with them. If philosophy were like science, then although we might expect people with different personalities to come up with different ideas, ultimately we would expect the philosophical community to settle on one explanation as the true one. But we do not find this. Although there is often more convergence than might be expected, in most areas of philosophy, there is nothing like consensus. 'Disagreement in philosophy is pervasive and irresoluble,' says Peter van Inwagen. 'There is almost no thesis in philosophy about which philosophers agree.'[7]

This has been empirically verified by the PhilPapers survey conducted by David Bourget and David Chalmers, in which 1,803 philosophy faculty members, as well as PhDs and graduate students, were questioned about where they stood on 30 central philosophical debates. As Chalmers notes, only one view attracted over 80% support, and three more over 70%. In 23 out of 30 cases, the leading view had less than 60% support.[8] I have mentioned the disagreement about the nature of abstract objects in chapter three. Another example is the question of whether believing something is right or wrong provides an inherent motivation to act on that moral principle: 34.9% thought it did, 29.8% thought it did not and the remainder took another view or were undecided.[9] As Chalmers concluded, 'there has not been large collective convergence to the truth on the big questions of philosophy.'[10]

The arguments alone are clearly not enough to persuade all clear-thinking minds to come to same conclusion. Either a large number of philosophers are not thinking straight or some factors other than brute strength of argument must be playing a role. The PhilPapers survey provides more evidence that the latter explanation is correct in the form of correlations between the views people take and where they were born, did their PhDs and currently work, as well as their their age and gender. For instance, almost twice as many male philosophers describe themselves as political libertarians (13.7%) as women (7.5%). On the issue of whether actions are right or wrong in themselves, irrespective of whether they happen to result in good or bad consequences, 34.4% of Americans endorse this position compared to only 23.3% of non-Americans. In deciding which arguments are stronger, philosophers are clearly bringing their own temperaments and cultures to bear on their judgements.

Philosophical autobiography provides strong evidence that philosophy is not a purely objective discipline, the products of which have nothing to do with the people who produce them. Philosophy is in an important sense a personal pursuit and we do not undertake it with an impersonal faculty called 'reason'. Rather, how we reason is coloured by who we are and the commitments we already have. One might want to go even further and endorse Wittgenstein's belief that 'Work in philosophy [. . .] is really more work on oneself. On one's own conception. On how one sees things.'[11]

I said that philosophical autobiography provides *evidence* in support of these conclusions, but it does not force us to accept them. How could it, when the thesis being proposed is precisely that rules of reasoning and evidence alone are not sufficient to force all rational souls to the same conclusion? Nonetheless, the evidence is strong and demands a response. Anyone who wished to maintain, in the face of this evidence, that philosophical arguments and principles should always be considered entirely impersonally needs to explain how this separation of life and thought can be achieved. Philosophical autobiography, I suggest, shifts the onus of proof onto those who deny the personal nature of philosophising.

There are philosophers who are fully prepared to acknowledge this, but not enough. Ted Honderich was unusually candid when he wrote, 'In my stubbornness, though, I am one with most philosophers, who for the most part are impervious to argument. There is a truth about philosophy in this. At the bottom of philosophy are things underdescribed as commitments. They are better described as grips that the world gets on us early.'[12] Yet 14 years later, even Honderich repeated the standard line that 'who wins in philosophy will be decided over time by those final judges, Fact and Logic.'[13] Perhaps Honderich should have written earlier that philosophers are ultimately impervious to arguments for the imperviousness of argument.

In conversation, we might find philosophers more willing to endorse Honderich's less bullish verdict. When I spoke to Saul Smilansky for my book on free will, for example, he told me that part of the intractability of the debate is explained by the fact that

> philosophers are human beings and they come from different places and have different values. Even if there is agreement about different notions of free will, some philosophers will be – I think there's no other word – temperamentally inclined to set the bar high and therefore say that there is no free will, and others set the bar lower and say obviously there is free will, and some people like me will say it's complex and we have various bars. I'm even inclined to think that to some extent some people have an optimistic or pessimistic temperament and therefore they tailor the bar that they intuitively feel will satisfy them.

Smilansky is sanguine about this:

> You cannot be somebody else, you can try to understand people with different views but in the end maybe the most productive thing is that you be obsessive and try to develop your position in the best way possible and then see what happens, whether it seems plausible to other people and what objections they have to it.[14]

For the most part, however, you will not find much public acknowledgement of the role of personality in philosophy. I think this is partly down to an understandable defensiveness about the philosophical enterprise. Philosophers know that many view their subject as speculative at best, bullshit at worst. They are therefore at great pains to emphasise the extent to which philosophy is hard-nosed, rigorous, analytic, logical. To allow that personality might play an important role in determining which philosophical position you take would potentially undermine all these protestations of stringency. It would also play into the hands of the many skeptics in wider society who would jump on any evidence that philosophy is unscientific, opinionated balderdash.

But perhaps this merely reflects an unwillingness among philosophers to accept that what they do is indeed inherently somewhat speculative and always in danger of collapsing into bullshit. As Simon Glendinning perceptively put it, 'It's always a tricky moment for any philosopher to acknowledge that what you are doing, what you think might be worth doing, might be just a spinning in the wind or just a kind of doing nothing at all, or doing something very badly.' Glendinning proposes an intriguing hypothesis that it is precisely the unwillingness to confront this possibility which leads many anglophone analytic philosophers to think of 'Continental philosophy' as its 'other', as a 'false personification by self-styled analytic philosophy of a possibility which is internal to and which threatens all philosophising, that is the possibility of being empty, the possibility of sophistry'.[15]

I'm inclined to think there is a great deal of truth in this, but you don't need to go the whole way with Glendinning's 'otherisation' thesis to see that it is certainly true that philosophers have not to date been as willing to accept the role personality plays in philosophising as the evidence clearly suggests it does.

2. The stories of our lives

Philosophical autobiographies do much more than simply reveal the personalities and prejudices of their authors, however. They provide striking examples of just why such factors inevitably colour our thinking beyond the biographical.

Honderich raises the important issues here in the coda to his autobiography. He discusses the problem of causation and how the biographer faces the problem of deciding what caused what in a person's life. This is, in fact, simply a particular instance of a general philosophical problem about causation, as Honderich made clear earlier in the book, illustrating it with the example of striking a match.[16] When we strike a match and ask what caused it to ignite, it is natural to identify the cause as the striking. In counterfactual terms, we say if we hadn't struck the match, it wouldn't have ignited, and so the striking is the cause. However, it is also true that other things had to be true for the ignition to occur: if there hadn't been any oxygen, or if the match had been wet, the ignition would not have occurred. In order for any effect to occur, we need not just one cause but what Honderich calls a 'causal circumstance': the set of circumstances required for the effect to occur.

The problem is that the causal circumstance for any event can be extensive and include a large number of things. But when we ask what caused the match to ignite, we do not want to be told the full causal circumstance, we usually want to be told that it was struck or that it came into contact with a naked flame. We wish, in Honderich's words, to 'praise' or 'dignify' one aspect of this circumstance as *the cause*. But what justifies the isolation of this part of the causal circumstance as *the* cause? Honderich argues at length that nothing does and that, therefore, when we explain why anything happens, the only intellectually respectable kind of explanation is explanation-by-causal-circumstance. Explanation-by-cause is no more than an unjustified isolation of one part of the causal circumstance.

In the case of biography the problem is simply magnified. In explaining why a person acts in a certain way, the causal circumstance is vast: as well as the situation and thought processes just before the action we have the person's entire life to date and his or her inherited characteristics. Yet in understanding a life we feel the same urge to praise causes. Indeed, many philosophers have done so without apparently considering it to be a problem. For example, Russell recounts five minutes that, in his mind, completely changed his life, when he saw the sick Mrs Whitehead in extreme pain. 'At the end of those five minutes, I had become a completely different person,' he recalled.[17] The impact was political as well as personal: Russell claims that in those five minutes he went from being an imperialist to a pro-Boer pacifist. It seems certain that this change cannot be fully explained without reference to a causal circumstance that extends far beyond those five minutes. Yet Russell finds no problem in singling out that short time as the cause of his change of heart.

Honderich is critical of the idea of explanation-by-cause, saying 'what we name as a cause is just the particular bit of a causal circumstance *that interests us*'[18] and that '[a chosen cause] gives us no more knowledge at all of why something happened, but is indeed only a matter of our interest and our practical interests'.[19] But we can turn this on its head and ask why, rather than being criticisms, these observations can't be viewed as holding the key to the solution of his problem about causation.

We can start by questioning why there is a problem of explanation-by-cause at all. The reason there is a problem is because Honderich cannot identify any strictly objective reason to 'dignify' or 'praise' one part of a causal circumstance over another. Without such a reason, objectively all we have is the causal circumstance. The problem, however, disappears if we no longer believe that we need a *fully* objective reason to provide an explanation-by-cause. Can't we just accept sanguinely that in 'praising' one member of the causal circumstance we are reflecting our own interests or even desires? To be objective, isn't it enough to recognise what these interests and desires are?

I think it must be. As Honderich sets up the problem it seems that explanation-by-causal-circumstance can be the only fully objective explanation. Once we accept that an effect is only fully explained by the full causal circumstance, it follows logically that any explanation that appeals to fewer factors will not be complete. So the choice is between saying we should never provide an explanation-by-cause or accepting that an explanation-by-cause will never be a full causal explanation.

The first possibility must be rejected, since we cannot do without explanations-by-cause. We are often required to give such an explanation where an explanation-by-causal-circumstance would not do in its place. If, for example, I want to know the cause of a car crash, there is a sense in which the right answer would be 'faulty brakes'. Although, as philosophers, we may not be able to give a satisfactory account of why this component of the causal circumstance should be identified as '*the* cause', we cannot deny that to identify it thus is both reasonable and necessary. There may be a philosophical problem as to why this cause should be praised, but there is no doubt that it is and should be. There is no problem in justifying the existence of explanations-by-cause in general. The only problem is justifying why in each particular case we praise the cause that we do, and more often than not, we can understand very well why we do so.

Given that explanations-by-cause are indispensable, the only sensible route to take would seem to be to accept their limitations: such explanations are not complete, so we need to attend to what interests are guiding the praising of causes and not be deluded into thinking that any explanation-by-cause is the 'real' explanation.

Judgement is required to decide which cause or causes we pick out to 'praise'. This is not a random process: for instance, when an accident investigator asks what caused the fire, some answers ('someone dropped a cigarette') are better than others ('there was oxygen in the room'). The process is not random, but at the same time, the combination of the facts plus logic does not yield an answer to the question, 'What caused the fire?' or even 'Tell me what I need to know about how the fire started.' In the case of the second question, it is highly implausible that one could specify the conditions for something being 'a piece of information an accident investigator needs' in any way that would enable such information to be extracted from the evidence without the use of judgement.

This echoes the so-called 'frame problem' in the philosophy of mind and artificial intelligence. The frame problem can be understood by thinking about how chess computers work. They can beat humans because they can work through every possible move and calculate which has the highest probability of being successful many moves ahead. This is not, however, how a human chess grandmaster works. Chess players cannot possibly work out the consequences of every move. Nor would it be efficient to do so. Many moves can be ruled out almost straight away as silly. The puzzle for creators of artificial intelligence (AI) is working out how chess players narrow down the bewildering range of possibilities open to them. Traditional algorithms can't do this because they rely on working through everything systematically, which is precisely what framing avoids. Humans therefore appear to be making judgements about what is relevant or irrelevant which formal reasoning mechanisms cannot make.

Identifying the part of a causal circumstance relevant to a certain kind of causal explanation is a very similar problem. This is something the human mind seems to find very easy. But it is not something that can be expressed in formal logic. Even if it could be *modelled* in formal logic, it would not follow that the way we *actually* think about such things follows this formal pattern. It does then seem that judgement – the ability to reach conclusions or form theories, the truth or falsity of which cannot be determined by the appeal to facts and/or logic alone – is an indispensable feature of our thinking.

So where Honderich sees a metaphysically arbitrary choice to dignify some elements of the causal circumstances over others, I see a rational need to frame the causal story in the appropriate way, where 'appropriate' cannot be determined by an algorithm. One reason why it cannot is that, as philosophical autobiography shows, philosophy is a personal pursuit coloured by character and what Honderich calls 'commitments', as well as by impersonal, objective rationality. It should be no surprise that explanations-by-cause are coloured by the interests and values we bring to the explanation, since *any* philosophical account is coloured by such things. The sensible response is to recognise and be open about this limitation rather than reject any philosophical account that does not fully overcome it. This issue reflects the wider problem of skepticism. Skeptical doubts can never be entirely eradicated. The key to their resolution is to understand why it is that they arise, learn from this the limitations of philosophy and then work within these limitations.

It is vital to recognise that when we talk about the limits of objectivity we are not simply talking about gaps in the facts. Rather, we are pointing to the truth that facts alone do not comprise all that we need to know about and understand in many situations. In the case of autobiography, Honderich writes that accounts or summaries of a life 'are not summaries called up by the facts, but also and inevitably attitudes to a life, passing or settled attitudes'.[20] He continues a little later, 'Such things are not a matter only of truth.' The point being made here is that when one recounts a life one cannot but make judgements as well as parade the facts. Even if one avoids judgemental language, the selection of some incidents as significant and the omission of others is in a real sense a judgement about what is important in a life. Honderich's argument is that such judgements can never be fully determined by the facts.

The same is true for much more than autobiography. Causal accounts do not merely describe the facts but reflect our attitudes to them. Consider, for instance, how much emphasis we place on subjective motivation or social environment when explaining criminal behaviour. There are often real disagreements between those who want to stress individual responsibility and those who emphasise the social determinants of crime. But even when people agree on exactly how much each factor contributed to the full causal circumstances, one might still wish to emphasise one factor over the other because of nothing more than a value, such as a preference for forgiveness or for encouraging people to take responsibility.

I would suggest that we also overestimate our capacity to capture all the relevant facts in the first place. We fool ourselves into believing that we have assembled all the vital data, arranged them into premises and then drawn our conclusions accordingly. This is hubris. The reality is that we have always selected what we judge to be most pertinent at the time, and this is bound to reflect our values and attitudes as well as our raw reasoning power.

We can see this when we think about the historical development of debates. In modern theory of knowledge, for example, for centuries the problem was seen in terms of the relationship between the individual knower and that which is known. It was only in the 1980s that the notion of 'social epistemology' took off, largely thanks to the work of Alvin Goldman.[21] Social epistemology builds on the insight that human knowledge is a collective achievement rather than a purely individual one. This seems to be so obviously true that we might well ask why it took so long for philosophers to put the social into epistemology. In part at least, it seems credible that the supreme value placed on the autonomy of the rational individual blinded philosophers to the social dimension of knowledge. If we think other values are not now directing our attention towards some factors and away from others, we are surely deluded.

The selection of some data and the setting aside of other data is both necessary and desirable. No account can include everything. To use an old metaphor, a map that has the same detail as that which it maps is not a map at all, but the thing itself or an exact replica. A map has to be accurate to be useful, but to be a map it has to be selective about what it schematises, which is why geologists, walkers and motorists all need different maps.

That is why there can be no one account that is 'the truth', not because 'truth' is beyond us. We need to distinguish between an account which is 'the truth' and one which is 'truthful'.[22] If by 'the truth' of a life we mean the one, true, complete account of it, then no such truths can be told. But we can tell more or less truthful stories about our lives and those of others: ones that do not gloss over embarrassing facts, ones that reveal many sides of a personality and not just those we wish to promote. Relating such a truthful story is not about cataloguing the largest possible number of true facts about a person. That is why our commitment to truth and rationality requires that our conceptual maps only include genuine features of what we are mapping and do not leave out anything that a user of that map might reasonably be expected to find useful. But the idea that we can come up with any kind of conceptual map that does not reflect our values and interests is a mirage. Philosophical autobiography helps us to see that behind all reasoning is a reasoner who can never drain away all her individuality.

This is no philosophical disgrace. It does not mean that our philosophising adds up to *no more than* a reflection of prejudices or received opinions. As I have been arguing, philosophy requires judgement. What we need to add to this is the adjective 'personal', thus accepting that philosophy requires *personal* judgement. Philosophical autobiography provides strong evidence that the ways in which we reason are inextricably tied up with our personalities and our lives. Styles of thinking are too deep-rooted in our individuality. So we have to recognise that, whatever judgement is and its role in reasoning, it is personal in the sense that it will differ from person to person, and it is unrealistic to expect that any argument that involves judgement will persuade every rational agent.

Quine began his autobiography with the sentence, 'My birth in a modest frame house on Nash Street in a south-east-central quarter of Akron on Anti-Christmas, June 25, 1908, brought the population

of that industrial city to a figure in the neighbourhood of sixty thousand.'[23] Quine is more concerned to give us facts about his life, many
more than a reader needs, than most of his fellow autobiographers.
But in launching straight into an account of his life without pausing
to consider if the very attempt to do so raises any philosophical
issues, his memoir is typical of those of other philosophers. Ayer, for
instance, features in Honderich's autobiography, but whereas that
book does examine the purpose, scope and limitation of the genre,
A.J. Ayer managed to write two volumes of autobiography without
even scratching these issues.[24] The neglect is to be regretted, since
philosophical autobiography provides a particularly well focused
medium for the examination of the interplay of life and thought and
the need to accept and understand the role of personal judgement,
not only in philosophy but in all reasoning.

CHAPTER FIVE

The challenge of psychology

Soon after Sigmund Freud died in 1939, W.H. Auden wrote a poem to his memory in which he described the founder of psychoanalysis as not so much a person as 'a whole climate of opinion' under which we live our lives.[1] This is one form of man-made climate change that no one could deny. Freud did not discover the unconscious, but he formalised and popularised the idea that the conscious mind is just the tip of the iceberg and that most desires and beliefs are unnoticed by those who have them. Hidden psychic forces propel us forward while what we call reason tells us a more palatable but largely fictional story of what we do.

Many are now skeptical of Freud's theory – and of psychoanalysis in general – but the broad idea that the unconscious is in the driving seat has become widely accepted and has been given empirical support by contemporary research in psychology. Experimental psychologists might be less convinced by the primacy of Freud's *eros* and *thanatos* – the sex and death drives – but they have catalogued a large number of biases and distortions of thought that affect each and every one of us. They may have abandoned Freud's specific ideas but they have only added to the general picture of human nature he painted in which we are not so much rational as *rationalisers*, using reason to make sense of our beliefs and actions after the event. Must we therefore accept that reason is a mere veneer for irrational impulses, or can can psychology justify giving rationality an important role in human thought and judgement?

1. Hot heads

In 1967, Philippa Foot devised one of the most famous hypothetical moral dilemmas in twentieth-century moral philosophy.[2] A runaway train is hurtling towards a narrow tunnel where five people are at work. If it continues, they will certainly be killed. There is no way to warn them or to stop the train. The only thing you can do to alter the outcome is pull a lever and divert the train into another tunnel, where only one person would be killed. Should you pull the lever?

The dilemma – known as the trolley problem – caught the imagination of moral philosophers because it dramatised an important difference in ways of thinking about morality. According to the *consequentialist* tradition, what matters is creating the best possible outcome overall, which in this instance clearly means pulling the lever so that four fewer people die. But according to the *deontological* tradition, the end does not always justify the means because we have duties to avoid certain actions, such as killing others. The trolley problem is designed to elicit our intuitions about whether the consequentialist or the deontologist is correct. In this scenario, it seems most people are drawn towards the consequentialist position: they think that pulling the lever is justified because it saves more lives, even though it means the action directly causes one death.

However, if you describe the trolley problem a little differently, it can elicit very different intuitions. In another version, the only way you can stop the train is by pushing someone else onto the track, knowing as an expert on the railways that this would be enough to stop the train. The same basic moral calculation applies: intervene to cause one death in order to save five others, or let the disaster unfold. But in the latter case, people are much less likely to say that the right thing is to cause the single death. People who, albeit reluctantly, would pull the lever are generally speaking not so willing to push a man to his death.

There is now an entire literature on 'trolleyology' and various explanations have been put forward as to what explains, if not justifies, the different responses to different versions of the problem. Although no single explanation commands anything like universal assent, most would accept that one very important reason for our differing intuitions comes down to psychology, not any moral principle.

The psychologist who gave us the theoretical model to understand this was Daniel Kahneman. Kahneman has argued persuasively that we have, in effect, two different ways of thinking. 'System 1 operates automatically and quickly, with little or no effort and no sense of voluntary control,' he says. In contrast, 'System 2 allocates attention to the effortful mental activities that demand it, including complex computations. The operations of System 2 are often associated with the subjective experience of agency, choice, and concentration.'[3] The most vivid way of summing it up is that System 1 is 'hot', emotional, quick thinking whereas System 2 is cool, calm reasoning.

The uncomfortable truth for those who like to think of human beings as being governed by System 2, with System 1 a mere occasional annoyance that kicks in when we're tired and emotional, is that it seems our thinking is much 'hotter' than we believe. Anything that provokes an emotional response is likely to fire up System 1, the conclusions of which System 2 will merely rationalise. In contrast, when thinking about larger numbers of people, they become just numbers and we use System 2, ceasing to respond emotionally to them. That is why charities routinely focus on stories of individuals in their fundraising rather than on numbers. It's also why the quote attributed to Stalin – 'The death of one man is a tragedy, the death of millions is a statistic' – is so chillingly accurate.

In the case of the trolley problem, when we talk about numbers of casualties and pulling levers, the problem seems purely practical and quite abstract, so most people will try to solve it using System 2. But when we have to imagine pushing someone on to the tracks, that triggers an emotional response. System 1 kicks in and we find ourselves repelled. But, of course, if asked why we should not push the person, we don't say, 'I don't know, it just feels wrong.' Rather, we come up with various rational justifications, such as the idea that it is wrong to use a person as a means to an end – even when this is just what we were prepared to do in the lever case. Evidence of the extent of our blindness to the ways in which System 1 dominates thought is that it took decades of 'trolleyology' before anyone even took seriously the idea that the real explanation for our different intuitions was simply emotional.

For cool reason, it gets worse. Kahneman and his peers in psychology have documented all sorts of ways in which even the smartest of us operate on the basis of unconscious, non-rational mental processes rather than conscious, rational thought. When it comes to thinking, we are all essentially lazy, relying on automatically processed rules of thumb – 'heuristics' – which save us the bother of actually having to compute. After a recent election, for example, I shared on social media a statistic which showed that although only 7% of the population have been privately educated, among Conservative members of Parliament the proportion was 48%, 17% for Labour, 14% for Liberal Democrats and 5% for Scottish Nationalists. Depending on your background assumptions, very different conclusions would leap out from these very same facts, each one seeming obvious to the person making the inference. If you are to the political left, you don't need to do any thinking to see the statistics as confirming your belief that society continues to give too much privilege to the children of the rich. But if you are more conservative, this might not seem obvious at all. That's why someone responded to my post by commenting, 'Proof that public schooling instils a sense of public responsibility'. This led to all sorts of confusion, since in Britain a 'public school' is in fact an elite private one. But in the confusion it became clear that for some what seemed immediately obvious was how marvellously private schools instil a sense of civic duty in their students. Of course, we all know that people draw different conclusions from facts, depending on their prejudices and prior beliefs. But what Kahneman shows is that we do not do so because our calm, System-2 thinking is distorted. Rather

System 1 just leaps to a conclusion on the basis of no real reasoning at all.

There are whole books detailing the various ways our minds work that provide endless other examples of this kind of absence of rational thought – 'rational' as understood by philosophers, anyway. Kahneman's *Thinking Fast and Slow* is essential reading for anyone who doesn't already know this work. You might rush out to buy it believing that if you can understand all these processes you can override them, but Kahneman himself is quite pessimistic about this. When once asked if it was possible to master System 1, like Plato's charioteer, he replied by saying, 'Anchoring is one of the few examples where you can defend against it.' Anchoring is where you interpret a number differently depending on which other numbers are presented alongside or before it. So, for example, a £20 dish at a restaurant will look expensive if all the other options are around £15, but if there are many options priced £25 or more, you will think it quite cheap. Many people trying to sell us things use tricks like this, such as creating an artificially high price and then 'discounting' it. Kahneman thinks we can guard ourselves against this 'because there is a very simple question to ask: where did that number come from? If you suspect the numbers you may be able to rid yourself of the illusion.'

Even this relatively simple liberation, however, 'requires special effort' and in most other cases there is little we can effectively do. So even Kahneman, when asked if his 45 years of study had changed the way that he makes decisions, had to reply, 'They haven't really, very little, because System 1, the intuitive system, the fast thinking, is really quite immune to change. Most of us just go to our graves with the same perceptual system we were born with.'

His interviewer clearly didn't quite believe this, and said, 'But do you sometimes think to yourself, "That was fast thinking, that was intuition, I'm just going to check that"?'

'I occasionally do,' he replied, but 'not enough. I do it much more effectively when it's the mistakes of other people. When it's my own mistakes I'm far too busy making the mistakes to overcome them.'[4] On another occasion, Kahneman summed up his pessimism by saying, 'If we think that we have reasons for what we believe, that is often a mistake. Our beliefs and our wishes and our hopes are not always anchored in reasons.'[5]

2. Not so fast

Interestingly, our philosophical response to findings like these may itself be influenced by an anchoring effect. The anchor here is our prior assumption about how much of our thinking is conscious and logical. If we think most of it is, then the news from psychology is going to look very bad indeed. But if we have a more modest view of human rationality and have already got used to the idea that non-rational forces shape our thoughts at pretty much every moment, then we are less likely to be shaken.

More importantly, if we have a narrow view of what rationality is, defined by logic and formal reasoning alone, System 1 will be an intolerable interloper. But if we have a broader conception of rationality, we might not be so quick as to see it as a pure enemy of reason. Kahneman himself seems inclined to take this view. 'People are quite reasonable,' he once said. 'It's not that people are irrational – I really hate that characterisation.'[6] How can that be?

The key is that conscious, systematic reason can license the use of some unconscious, automatic mechanisms. To put it another way, there can be rational justifications for what is usually thought of as non-rational because it involves no conscious reasoning. There is a wonderful fictional example of this in D.H. Lawrence's short story 'The Rocking Horse Winner', in which a child repeatedly and reliably backs the winners in horse races without having any idea why he knows which horse will win, and so obviously also without having any justification for his choices. Since we know that even professional tipsters rarely do significantly better than chance over the long run, would it not be more rational to follow the tips of the boy than those of anyone else alive? Reason tells us that he is a more reliable tipster than anyone else, so we follow his advice, even though there is no clear thought process in his method.

In real life, the best example of this kind of thing is when we don't go ahead with something because it doesn't 'feel right'. On paper, everything looks fine but something is making us wary, and we don't know what it is. We do not need to believe that this kind of intuition is infallible to believe that it can be well worth paying attention to. As long as we have good grounds to believe that when we feel this way in this kind of situation, usually it does indicate that something is amiss, then we have rational grounds to follow our hunches, even though the hunches themselves are not the result of rational deliberation.

It should now be clear why System 1 is not always the enemy of reason. It has evolved because we often need to make quick, snap judgements when there is no time to sit down and think things through. Heuristics are cognitive shortcuts, and the key is that they wouldn't have evolved if they didn't work more often than not. The problem is that they are so deep rooted that we often find ourselves using them even when we don't need a quick, snappy solution but cool, calm reasoning. But that is a far cry from saying we would be better off without them. If we could try living for just one day without using any heuristics, we would be a complete mess, paralysed by the need to check if everything was safe or dangerous, rash or sensible, fair or unfair. If System 2 sat down and thought about it, it would certainly opt to keep System 1, for it could not survive without it. It may be far from perfect, but it is rational to want to use it.

There is also a second reason why 'hot' thinking might complement rather than conflict with the cool variety. Consider the trolley problem again. There are those who take the view that the rational thing to do is to sacrifice one life to save five and that when we refuse to do so, because it requires pushing someone, that is because our emotions are clouding our judgement. But why should we assume that the optimal moral judgement is a 'cold' one? Indeed, we have various reasons to think it is not. First, as we will see later (in chapter seven), there are good reasons to think that morality is rooted not in principles of pure reason, but in 'moral sympathy' or empathy. It is only because we feel for people, care for them emotionally, that we have any reason to be moral at all. There will be much more on this later.

Second, far from being morally superior, there are reasons to think that people who are more inclined to maximise the greatest good by all means necessary are morally deficient. The psychologists Daniel Bartels and David Pizarro conducted a study in which they presented people with versions of the trolley problem. They found that 'Participants who indicated greater endorsement of utilitarian solutions had higher scores on measures of Psychopathy, Machiavellianism, and life meaninglessness.' This implies the 'counterintuitive conclusion that those individuals who are least prone to moral errors also possess a set of psychological characteristics that many would consider prototypically immoral.'[7]

Note here the question-begging use of the phrase 'moral errors', which assumes that emotion distorts correct moral judgement, when it could be argued that it is essential for it. We do indeed have good reasons to think that moral reasoning really does require the input of feeling in ways which sabotage any attempt to make morality a matter of clear rules and principles. Although it is of course good to have a scientific paper to back up an argument, without any empirical evidence other than the general data of experience we can see that there is often a tension between always doing what a calculation suggests produces the greatest welfare of the greatest number, and behaving in a way that is consistent with our generally positive emotions of love and care. The clearest example of this is parental love. Would the world be a better place if parents considered the interests of all children equally, giving their own no preferential treatment? It would seem not. And yet because parents lavish so much love on their own children, money that could save a child from dying from malaria is spent instead on frivolous toys and treats that the child doesn't need.

It is not at all obvious how to resolve this tension, but I think most would accept that it requires balancing hot and cold reason rather than eliminating one of them. And hot reason does indeed deserve the name 'reason'. Living according to reason requires us to give due weight to the unconscious, non-deliberative and affective aspects of living, which we depend on not just for practical purposes but for ethical ones too. Pascal famously said, 'The heart has its reasons of which reason knows nothing', but this remark betrayed an all-too-common narrow-minded conception of what reason is and what it can understand.[8]

Psychology is informing our cool, cognitive reason about the heart's reasons. That means we are one of the first generations to be able to judge which of these reasons we should take as legitimate and which we should challenge. Of course we are finding out that sometimes our automatic and emotional responses are just wrong and misleading, but that does not mean they all are. As the psychologist Dan Ariely said in response to Kahneman's work, 'We are limited, we are not perfect, we are irrational in all kinds of ways. But we can build a world that is compatible with this that gets us to make better decisions rather than worse decisions. That's my hope.'[9] And mine too.

3. Gendered reason

I think we should accept the fact that our reason is not pure, but is subject to all manner of psychological influences. But what if those influences are systematically divergent in different populations? In particular, what if the way we think differs depending on our gender? Must we think not of reason in the singular, but of masculine and feminine reason?

The French philosopher Luce Irigaray thinks we must.[10] 'Men and women do not generate language and structure discourses in the same way,' she has said. 'And they cannot understand one another, nor even listen the one to the other, without first becoming conscious about such differences.' Irigaray's thesis is not the now widely accepted one that men and women *tend* to think differently. The controversies that surround this claim centre purely on whether these average differences are rooted in biology, culture or some mixture of the two. Even those who claim that the differences between male and female brains are hard wired, such as the British psychologist Simon Baron-Cohen, are keen to stress that these differences are no more than typical and so, rather confusingly, 'not all men have the male brain, and not all women have the female brain.'[11] Irigaray rejects this as an impossibility.

'To be man and to be woman does not correspond to a simple biology, nor a simple social stereotype,' she says. 'It corresponds to a relational identity. This relational identity exists. It is not the same to be born a girl from a woman, that is from the same gender, the same sex, to be capable of becoming a mother, to be able to generate in oneself the same as the other, to make love in oneself.' This is perhaps where the psychoanalytic influences on Irigaray's thought become apparent: she is a trained analyst of the Lacanian school. For her, it must make a critical difference that women are born from humans who share their sex, while men are not. 'The first other in the life of a man,' she writes, 'the first human you with whom he is in communication is a feminine-maternal you.'[12]

When I interviewed her, I suggested that this means that in a sense I was not meeting her at all, since we could not share the same understanding. She agreed. 'In this moment we seem to be in the same place, inhabiting the same space, the same time, the same country, the same culture, the same language. In a way it is only an illusion.'

Irigaray's position is an extreme one, which is frankly not supported by the best evidence of psychology. Nor, thankfully, is any serious field of academic study in which gender apartheid is routinely practised, with men and women using their own versions of reason separately. Feminist philosophy, for instance, is not separate from all other philosophy. A feminist critique of epistemology (theory of knowledge) has its force because it suggests there is something epistemology is missing because of distortions rooted in gender, distortions it seeks to remedy. Such a critique would lack any power if it amounted to the claim that there is male epistemology and female epistemology, and each of the two should mind their own business.

If reason is to have any potency at all, it must in a substantive sense aspire to some kind of universality. I will be saying more about this in the next chapter, but for now it should at least be clear that an argument that simply has no possible purchase for one half of humanity is not a rational one. So to accept the extreme claim that masculine and feminine reasons are separate and cannot be reconciled is to give up on rationality. This would seem perverse, since we have numerous examples of knowledge and theories that clearly do cross the genders. Science is the clearest case: Newton's Laws apply equally to all genders, and women are not free from the pull of gravity just because a man wrote the equations that describe it.

However, to say that reason is in essence gender-neutral is not to deny that there are many ways in which awareness of the ways in which gender might affect the use of reason is vital, if we are to think properly. Nowhere is this more obvious than in philosophy, where, compared to other disciplines, women are especially underrepresented. The most recent systematic study showed that although nearly half of undergraduates in philosophy in the UK are women, that proportion goes down to 30% at PhD level, 21% for permanent and junior lecturers, and only 15% at professorial level.[13] The situation in the USA is very similar.

To say that many are not happy with this is an understatement. Sally Haslanger has described how, when she entered philosophy, she

had a budding feminist consciousness, and I thought then that there weren't enough women on the reading lists in my classes or among my teachers. But I thought things would certainly change, given the importance of the feminist movement. I've been though the profession now and worked hard on the Committee on the Status of Women. I've worked hard in other forums like SWIP – the Society for Women in Philosophy – that were trying to advance women's interests. After 30 years I was seeing that there wasn't really that much change, and that made me mad.[14]

Philosophers like Haslanger, Rae Langton, Jennifer Saul and Helen Beebee do not believe that the reason for this is that philosophy is inherently masculine. Rather, they see the roots of the problem in psychology.

'There's a lot of empirical research showing that almost all human beings are subject to a range of biases against certain stigmatised groups – like blacks, gay people, women, disabled people and so on and so forth,' said Saul. 'These biases operate at an unconscious level. They're often totally contrary to the person's explicit, genuine conscious beliefs: they may devote their lives to fighting racism and sexism, and yet still there are tests that reveal in the laboratory that they do have these biases. Even psychologists, who know about this stuff, are subject to these biases.'

One such bias is stereotype threat, which, Saul explains,

occurs when members of a stigmatised group in some particular area are presented with a situation that's said to be threat provoking, where they become preoccupied with fear of confirming stereotypes about their group, and they actually under-perform as a result of this. So black students in any test which is presented as a test of intellectual ability will under-perform; women who are asked to tick a box indicating their gender before taking a maths test will under-perform; five-year-old girls will do worse on a maths test if they first colour in a picture of a girl holding a doll rather than a picture of a sunset. Anything that reminds you of the stereotypes about your groups will cause you to under-perform in the area that your group is stereotyped as performing badly in.

One reason philosophy has been less successful than other disciplines in overcoming these biases could be that the subject's self-image actually makes a philosopher more vulnerable. 'Philosophers have this special relationship with objectivity,' says Saul, 'where we think that we're better and more rational than everyone else. It's very well confirmed that people are really bad at judging their own objectivity and systematically overestimate it. But really interestingly, it's also been shown that thinking about how objective one is increases bias rather than decreases it. If you form the explicit intention to be unbiased and not affected by gender and race, you will be more affected by these things.'

So in a sense, philosophy has been so bad at involving women because of, not in spite of, its strong desire to be gender-neutral. 'Many philosophers have the view that in order to be objective you have to be value-free or value-neutral and feminism is by its nature not value-free or value-neutral,' explained Haslanger.

> So there are a lot of philosophers to this day who think there's an inherent contradiction in the idea of feminist philosophy or feminist epistemology. But one of the aims of objectivity, I think, is to get multiple perspectives on a phenomenon so that you can better understand it. If you just have a single perspective on the phenomenon, then that doesn't protect you against bias. I think feminists have shown that knowledge practices in the contemporary West and throughout the history of philosophy have been exclusionary and have been problematic and have prioritised some kinds of knowledge at the expense of other kinds of knowledge in ways that reflect a bias. So what we're saying is that we can achieve greater objectivity by bringing women and feminists into this conversation.

I couldn't put it better than Haslanger and Saul. They eloquently explain how psychology does not debunk the idea that reason is gender-neutral, it simply points to the ways in which its practice is not. The case of women in philosophy also illustrates another oft-neglected feature of rationality. Philosophers understandably focus on the nature of reason itself. However, in order for reason to flourish, it needs to be practised in the right environment. And that is sadly often lacking in the very places where reason is held in the highest esteem.

So, for instance, in order for philosophy to maximise the rational input of all its most skilled practitioners, it needs to create an environment in which all are equally able to contribute. Many doubt this is in fact what we see. Beebee points her finger at 'the kinds of highly aggressive discussion that you can often get at philosophy seminars – this is at professional and postgraduate level but maybe to some extent at undergraduate level as well. I think in seminars, at least in a lot of my experience, there is a very adversarial, confrontational approach that the audience has towards the speaker. It's like: this is a fight we're having now, and I want to win the fight and I want you to lose the fight. That can be very off-putting.'

Some have objected that this suggestion undermines women, because it implies they are not up to the cut-and-thrust of first-rate philosophy. Beebee rejects that charge. 'I don't think it's undermining of myself to say that I don't actually find a bunch of people being extremely aggressive towards each other and trying to win the fight all that comfortable. To say that what I'm saying is that women can't cut it in this discipline is to mistake the nature of the discipline for the contingent nature of certain social interactions that philosophers tend to fall into.'

Beebee's point is that the aggressive nature of philosophical dispute is bound to work against any group that happens to find itself in a minority. 'If you behave in a very aggressive and competitive way towards someone who is already in a marginalised group, that's going to make them feel uncomfortable, even if they're just as competitive and aggressive as you.'

Langton highlights an even worse problem than seminar styles. 'You mustn't ignore the level of sheer hassle that many women put up with in philosophy,' she says. 'The problems have been emerging recently in a new blog, "What is it like to be a woman in philosophy?". A lot of the stories are really horror stories about departmental parties where sexual harassment and attempted rape took place.'

The blog is a sobering read for anyone under the illusion that philosophy is inherently self-improving. One woman talks of a male professor who arrived to talk at a conference and the first thing he said to his host was, 'Show me a graduate student I can fuck.'[15] Another female professor recalls being told by her male superior that despite an impressive publication record, her promotion prospects were poor. Pointing to her pregnant belly, he explained, 'I just don't think *that* is a very good idea.' The woman had the wit to reply, 'This isn't an idea at all. It is a conception,' and left.[16] The problem for women in philosophy is not that reason is masculine but that too many men are not nearly as good at using it as they think they are.

4. One-trick ponies

At first sight, Daniel Kahneman's distinction between System 1 and System 2 might sound a lot like Plato's allegory of the 'charioteer of the human soul'. The noble horse is of course our rational part, while the unruly one is our irrational appetites and impulses. The allegory contains a germ of truth, in that we are not driven by pure intellect alone and our more instinctive, intuitive responses often lead us astray. But they can also keep us on track, since our conscious, deliberative part simply could not cope with every detail of navigation. They also give us much-needed momentum, since reason alone has no motivation to go anywhere at all without some affective desires.

Modern psychology is humbling, especially if you believed that it was possible to drive the chariot of the human soul by pure reason alone. But if we are to be more realistic, we need a different image. Plato's chariot and horses is both too complicated and not complicated enough. It is too simplistic because reason and emotion are not neatly divided, and to become more rational we should not seek to subjugate those parts of our minds that are outside conscious deliberation. Plato's problem is that his noble steed is too pure bred, able to use reason only in its traditional, narrow sense.

His model is also too complicated, since even Kahneman describes Systems 1 and 2 as 'fictitious characters', which 'are not systems in the standard sense of entities with interacting aspects or parts'.[17] So we would do better not to think of the human soul as comprising two wildly different horses and a controlling charioteer, but as being one single equine which draws on all sorts of cognitive tools, from the conscious, systemic and deliberative to the automatic, unconscious and affective. As I suggested at the opening of this part of the book, to avoid hubris we ought to think of this beast as more like a mule than a thoroughbred. Our rationality is a somewhat messy thing that cannot be captured only in the formal processes of logic. But in many ways we mules are superior to Plato's pedigrees, because whereas his cannot bring reason and emotion together, we can. Better to be a many-skilled mule than one-trick pony.

CHAPTER SIX

Guided by reason

We have many reasons to dismiss the ideal of rationality as an impersonal, impartial sovereign that will lead us to the truth. As we have seen, reason is unable to determine for us what we ought to believe about the big issues of religion and to a lesser extent about science. Rational agents may agree about a great deal but there is always an element of judgement in drawing conclusions that cannot be reduced to anything like a logical algorithm. The way we think is deeply affected by our own personal dispositions, commitments and values. Many non-deliberative factors influence our reasoning and it would be unrealistic to believe we could ever fully overcome them.

If we imagined reason to be our absolute ruler, then it would be right to use considerations like these to dethrone it. But to demote our erstwhile sovereign is not the same as to decapitate it. To work out what best to do with our not-so-omnipotent leader we need to think a little about our assumptions of what the leadership role entails.

Our problem is that we have looked to reason to provide guidance from a privileged, external, impartial standpoint. This is a form of rule that is *heteronomous*: coming from outside ourselves. Reason is, if not quite personified, then at the very least 'reified': turned into an abstract thing with a life of its own. On this conception, all we need to do is find out what reason demands and follow it. But we can't do that, because reason is a human faculty that is shaped and limited by its hosts. We can formulate laws of logic that exist outside of us and even come up with some principles of inductive reasoning, but in order actually to use reason we cannot leave us reasoners behind.

Reason therefore has to be autonomous, not heteronomous. It has to be something we use for ourselves and fully own, taking responsibility for how we use it. There is, however, something almost paradoxical about this, which Kant's account of the autonomy of reason illustrates. Kant argued that when we reason we must never submit to an external authority but must think for ourselves. Only this is appropriate to the dignity of the human individual. At the same time, however, Kant believed that if we think truly for ourselves, we will come to see what reason demands and freely submit to it. So whereas the person who accepts $1 + 1 = 2$ because a teacher says so is thinking heteronomously, someone who understands why the sum must be so is thinking autonomously. But in so doing, one form of obedience is being substituted for another: we bow down to reason, not to those who tell us what to think.

Kant's autonomy could therefore be seen as another form of heteronomy, in which the external authority is not human but the pure, abstract nature of reason itself. The autonomy of reason I propose goes further. We have to accept that reason does not stand outside ourselves but must work within us. Reason is not a guide we can simply entrust ourselves to, expecting it to take us along the road to truth without our having to make any decisions at all. Reason is the kind of inner guide that informs but does not dictate our decision-making, rather than an external one that makes our decisions for us. Nevertheless, Kant was on to something, because there is a sense in which reason does require us to accept heteronomous demands. Our guide is useless if it is merely a form of self-determination which pays no attention to the brute reality of the external world. When we are presented with arguments or given reasons for belief, the way things really are must determine whether they are rational or not. In short, reason is nothing if it does not aspire to objectivity. That is the heteronomous aspect of reason and it brings us to the heart of my account of rationality: rational argument should be defined as *the giving of objective reasons for belief.*[1]

1. Objectivity

Given what I have argued so far, the demand for objectivity might appear to set too high a bar for rationality. Doesn't objectivity require precisely the kind of impersonal certainty that I have consistently argued is beyond us? But just as I am arguing that we need a more modest conception of rationality, so our concept of objectivity must not be so austere as to be beyond us. As it happens, we have already available just the kind of realistic conception of objectivity we need, one developed by Thomas Nagel.[2]

Nagel describes an unattainable ideal of objectivity as the tautological 'view from nowhere'. Described as such, its impossibility is self-evident, but of course it is not always so conceived. Objectivity has been more typically described as taking a 'God's eye view', which is not obviously paradoxical, even though it is so heavily metaphorical that it is not at all clear what a literal translation of the idea would look like.

The most credible version of the kind of strong objectivity Nagel rejects does away with the metaphor of 'views' or 'perspectives'. An objective fact or account would be one that was true for anyone at any time, regardless of what particular perspective on the universe they take. Perhaps the most ambitious human attempt to express such objective truths are the gold-anodised aluminium plaques sent on two Pioneer spacecraft in 1972 and 1973. These were the first human-made machines to be sent beyond the solar system. The idea was that if the craft were intercepted by aliens, the plaques would enable them to understand who we are and where we came from.

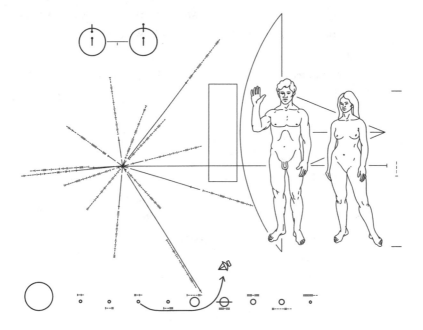

The designers of the plaque were trying to find what Bernard Williams called 'concepts and styles of representation which are minimally dependent on our own or any other creature's peculiar ways of apprehending the world',[3] and hence to communicate in a truly objective way. Human language wouldn't do, since it would be incomprehensible even to aliens who had oral and written languages like ours, let alone any that communicated in different, perhaps unimaginable ways. So instead, they settled on images, diagrams and mathematics. A man and woman were pictured, along with a schematic map of the universe and a diagram representing the hyperfine transition of the hydrogen atom. Binary numbers accompanied the diagrams.

The reasoning behind this was that, however different aliens might be from us, if intelligent, they must be familiar with hydrogen, the most abundant element in the universe, and they must also have some conception of mathematics, which appears to be fundamental to understanding nature. Although they may have different ways of representing these things, there must be a strong chance that they would be able to make sense of our entirely schematic representations of them.

Whether aliens could make sense of the plaques is moot. The question as to why they would know raising an open palm is a symbol of welcome is only the most obvious problem. The diagram of the universe, for example, includes an arrow. The meaning of this appears so self-evident to us that we forget that its ubiquity today depends entirely on the fact that it was initially recognisable as an analogue of the real arrows of hunters. The idea that any species would understand a mark such as '→' to be a directional pointer without this human history seems baseless. There is nothing which makes '→' more objectively a pointer than '1', '!' or 'Y'. Even more fundamentally, why should we assume that aliens would know that the visual markers were important at all? If they did not have eyes, they might not even notice what to us seems obviously to be 'on' the plaque.

Still, although we might have failed to come up with a truly objective way of communicating, isn't the information on the plaque still a decent shot at objectivity? After all, hydrogen is the most fundamental element in the universe and mathematics is universal. There are two problems with this response. First of all, it is really difficult to be completely confident about what the most objective view of the universe will look like. With hydrogen, for example, we already know that elements are far from the most fundamental building blocks. Who knows whether to an advanced civilisation dividing matter (another concept they may have done away with) according to elements is as primitive and misguided as dividing the human body up into the four humours of black bile, yellow bile, phlegm and blood?

Second, there is a sense in which this is beside the point. Even if the truths we latch on to are indeed objective, they are always framed within our human ways of understanding, by our language and our senses. This means even objective truths are never conceived in their pure, objective state, but always as seen through the human lens. Truth has to be seen from *some* perspective or other, even if it is in itself purely objective.

But rather than despair that this makes absolute objectivity unattainable, we should rather ask whether it makes sense to talk of something less than absolute objectivity. This is where Nagel's account comes in. For Nagel, knowledge does not divide neatly between the either/or of 'objective' and 'subjective'. Rather, there is a spectrum, with absolute objectivity and subjectivity at opposite ends, and degrees of each in between.

Our understanding is subjective to the extent that it depends on idiosyncratic features of our viewpoint, reasoning, conceptual framework or senses. It becomes more objective the less it depends on these factors and the closer it gets to the unachievable 'view from nowhere'. The value of objectivity is that it takes us away from subjective viewpoints which are more partial, both in the sense of reflecting our biases and preferences and in the sense of invoking a more limited range of reasons and experiences. Understood in this way, we can see how the Pioneer plaques did represent knowledge that was not merely human understanding but had a high degree of objectivity. Perhaps we did not put it in such an objective form that all aliens could comprehend it, but at least they did not need to be human to have a chance of understanding it. So both the content and the means of expression of the plaque achieved a high degree of objectivity.

That is the notion of objectivity we need to use when we say that rational argument is the giving of objective reasons for belief. It entails appealing to reasons which do not depend on others sharing our own particular perspectives in order for them to have force. It does not mean appealing to reasons which are of such a form that any intelligence anywhere would be able to see their force.

One thing that is worth noting at this point is that 'objective' is often taken to be synonymous with, or at least implying, 'true'. This is a mistake. To say an account, reason or observation is objective or subjective is to say something about its character, not its truth value. I can report a fact about my subjective experience truly – for instance, that I perceive a sound to be yellow – and I can report an objective fact falsely, such as the distance between two planets. The degree of objectivity a claim has relates only to the extent to which it does not require a particular perspective to be understood. That is why it is right that we talk of 'objective truths' or 'objective facts' and don't merely say that statements are 'objective'.

Rationality and objectivity are usually seen as natural bedfellows. My suggestion is that their link is more intimate than this. To offer a rational argument just is to provide objective reasons for belief, reasons which can include both evidence and argumentative moves. This is a deliberately catholic definition of rationality. It allows that an argument can be rational but can fail, which is surely right: there is a difference between someone who argues irrationally and one who argues rationally but makes mistakes. It is also broad enough to encapsulate both reason's deductive and non-deductive aspects, and to appeal to those who think rational argument aims at truth and to those who think there is no such thing as The Truth. I'll say more about this towards the end of this chapter. First I need to say more about how we recognise those reasons and arguments that are objective. I would argue that they have five key characteristics. They are comprehensible, assessable, defeasible, interest-neutral and compelling.

2. Five characteristics of the objective

(i) Comprehensibility

Art appreciation is usually thought of as quintessentially subjective. Nonetheless, some judgements are clearly more objective than others. Consider, for example, how we might respond to Goya's painting *Perro semihundido* (Half-submerged Dog). You could say things such as 'I like it' or 'It makes me feel sad'. These comments don't tell me anything about the work. If I share your reactions then your remarks just happen to describe how I feel too, but if I don't they only tell me about how you are feeling. But if I push you, you might say more. You could point to the dog's eyes and how it seems to express a kind of resigned helplessness, a sense heightened by the way in which the huge wave dominates the picture. You might muse on how depicting a dog deepens the pathos, since we are being made in some sense aware of the helplessness of all living creatures in the face of nature.

In comments like this we get nowhere near to perfect objectivity. Many people would still find themselves unilluminated. Nonetheless, there is clearly a move towards greater objectivity in such remarks. The characteristic feature of objectivity is that it moves from a particular viewpoint to a more general one, one that can be shared. The move from reporting a purely personal reaction to describing features of the work itself and explaining why they provoke such reactions is one such move from the individual to the more general. One key feature of this move is that the terms of explanation offered in the more objective account are in principle comprehensible by more rational agents than are those in a subjective account.

To take another example, a physics which is in principle compre-hensible by Martians who lack the typical sensory apparatus of humans is more objective than one that depends upon a specifically human way of experiencing the world. I would conjecture that this kind of increased comprehensibility is a constitutive feature of rational argument. An argument that is in principle comprehensible by any rational agent is more rational than one that is comprehen-sible only by certain types of rational agent.

This is not to be confused with clarity or difficulty. Theoretical physics is one of the most objective sciences we have, but it is mysti-fying to the layperson and extremely hard to grasp. To say something is 'in principle' comprehensible is not to say everyone has the intel-ligence, knowledge or application to understand it. 'In principle' here means that there are no obstacles to understanding other than intelligence, knowledge and application, obstacles that in the real world might indeed prevent many from ever understanding.

If we think about how we use the term objective more widely, we can see that comprehensibility is at the heart of it. Inspection and assessment of schools and businesses is one clear example. Inspection can be defended as objective when it is perfectly clear to everyone what the criteria are and how they have been assessed. It can be criticised as subjective when there is no way of really knowing what could be done to get a higher mark or avoid being docked points. All other things being equal, the more comprehensible any description or explanation is, the more objective it is.

(ii) Assessability

Comprehensibility is the most basic characteristic of the objective. However, it is not enough that a rational argument is comprehensible by any rational agent. It must also be assessable. If there is no way in principle that others could judge the truth of what is claimed, it remains in the domain of the subjective. As Michael Lynch puts it, objectivity 'is a matter of openness to evaluation from a common point of view.'[4]

This is in a sense an extension of the criterion of comprehensibility. Think again of the example of inspection. Criteria like 'cleanliness' or 'good record keeping' are clear enough for us to understand what they mean in general, but to truly understand them in context you must know how to judge whether they have been met. Knowing how to assess whether the conditions have been met is part and parcel of understanding what the conditions are.

But there are times when we have comprehensibility without assessability. This is one reason why the kind of art appreciation I discussed only reaches a limited degree of objectivity. If I just don't see resignation in the dog's eyes, for instance, there is no way of assessing whether I am wrong or you are projecting emotions that aren't there. My judgements are objective to the extent that they can be understood, but less objective than other kinds of judgement to the extent that there is no clear way of assessing their validity.

There is an another important link between assessability and comprehensibility. One key feature of any objective account is that everything in it is out in the open. Whenever people appeal to inner convictions, esoteric revelations or diktats from authorities they are evading objective scrutiny by keeping key elements of their justification hidden. To give an objective account requires you to hide nothing. This means making your evidence and arguments open to the closest possible examination, in terms that make sure that they can be both understood and assessed by any rational agent.

It might be objected that in invoking the concept of a rational agent in my explanation of what rationality is I am guilty of arguing in a circle. To some extent this is true, but the circularity is not vicious. A rational agent is one who can understand and assess objective arguments, and an objective argument is rational if it can be understood and assessed. These terms all hang together. Words can only be defined using other words, so definitions always end up going round in circles. What one person criticises as circularity another accepts as the holism of language.

The idea that anyone ought to be able to assess claims to objective truth has been a deep assumption of Western philosophy since its origins in ancient Greece. What distinguishes philosophical claims from theological ones is that the philosopher making them does not do so by appeal to any authority other than that of the evidence and arguments themselves. However, it has proven extremely difficult to specify in more detail exactly what distinguishes the assessable from the unassessable. David Hume managed to divide the assessable up 'into two kinds, to wit, Relations of Ideas, and Matters of Fact'. Relations of ideas are 'the sciences of Geometry, Algebra, and Arithmetic', to which we might add formal logic. Claims within these disciplines can be shown to be 'either intuitively or demonstratively certain'.[5] Matters of fact, on the other hand, are shown to be true by experience. Hume, however, says little about how we show this, being mainly concerned with the question of how we establish the relation of cause and effect, upon which 'all reasonings concerning matter of fact seem to be founded'.

In the early twentieth century, attempts were made to come up with a more robust test for what might pass as a genuine matter of fact, rather than of mere speculation. The so-called logical positivists of the Vienna Circle proposed various versions of the principle of verification, according to which propositions are only meaningful if there is some empirical method of demonstrating their truth. Assessability is thus cashed out as provability. Karl Popper would later come up with a mirror-image alternative according to which hypotheses are scientific if there is some way of testing them such that failing to pass the test would falsify them.

Verificationism and falsificationism both failed, largely because they were seen as self-defeating. There is no way to verify the principle of verification or to falsify the principle of falsification. Therefore by their own criteria they are meaningless or unscientific respectively. However, in rejecting these attempts to put more flesh on the notion of assessability we must not throw out its vitally important bones. Both verificationism and falsification overreached, but they were reaching in the right direction.

A.J. Ayer, who brought his version of logical positivism to Britain, shows how close the school got to the nub of the issue. In the preface to *Language, Truth and Logic*, he wrote 'I require of an empirical hypothesis not that it should be conclusively verifiable, but that some possible sense experience should be relevant to the determination of its truth or falsehood. If a putative proposition fails to satisfy this principle, and is not a tautology, then I hold that it is metaphysical and that it is neither true nor false but literally senseless.'[6] (In the context of British empiricism at the time, we need to understand 'sense experience' as including all empirical evidence gathered from the sciences, which were understood ultimately to rest on observations dependent on sense experience.)

The demand of an empirical hypothesis 'that some possible sense experience should be relevant to the determination of its truth or falsehood' is an extremely modest one, far short of the demand for verification or falsification. Had Ayer stuck with this modesty, he would not have got into the terminal difficulties that mean *Language, Truth and Logic* is now largely ignored, an increasingly rare sight on undergraduate reading lists. But at the same time, the right modesty would also have meant that the book would never have created a storm on publication, making its author one of the pre-eminent philosophers of his generation for the rest of his life.

Ayer's central mistake was to think that his principle could distinguish between the meaningful and meaningless. This error has two parts. First, a better distinction would be between the objective and subjective. If I say to you that a piece of music, for example, makes me feel like I am floating on air, there may be no way for you to verify or falsify that claim. But that doesn't make it meaningless. It simply makes it subjective.

The second part of the mistake is to make the distinction binary where it should be spectral. If you accept that what makes a claim meaningful (or objective) is 'that some possible sense experience should be relevant to the determination of its truth or falsehood', then it should be obvious that you are not going to be able to draw a sharp line between those claims which meet this test and those that don't. Even if you could determine a threshold, it would still be the case that some claims are easily settled by sense experience, while for others evidence is relevant to assessing its truth but cannot determine it.

Ayer found himself caught in a classic philosophical predicament. If an idea is too vague it will be dismissed as woolly and hand-waving. Too precise, however, and the logic-choppers will be out to unpick its contradictions and inconsistencies. As Aristotle's immortal adage states, 'It is the mark of the trained mind never to expect more precision in the treatment of any subject than the nature of that subject permits' – nor less, we might add. The Goldilocks state of philosophy is to be precise enough to be saying something substantive but not so precise as to ride roughshod over the complexities and ambiguities of the real world.

Do we have this 'just right' understanding of assessability? For my purposes, I think we do. As I will argue in more detail shortly, the conception of rationality I am putting forward here is a minimal one, and in that sense its key terms are place-holders for various more precise ones which different schools might fill out. Furthermore, I have not so much argued that claims to objective truth must be assessable as invited us to attend to the nature of objectivity and notice that it has this feature. It is not for me to legislate here how exactly rational arguments are to be assessed. But it should be obvious that an argument cannot be rational if there is no way of assessing it at all. The only *a priori* restriction on the types of assessability that are admissible is that they should be methods of assessment which are in principle employable by any rational agent.

(iii) Defeasibility

Popper also got close to the truth with his principle of falsification. Once again, however, the mistake was to over-specify something which, if stated in more general terms, should be uncontroversial.

Popper's central insight, still widely accepted by scientists today, is that if a hypothesis is genuinely scientific then other scientists must be able to conduct experiments to test it. These experiments might not be able to prove beyond all doubt that the theory is correct, but there are possible experimental results which would show that it is false. To give a simple example, the hypothesis that you cannot transform base metal into gold can never be decisively verified by repeated failures to achieve just this transformation. An experiment that did turn lead into gold, however, would show it to be false.

As a mark of a rational argument, falsification has various problems. First of all, Popper intended it as a criterion for demarcating between science and non-science. So even if the principle works, it does not allow us to to distinguish between the rational and the non-rational, unless we make the further claim that the only form of rational discourse is the scientific one. This is impossible, since such a claim would not be a scientific claim but a philosophical one, and so would be self-refuting.

Second, it is unclear that all scientific claims are actually falsifiable. Hilary Putnam, for example, has argued that 'The Law of Universal Gravitation is not strongly falsifiable at all; yet it is surely a paradigm of scientific theory.'[7] How can this be so? For Popper, falsifiability is possible because theories imply predictions, and we can see if these predictions are borne out or not. For example, Einstein's theory of general relativity predicted that light does not travel in a perfectly straight line. On 29 May 1919, Arthur Eddington performed an experiment during a total solar eclipse to test this. The Astronomer Royal, Frank Watson Dyson, had realised that the sun would cross the Hyades star cluster during the eclipse, and so the light from these stars would have to pass through the sun's gravitational field, which Einstein's theory predicted would bend their course. Because of the eclipse, however, they would be visible. By comparing the apparent position of the stars at this moment with their true position, Eddington was able to show that the light had indeed bent.

But had the experiment not detected the bending, would this have disproved Einstein's theory? Other failures to confirm predictions in the history of science suggest not. Often experiments do contradict existing findings, but they are not automatically assumed to disprove them. The possibility often remains open that there was something wrong in the experimental design or that some false assumptions have been made. Putnam cites the example of the orbit of Mercury, which was not completely explained by Newton's theory. But this did not lead to Newton's theories being rejected. Rather, Mercury was set aside as an anomaly. This kind of toleration of unexplained anomalies is not untypical in science.

According to Putnam, one reason for this is that 'Theories do not imply predictions' in the straightforward way Popper believed. 'It is only the conjunction of theory with certain "auxiliary statements" (A.S.) that, in general, implies a prediction,' he says. This means 'we cannot regard a false prediction as definitively falsifying a theory' since there is always some uncertainty of the status of the auxiliary statements and their link with the theory being tested.

As with assessability and verification, we need to make sure we do not throw out the baby with the bathwater, the baby in this instance being *defeasibility*. A rational argument is always in principle defeasible – open to revision or rejection – by public criteria of argument and evidence. I think this is just a corollary of the criteria of comprehensibility and assessability. To give a rational argument is to say that others can understand and assess it, and this leaves open the possibility that their assessment might be negative or that their understanding might be superior to one's own. It certainly seems contrary to the spirit of rational inquiry to rule out the possibility that what one has decided is true could not possibly be false. And even if there were some indefeasible rational arguments, they would form a very narrow set of non-empirical *a priori* tenets.

Defeasibility is a property of all propositions with any degree of objectivity, however small. Think, for instance, of someone who insists that Goya's *Perro semihundido* was the greatest painting of the nineteenth century. Such a person could reasonably maintain that this is just a matter of opinion and is not intended as an objective claim. Nonetheless, if they accept that there is any sense at all in which the claim rests on some objective judgements about the work, it would be indefensible to make it indefeasible. At the every least one should be open to the possibility of being persuaded that another work is superior. Whenever any claim involves something that is assessable by others as well as ourselves, we ought to keep it open to refutation or revision, no matter how certain we are that something is true, no matter how impossible we find it to imagine its refutation.

(iv) Interest-neutrality

Imagine a deranged super-villain who is on a mission to defeat the forces of rationality. He kidnaps a philosopher and is determined to make her sincerely believe something irrational. So he says that he will destroy the Earth unless she is able to say with sincerity that $1 + 1 = 3$ and pass a lie detector test while doing so. Our philosopher thinks hard and realises that there are in fact assessable, comprehensible and defeasible reasons for her to believe that $1 + 1 = 3$, since believing this is the only way to save the universe. Do we not then here have objective reasons to believe something that is false? And given that I define rational argument as the giving of objective reasons for belief, does that not also mean that there can be rational arguments to believe something false?

The question is likely to provoke contradictory responses. On the one hand, it does seem undeniable that in such circumstances it is rational to believe a falsehood – if you can make yourself do so. On the other, it might seem equally undeniable that rational arguments ought to lead us towards the truth, rather than to what is merely expedient.

The tension is resolved by attending to an ambiguity in the notion of rationality. Rationality can be used in the service of an end or as an end in itself. Call the former kind practical rationality. If our kidnapped philosopher has a desire, interest or value which favours the universe continuing to exist, then it is in an important sense rational for her to (at least try to) believe sincerely that $1 + 1 = 3$. But we can easily see that this kind of practical rational ground for belief is very different from the usual rational grounds for believing that $1 + 1 = 2$. It does not provide a rational argument to believe that $1 + 1 = 3$, but a rational argument why it is *prudent to believe* $1 + 1 = 3$. Because such practical reasons appeal to our desires, values and interests, they are less objective than ones which make no reference to the particular interests, values and desires of living creatures.

Practical rationality, which involves what we ought to believe, given our goals and values, can therefore be contrasted with what I'm going to call *epistemic rationality*, which solely involves what we ought to believe if we set aside our goals and values. Epistemic rationality needs more than assessable, comprehensible and defeasible reasons for belief; it also needs its reasons to be interest-neutral. Any reasons which appeal to what people desire are not interest-neutral, since they only have any purchase if we think that people's desires are a reason for doing something.

This interest-neutrality of rational argument is central, since the whole point of a rational argument is that it does not resist brute reality and cannot be bent at will. This does not imply any metaphysical commitments concerning the real existence of an external physical world. (In fact, it is essential that our conception of rationality is free from such commitments, since it is by means of rational argument that we attempt to determine which metaphysical stance it is appropriate to take.) Accepting the resistance of an objective, rational account of the world to our will is simply a precondition for any rational inquiry into the nature of that world, whatever its ultimate nature.

Although the demands of practical rationality might ultimately conflict with those of epistemic rationality, it is important to notice that practical rationality rests on epistemic rationality. Consider our kidnapped philosopher again. In order to conclude that from a practical point of view she ought to believe that $1 + 1 = 3$, it is important that all the data she uses to base this conclusion on are supported by the proper use of epistemic rationality. In other words, her reasons for believing that the villain will blow up the world and that she must pass the lie detector test must be of such a kind that any rational agent should accept them. In order to make the right decision, she must assess the evidence in an interest-neutral way, and only then decide what she ought to do in order to serve the interests she takes to be most important. In this case, that means taking the survival of the planet as being more important than preserving a small corner of true belief.

We can now see clearly why the apparent paradox that it can sometimes be rational to believe what is irrational is no paradox at all. A better description is that it can sometimes be practically rational to believe what is epistemically irrational, because epistemic rationality is interest-neutral but practical rationality is not. But it cannot be stressed enough that practical rationality is not an entirely different system. Practical rationality must work on the basis of epistemic rationality.

Having made the distinction, I want to set aside practical rationality and continue to discuss rationality on the assumption that we are talking about the epistemic kind. There is a lot of skepticism these days about the possibility that rationality can be interest-neutral. Perhaps most influential here has been Michel Foucault, who argued that truth and power were intimately linked. To get the full sense of what this means, 'truth' needs to be put in inverted commas, as Foucault himself did when trying to sum up the basic proposition he was putting forward: ' "truth" is linked in a circular relation with systems of power which produce and sustain it, and to effects of powers which it induces and which extend it.' On this understanding, 'truth' cannot be detached from relations of power and so has no neutral meaning: 'It's not a matter of emancipating truth from every system of power (which would be a chimera, for truth is already power), but of detaching the power of truth from the forms of hegemony, social, economic, and cultural, within which it operates at the present time.'[8]

There is surely an important insight here that Foucault is trying to grasp. It is certainly true that whenever we see people claiming to present disinterested knowledge we should ask whether this is not in fact ideology disguised as empiricism, value in the guise of fact. The state will use the claim that something is scientific, for example, as a justification for a policy that suits its ideology. But it does not follow that whenever you see something claimed to be knowledge, you will always find someone using that knowledge claim as a means of exerting power. The idea that claims to disinterested fact are often no such thing is not the same as the claim that there is no such thing as a disinterested fact. Whenever thinkers have tried to go this far, they have always ended up in absurdity. Luce Irigaray, for instance, notoriously suggested that perhaps even $E = mc^2$ is a 'sexed equation', expressing masculine dominance. Why?

Because 'it privileges the speed of light over other speeds that are vitally necessary to us'.[9] But the fact is that scientists, East and West, male and female, all have equally good reasons to accept the equation. This is interest-neutral science, pure and simple. As the physicists Alan Sokal and Jean Bricmont put with almost comical plainness, 'Whatever one may think about "the other speeds that are vitally necessary to us", the fact remains that the relationship $E = mc^2$ between energy (E) and mass (M) is experimentally verified to a high degree of precision, and it would obviously not be valid if the speed of light (c) were replaced by another speed'.[10]

A common retort to this is to say that the practice of science is never value-neutral, because at the very least there will be decisions about what to focus research on – whether to spend money flying people to Mars or curing breast cancer. But this claim that there is no such thing as the value-free practice of science is an importantly different claim to the one that there are no value-free scientific truths. A scientist may well be led by ideology to investigate the harmful effects of pesticides on human health, but if she is a good scientist, and if her findings are corroborated by others, the truths she discovers can still be value-free.

Tim Lewens provides a very clear example of this. He argues that Marx and Engels were correct when they claimed that Darwin's thought was 'steeped in the industrial capitalist milieu' that surrounded him. But that did not invalidate his conclusions. 'What matters is not, in this case, whether Darwin's views are influenced by his bourgeois ideology, but whether that ideology acts to distort, or to reveal, the workings of the natural world.'[11]

The key distinctions here are very simple but so often overlooked. The following four statements are equally true and entirely compatible.

Many value-laden beliefs are presented as disinterested truths for purposes of ideology and power.

Disinterested knowledge is often used to promote value-laden ends.

The practice of science is value-laden.

Rational argument requires the giving of reasons which are
interest-neutral.

To deny that interest-neutral reasons for belief exist ends up in
either absurdity or emptiness. It is absurd if it means that, for
example, there is no fact of the matter about how far one point on a
map is from another. It is empty if it simply means that every time
we assert a fact, we must also be asserting some kind of value,
such that we desire the truth, or that we think it is important to know
the distance between two points on a map. Of course values
and interests infuse how we live and how we think. But that does not
mean values and interests permeate the content of every knowledge
claim.

(v) Compulsion

It is, however, more than possible to have a weak argument that
offers assessable, comprehensible, defeasible and interest-neutral
reasons for believing X. For the argument to have objective force it
must in some way be *compelling*. Turned over and examined on all
sides, any rational agent who understands the argument should find
herself feeling forced – or at least strongly pushed – to accept the
conclusion, whether she likes it or not. Furthermore, this compulsion should be a consequence only of the kind of features of the
argument already set out: i.e. the assessable, comprehensible and
interest-neutral ones. If something else, such as personal incredulity
or wishful thinking, makes someone feel compelled to believe something, then this is not the kind of compulsion which is to be sought
in a rational argument.

This idea is captured in the notion that a strong argument
carries *objective weight*. In using the term 'objective' here, we are
reporting the sense that the force of the argument comes from somewhere outside ourselves. And the metaphor of 'weight' captures the

sense we have that something other is placing a burden on us to accept it.

This is plain enough, and evident in any example of a good objective argument. When you understand that 1 + 1 = 2, for example, you realise that you can't but accept it as true. When you accept the evidence that, say, smoking is a major cause of lung cancer, you feel that you must accept the argument, not that you are choosing to do so of your own free will.

It is, however, very difficult to explain just what makes an argument compelling in this sense. Any explanation is likely to be somewhat circular, although, as I have argued before, this needn't be vicious. In this case, we can see that the idea of compulsion is a necessary corollary of the other features of rational argument. If you can see that an argument is assessable by all, and that assessment has not raised any major problems with it; if you also understand it; and if you can see that it does not require you to share any particular agent's interests to accept it: such an argument must carry with it a certain degree of force.

There is a sense here in which there is simply nothing left for a rational agent to say to someone who claims to have followed all these steps but is still not convinced. Take the smoking example. Imagine someone saying, 'Yes, I can see the evidence. I clearly understand it. I know how to assess it and I see nothing wrong with it. I can also see that the case does not require you to have any kind of personal interest in the destruction of the tobacco industry. But I'm not convinced.' In such a case you would be justified in concluding that the person was just not being rational. Whatever was stopping the person from feeling the force of the argument, it wasn't reason. The fact that there is nothing left to say to such a person could be seen as dispiriting, but it is not realistic to suppose that we can always make a case for reason or a reasoned case that everyone is bound to accept. If someone is not rational, no rational argument that they ought to be is going to work. It's like trying to convince someone with no taste buds that something is delicious by getting them to taste it.

To understand the particular character of what we might call this 'rational force', it is worth distinguishing it from 'psychological force'. In one sense, rational force is of course psychological: it is something we experience in the mind. But there is a specific sense of psychological force which is a little different. This is the sense in which we find ourselves strongly inclined to believe something and to act accordingly. This is often in spite of or even contrary to what we can also see has rational force.

The smoking example is again helpful here. The person I have described simply doesn't feel the rational force of the argument that smoking causes lung cancer. More common, however, is the person for whom the rational force just doesn't translate into psychological force. Such a person understands fully that smoking is very bad for her health and that she ought to give up, but for any number of reasons, although she sees that the rational argument for giving up is compelling, it does not move her to do anything about it. The compulsion remains purely rational and does not have any psychological effect, in this particular sense of the term.

This kind of distinction seems to be extremely common when it comes to moral philosophy. I know many people who claim that they find the rational argument for ethical vegetarianism unanswerable, but they still don't feel inclined to give up meat. Similarly, many are persuaded by utilitarian arguments of the kind offered by Peter Singer, arguing that we ought to give up almost all our wealth, and yet rational conviction does not translate into psychological motivation.

These examples are clear enough, I think, to point us towards the phenomenological character of the kind of rational compulsion I am describing here. It is a very specific sense that an argument is unanswerable, or that a reason has no defeating counter-reason, a sense which is independent of any desire or inclination we might have to use the argument or reason as the basis of action. To be rational entails having the ability to recognise that a rational argument has conclusions that are in some sense demanded by it, not merely invited.

3. The boundaries of the rational

As a way of both testing and illustrating how this account of the objectivity of rationality works, it is worth looking at two examples of forms of understanding that stand at best on the fringes and at worst outside the domain of the rational: anecdotal evidence and mysticism.

To say that the evidence for something is 'merely anecdotal' is to dismiss it as inadequate. For that reason, few explicitly claim to base their beliefs on anecdotal evidence. In practice, however, that is exactly what many people do. This is perhaps clearest in the case of homeopathy. There has been much research into the efficacy of homeopathy and the overwhelming scientific consensus is that it just doesn't work. And yet, as I am soon reminded whenever I write or talk about this topic, many otherwise sensible, intelligent people remain convinced that it does. None believe that their convictions rest on blind faith. All offer reasons for belief, and in so doing they purport to place their claims in the domain of the rational.

These reasons tend to be of three sorts. First, there are those of personal experience. 'I have seen how much people have benefited by the care and expertise of homeopathic doctors' is a typical testimony. Second, there are claims of impressive historical successes. Pre-eminent in the lore of homeopathy is the Soho cholera epidemic of 1854, where victims who were admitted to the London Homoeopathic Hospital had a mortality rate of 16%, compared to 53% for those who ended up at the Middlesex Hospital. Finally, they will cite selected studies.

We can see why these reasons deserve to be considered as attempts to provide a rational case for the efficacy of homeopathy. They appear to be comprehensible and assessable, and in turn defeasible. Those who offer them also see them as interest-neutral and compelling. We should reject them, however, because when we examine these supposed characteristics more carefully, they are not present to a sufficient degree.

Assessability is the key here. Claims are made which appear to be assessable, but when they are indeed properly assessed, they fail the test. Obviously, a claim such as 'I have seen how much people have benefited by the care and expertise of homeopathic doctors' is not in itself assessable as it is a first-person report. It becomes assessable if it is supplemented by the likes of 'and you too could see this for yourself if you bothered to look', which is the usual follow-up. But of course one cannot know anything about the efficacy of a medical treatment merely by first-person observations. You need proper trials which compare outcomes using different treatments. So the claim to have 'seen for myself' turns out either to be unassessable after all, or merely a pointer towards proper research.

The appeal to historical examples is flawed in the same way. The statistics concerning the two hospitals in 1854 may well be correct, but we cannot know whether this provides any good reason to believe homeopathic treatments were the cause of the difference unless we know the full circumstances. In this case, it has been suggested by Ben Goldacre that the homeopathic hospital probably did better because it simply did no harm, while the interventions such as blood-letting practised elsewhere only made matters worse.[12] This may or may not be correct, but the mere presentation of the different death rates by itself does not provide properly assessable data.

So we are left with studies, and these overwhelmingly show homeopathy to be no better than placebos. If you look at the evidence against the efficacy of homeopathy, it is rationally compelling. Those who argue otherwise look guilty of approaching the evidence in a non-interest-neutral way, selecting those studies which are favourable and rejecting those that are not. Their reluctance to back down when other reasons are shown to be lacking also suggests, although it does not prove, that they do not see their reasons as genuinely defeasible at all.

This explanation for why we should not accept the purported reasons in favour of homeopathy's efficacy shows how the account of rationality I have offered provides a framework for distinguishing what we should rationally accept and reject. But crucially, it also shows why it is often unhelpful and inaccurate to accuse opposing parties in an argument of irrationality. The homeopathic community tries to make rational arguments but fails. It does not argue in a way which is inherently irrational, it simply fails to provide arguments that are compelling when assessed in an interest-neutral way. We should distinguish between arguments in two ways. To say they are rational or irrational is to describe their mode; to say they are good or bad is to distinguish them by their quality.

A second kind of argument is one based on what we can broadly call mystical experience. To give a simple example, there are those who claim to have achieved some form of knowledge by the use of LSD that the self is not real. Others claim to have seen the world 'as it really is'. I think such arguments are inherently non-rational. They are interest-neutral, in that there seems no reason to think that they are motivated by prior commitments or self-interest. They might seem to be assessable because anyone can take LSD and see for him- or herself whether this is true. But they are not properly assessable because they are not properly comprehensible. The nature of such experiences is that they cannot be adequately described: you have to 'be there'. So even the terms used to describe the claims made are taken to be imperfect proxies for a more direct kind of knowledge or insight. This makes them profoundly non-objective. An alien with a different brain chemistry, for example, would not be able to access the same state or thereby assess it.

Nor do such claims appear to be properly defeasible, in that people who have the experiences swear that they have seen the truth and are not open to being persuaded otherwise by rational argument, which they think fails to capture the experience. Finally, the reasons they offer for their conclusions are compelling only in the psychological sense. They are not rationally compelling because no rational reasons are given for them.

That does not mean that we can therefore conclude that mystical experiences provide no reasons for belief. The conclusion is the more modest one that they provide no *rational* reasons for belief. It remains an open question whether there are any good non-rational reasons for belief we should accept. But if there are, the case needs to be made.

4. Rational catholicism

I have argued that judgement is required at every level to construct or analyse a rational argument. But to say judgement is required is not a vague way of saying that everything is up for grabs or down to personal inclination. A rational argument must meet certain standards of objectivity. These standards ensure that judgement does not have free rein but plays a very specific role, providing a way to distinguish between arguments that are non-rational, such as those that are based on mystical experience, and those which are rational in form but fail to meet the standards of a good rational argument, such as those for the efficacy of homeopathy.

This account of rationality also explains why it is natural to see logical arguments as the paradigms of rationality. When an argument is set out in explicit logical steps it becomes clearly comprehensible and assessable, which also ensures it is defeasible. And if the premises are correct, that gives an interest-neutral reason to accept the force of the conclusion. But the fact that formal deductive arguments most clearly pass the test for rationality does not mean that no other form of argument does. Deduction does not define rationality, it merely exemplifies its virtues more clearly than is usually possible.

This view of rationality has important consequences for our conception of what reason is. It shows how it is possible to abandon the idea that we can arrive at the truth by appeal to objective facts and logic alone, without necessarily embracing total relativism, since the strong constraints on the requirements for objective rational arguments severely limit the range of possible rational accounts we can give of the world. It suggests that good judgement is much more than just opinion, and something less than the mere following of logical rules.

This conception of rationality might help us to explain some otherwise puzzling features of rational discourse in general, and philosophy in particular. In general terms, we might call this *the catholicism of rational discourse*. In every department of a typical university, we see rational inquiry. And yet the methods and assumptions of the different disciplines vary enormously. Sometimes, these differences can appear to mark fundamental disagreement about the nature of rationality. Some belligerent scientists, for instance, insist that anything being done in the arts and humanities which is not based on the empirical methods of science is just nonsense.

I think that, on the whole, these divisions are at least in part a product not of a different conception of rationality but of different judgements about what kinds of reasons satisfy the requirements of rationality. So, for instance, a lot of natural scientists think that only empirical scientific data are clear, assessable and interest-neutral enough to provide the basis for a compelling argument. Others would say that there are important questions which cannot be settled by scientific means, and that we ought to look for the strongest reasons to determine the answers to these that we can find. Such disagreements are inevitable, since what counts as an objective reason for belief in the end depends in part on judgement.

Similar divisions are found within disciplines, such as philosophy. Take that between those who see philosophy as being continuous with natural science and those who do not. Here again, the distinction can be seen to cut across a common conception of rationality. Put simply, the former are much more impressed by natural science than the latter and therefore believe that our most objective reasons for belief are grounded in natural science. If this is so, then there may often be no deep disagreement between the two camps about the nature of philosophy. This might also help account for why philosophers in both the 'analytic' and 'Continental' schools are basically doing philosophy but why, nonetheless, they sometimes appear to be doing quite different things. So it is not that there are different fundamental conceptions of rationality at work, it is rather that each tradition places emphasis on different elements of the rational toolkit.

Accepting the catholicism of rational discourse also means keeping our positions on substantive issues in philosophy separate from our position on the nature of reason, broadly construed. That is why my account has not tried to give any substantive account of what it ultimately means for anything to be true. In particular, when talking about objectivity I did not talk about the way things are independently of how we view them, as that would commit me to a kind of metaphysical realism. Nor do I describe true statements as those which correctly describe the world. My account of rationality solely concerns the process of reasoning. To be truly catholic it has to be thus constrained, or else it could not claim to describe the way in which even people with wildly different substantive views reason.

There is another odd feature of philosophy that I think my account helps to explain. That is how it is both the most rigorous discipline in its employment of arguments and yet one of the most indeterminate in respect of its findings. Consensus is omni-absent in philosophy yet the arguments of philosophers are among the most rationally rigorous in the humanities or the sciences.

I think my account helps makes sense of this because it shows how rationality is highly rigorous both in its demand for objective reasons for belief and in the way deductive logic is one of its most powerful tools. But unlike data in the natural sciences, the raw data of philosophy is not quantifiable data from empirical experiment. It is rather the whole of human experience. Philosophy also lacks the settled, agreed methods of a science that enable consensus. Philosophy, then, relies entirely on rationality and nothing but. This involves a high degree of commitment to the rigours of argument but also, ultimately, an acceptance that rational argument does not lead linearly to only one answer, since you cannot take judgement away from rationality. Our reliance on rationality as our sole resource makes us both rigorous thinkers and condemned ultimately to use our own best judgement.

Understanding how it is that philosophy demands the rigour of rational argument, but that rational argument itself demands the use of judgement, therefore helps us understand why it is that philosophy pushes us so hard intellectually yet cannot compel equally intelligent thinkers to agree. As I suggested at the beginning of this chapter, reason is the kind of guide that helps us find our way, but does not prescribe a single path. Reason is something we use, and while we cannot take it just anywhere without doing violence to it, nor does it simply carry us forward, like a self-driving car.[13]

5. Ending the truth wars

Freud once said, 'intolerance finds stronger expression, strange to say, in regard to small differences than to fundamental ones'.[14] The same point was made, perhaps better, in Monty Python's *Life of Brian*, in which the People's Front of Judea spat blood at the mention of the Judean People's Front and the Judean Popular People's Front.

The problem is that if you look at anything very closely, including ideas and ideals, differences which appear small from the wider perspective suddenly appear very large indeed. And so it should be. It is precisely our ability to examine the objects of intellectual endeavour closely and discern differences invisible to the naked mind's eye which allows us to deepen and extend our learning in the humanities and the sciences.

However, if we never step back and examine the broader picture, we can become blinded to some important features of intellectual life that should be obvious to us. And while intellectual hyperopia gets in the way of first-class, specialised academic work, intellectual myopia is, I would argue, a more pernicious and widespread affliction of intellectual life today.

I have argued that this myopia blinds us to the shared sense in which almost all of us are committed to reason. This affliction has increased the intensity of what Simon Blackburn has called 'The Truth Wars' in his book of the same name. The general history of this conflict has been chronicled many times. First came the Enlightenment, and the championing of reason, truth and science over authority, falsehood and superstition. Then, in the twentieth century, many lost faith with the Enlightenment project. Some, such as Adorno and Horkheimer, went so far as to suggest that Auschwitz was the logical conclusion of the Enlightenment. 'Enlightenment is totalitarian,' they argued, and the 'unconditional realism of civilized humanity' it engendered 'culminates in fascism'.[15]

Reason has been one victim of this backlash, but arguably truth has suffered even more. The result is now a stand-off between what Bernard Williams called the 'deniers' – those who deny that there is such a thing as 'the truth' that reason aims at – and the 'party of common sense', those who claim that the truth really is out there. Williams wrote that 'the deniers and the party of common sense, with their respective styles of philosophy, pass each other by'. This diagnosis is correct. The gulf of mutual comprehension is greater than that of any fundamental difference. What we have here is a case of both sides getting very worked up about what are, in the grand scheme of things, small differences. And as with the freedom of Judea, so here the tragedy is that a greater cause, one that both sides support, is suffering as a consequence of internal divisions. That greater cause is a commitment to reason, no matter what reservations some may have about the history, use and connotations of that term. Despite their apparent differences, it should be obvious that both 'deniers' and the 'party of common sense' share something like the thin conception of reason and rationality that I have been defending.

I think the disagreements over the nature of truth can also be seen as relatively minor. Take as an example where Williams disagrees with his old sparring partner Richard Rorty. Their official disagreement is that Williams thinks there is a thing called the truth, and Rorty doesn't. The real disagreement, however, is essentially that Williams thinks that it *matters* whether or not there is a thing called the truth, whereas Rorty doesn't. Williams thinks it is inconsistent and dangerous to deny that there is a truth; Rorty thinks it pointless and immature to insist that there is. Both Williams and Rorty are committed to what Williams calls the two virtues of truth: sincerity and accuracy. However, Williams thinks that Rorty is just wrong if he thinks he can be committed to the virtues if he is not also committed to the idea of truth.

There are, of course, major disagreements here. And if you are serious about intellectual work, they matter. But it is worth remembering that there is a great deal agreed before the disagreement arises. Being committed to the virtues of sincerity and accuracy is no small matter. For though what that entails in terms of commitment to the truth is highly contentious, what it means with regard to commitment to rationality is, I would argue, much less controversial.

Similarly, although both sides of the debate probably disagree in their thick conceptions of rationality, they will agree on the thin one. You just cannot have a sincere intellectual debate unless you in some sense attempt to provide what I have called objective reasons for belief, even if you refuse to use the word 'objective'.

The debate about whether there is such a thing as the truth is therefore largely a bogus one. Deniers of truth are as quick as anyone else to call out liars, especially in politics, or to feel aggrieved at being libelled or misrepresented. Critics mock them for this, claiming that it shows their denials are insincere. That is a mistake. Their denials are not insincere but *technical*. And the fact that these technicalities might matter some of the time doesn't mean they matter in most ordinary cases. We ought to recognise the 'truth wars' for what they are: a dispute over details.

In our disagreements we sometimes forget that, as a community of rational inquirers, we share many core values. Perhaps we don't like the connotations terms like 'reason' and 'rationality' have, thinking that they suggest a false objectivity or authority. But it is only within the domain of rational inquiry that we can sensibly express these concerns. Those who urge us to reject the idea of truth, for example, do so by offering comprehensible, assessable, defeasible reasons for doing so, reasons that aim to speak to people regardless of their own interests and which have some force.

Think of any serious participant in intellectual life. Is there any who does not try to be as comprehensible as is possible? Many are so incomprehensible that we doubt them, but this is almost always a failure of execution, not a success born of intent. Does anyone assert that it is not possible for anyone else to assess the merits of their claims? Very few, and the whole *raison d'être* of publishing and discussion is precisely that others are, in principle, capable of assessing what they have read or heard and sharing these assessments. Does anyone declare that what they have to say is wholly relative to the interests only of a particular sector of society? Surely not. Even as we acknowledge our biases and partial perspectives, we strive to overcome them as much as is possible. Does anyone think there is no way they could possibly be wrong about what they believe? We may sometimes feel this, but the fact that we nonetheless leave ourselves open to criticism and take those criticisms seriously shows we are committed to the idea that rational inquiry demands we treat our beliefs as defeasible. And finally, when you have seen someone provide what seem to you good reasons for their accepting their position, is your agreement not in some sense involuntary? Similarly, can you not help but dismiss arguments that seem to you weak or ill-founded?

As convinced as I am of the essential truth of my account, I am aware that there will be many objections. Every one of my five characteristics of the thin notion of rationality can be understood in many ways, and even rejected. But I would maintain that this unease is not a symptom of any inherent flaw in my account. Rather, any intelligent, reflective reader is going to be concerned with how to thicken such conceptions, and also to challenge them. But unless I and my readers shared some thin conception of what rational debate looks like we could not come together to discuss them in the first place.

PART III: THE MOTIVATOR

The third myth of rationality is that reason can give us our primary motivations for acting; in particular, acting well. Plato once again can be seen as the founder of this myth. In the *Protagoras*, Socrates suggests that no one chooses to do what is worse for them knowingly. 'It's not, it seems to me, in human nature to be prepared to go for what you think to be bad in preference to what is good,' he says. 'And when you are forced to choose one of two evils, nobody will choose the greater when he can have the lesser.'[1] This sounds like common sense, but common sense would add that what we judge to be best could be any number of things, most obviously the morally right thing or our own self-interest. What's more, we can misjudge such things and there can be conflicts between them.

For Plato, however, all this mess can be tidied up. Plato believed that there is an eternal unchanging 'form' for every thing and concept, including the Good. If we had knowledge of the Form of the Good, we would see that self-interest and what was right perfectly coincide. Given that we would never knowingly do what we thought worse for us, it follows that with this knowledge, we would be perfectly motivated to do what is right.

J.L. Mackie sums it up clearly and succinctly. 'In Plato's theory, the Forms, and in particular the Form of the Good, are eternal, extra-mental, realities. They are a very central structural element in the fabric of the world. But it is held also that just knowing them or "seeing" them will not merely tell men what to do but will ensure that they do it, overruling any contrary inclinations.'[2]

This is a strong theory, stronger than the idea that if you believe something is right then you necessarily have a motivation to do it. What Plato adds to this theory of the 'internalism' of moral motivation is that you can know what is right by the use of pure reason alone. Disinterested rational inquiry can lead you to discover moral principles which you will then be motivated to follow. Morality and moral action are therefore the fruits of disinterested reason.

Our concern in Part Three is not the question of whether holding a moral principle is intrinsically motivating, but whether it is true that we can arrive at motivating moral principles by the use of the disinterested intellect alone. Can reason motivate us to act, and to act well? I will argue that it cannot and that Plato's myth of reason as the motivator needs to be rejected, along with the myths of reason as the judge and guide.

CHAPTER SEVEN

Rational morality

One of the most long-running disputes in moral philosophy concerns the relationship between ethics and rationality. On one side, there are those who, in agreement with Kant, believe that the requirement to behave according to moral principles can be established by disinterested reason alone. As Kant himself put it, 'The ground of obligation here must be sought not in the nature of the human being or in the circumstances of the world in which he is placed, but *a priori* simply in concepts of pure reason.'[1] I will here describe all who agree with this broad position as Kantians, with the warning that in this context it includes a wider group than those who agree with the specifics of Kant's particular position.

In the opposing camp are those who, following Hume, argue that reason can never provide the basis for morality and that at best it can only serve the desires and impulses, moral or otherwise, that arise in us from non-rational sources. On this view, as Hume put it, 'Reason is and ought only to be the slave of the passions.'[2] This view, and successors of it, is often known as sentimentalism. This has nothing to do with cooing over pictures of fluffy kittens but relates to the increasingly archaic meaning of sentiment as 'feeling' or 'emotion'. Sentimentalism should not be equated with emotivism, the crudest version of the theory, which says that moral judgements are no more than expressions of approval or disgust. Sentimentalism is a broader term for any theory that sees morality as fundamentally grounded in an emotional response of some kind, rather than in disinterested reason.

The disagreement between Kantians and sentimentalists is of much more than scholarly interest. In many parts of the world today there is a crisis of moral legitimacy. In the West, this has followed the decline of organised religion. Christianity used to provide the moral foundations for society as a whole, but as it has diminished in authority nothing else has come to take its place. This has left many worried that nothing *can* take its place. If we give up the idea that morality is handed down from on high by divine command, we are left with nothing more than preference and power to determine what is acceptable and what is not, what is permitted and what is prohibited.

In fact, in moral philosophy, divine command theory has not been especially popular for a very long time. It suffers from a major problem that Plato identified millennia ago.[3] The nub of the problem is this: if God's choice settled what is right or wrong, then surely he could make all that we think right wrong, and vice versa? This can't be right; a good God would not permit torture, for example. So that means God must command us to do good because it is good and not just because he tells us to do it. But that means the notion and nature of 'good' does not depend on God at all. So even if God is the cosmic boss, there is still a question of what makes things good or bad, right or wrong. The Kantian and sentimentalist answers are currently the best alternatives on the table.

So if we are to provide a rational justification for morality, we need to decide which side is right and be able to present a clear defence of it. In this, as in almost everything else, I believe Hume got it fundamentally right. That has not stopped many from dissenting over the 250 years since he set out his case. I think, however, there is a way to show why those who argue that morality can be established as a requirement of disinterested rationality must always be wrong. We can see how this argument works by looking at a recent attempt to produce such an argument in the Kantian tradition by John Searle. By seeing how Searle's argument fails we can see why all similar arguments must suffer the same fate.[4]

1. Rationally bound ethics

Searle wants to show that disinterested reason is sufficient to establish the demand for strong altruism. Before we look at his argument, there are several aspects of how he sets out the terms of the debate which are revealing. First, he distinguishes strong altruism from its weak variety. Weak altruism is where a person is 'naturally inclined to care about the interests of others'.[5] This is of course the kind of altruism that Hume, Francis Hutcheson and Adam Smith all believed we had out of a natural sympathy. For Searle, this kind of altruism is 'weak' because no matter how universal it is, it is ultimately grounded in nothing more than dispositions or preferences. As long as altruism is merely a matter of personal inclination, we can no more hope to give any rationally compelling reasons why someone should be altruistic than we can give rationally compelling reasons why they should like the taste of beer.

It's worth noting at this point how this formulation provides an example of what I call the importance of *intonation* in philosophy. Very often, important disagreements do not hinge on the facts, but on attitudes towards the facts. These attitudes are often revealed in the use of certain emphasisers and adjectives that do not alter the fundamental meaning of a proposition, but rather suggest a response to it. In this case, the plain fact, agreed with by both Kantians and sentimentalists, is that, according to sentimentalism, altruism is ultimately grounded in dispositions or preferences. You can state that as a fact of life to be accepted, or in a tone of disbelief that suggests it is a kind of outrage that must not stand. To capture the latter attitude in print, you can add some emphasis and punctuation: 'altruism is ultimately grounded in *nothing more than* dispositions or preferences!' This rhetorical effect of implied incredulity is often achieved by the use of phrases such as 'Nothing more than', 'just' or 'mere': 'altruism is grounded in *mere* sympathy' rather than plain 'altruism is grounded in sympathy', for example. Take away the 'nothing more' and you get 'altruism is ultimately grounded in dispositions or preferences', which you might still find objectionable but not quite as outrageous.

I stress this because it is an important and often overlooked example of how arguments often depend for their persuasiveness on factors other than their formal soundness. This is perhaps more common in public discourse than in technical philosophy. Think, for example, of how certain scientists are accused of conceptualising human beings as 'mere biological robots', when if we are biological robots we are rather remarkable ones and there is nothing 'mere' about us. Putting 'only' before a number is also a neat way of making it look small when actually it might be very significant. Which precise words you choose to describe ideas can also have an effect, as Searle illustrates. By calling the form of altruism he rejects 'weak' he is subtly loading the dice against it, belittling it by the very name it is given.

Rhetoric aside, however, there is still a meaningful distinction to be made between what Searle calls weak altruism and its strong version. Searle defines a strong altruist as someone who 'recognises the interests of others as a valid reason for acting *even in cases where he has no such inclination*.'[6] (My italics.) This is the kind of altruism that Kantians believe can be demanded by disinterested reason.

Before we go any further, it should be pointed out that sentimentalists can be strong altruists in this sense. The sentimentalist position is not that morality is simply what we are inclined to do on any given occasion. It is rather that the basis of moral judgement is emotional, not intellectual. One simple example should make this clear. A sentimentalist might believe that it is wrong to cause unnecessary suffering. The ultimate basis of this judgement is not that to do so would be irrational, but simply a recognition, rooted in empathy, that suffering is a bad thing, to be avoided if possible. Having adopted this principle, the sentimentalist might on a given occasion see reasons not to act in a certain way, despite being inclined to do so, such as when confronted with a juicy steak from a factory-farmed animal. Such a Humean, to use Searle's formula, recognises the interests of other animals as a valid reason for not tucking in, even though in this case he has no inclination to refrain and will in fact be left salivating by doing so.

This mistake by Searle is as significant as his linguistic sleight. What it reveals is that his argument is proceeding on a strong assumption about what counts as a reason. In assuming that Humean 'weak altruists' have no reason to refrain from acting against their inclinations, Searle is assuming that an empathetic moral sentiment, combined with certain factual knowledge, does not provide a reason to act. Why should he think this? The only explanation would be that for Searle, reasons are produced solely by disinterested reason, which acts independently of anything other than facts and logic. It should be evident that this raises many questions. Reason has been implicitly defined in a narrow way.

Before we have even got to the structure of the argument itself, we can therefore already see how the Kantian case sets out the terms of the debate in ways which prejudice the sentimentalist. I do not think this kind of 'pre-loading' of arguments is rare. As political spin doctors well know, the surest way to win an argument is to make sure it is conducted on your terms.

Let us, however, set aside all these concerns and see how Searle takes the argument further. Searle's variety of strong altruism is certainly not sentimentalist, since he concludes that there are 'rationally binding desire-independent altruistic reasons for action'.[7] The reasons are rationally binding because to disregard them requires one to act inconsistently and hence contrary to reason. They are desire-independent because they exist whether or not one wants them to exist. For reasons already given, if they are not to be sentimentalist, they must be fundamentally based on something other than desires too. So for Searle, to recognise that one has rationally binding reasons to help others whether one is disposed to do so or not is to accept the case for strong altruism.

Searle's argument for strong altruism requires three steps and is illustrated with the example of being in pain. Central to the argument – and something I will not question here – is what Searle calls the 'generality requirement'.[8] This is a version of the widely accepted principle of universalisability which states that to assert that something is the case is to assert that everyone in a similar situation should also assert that it is the case. So if I say 'Paris is the capital of France' I must believe that everyone else in possession of the key facts should assert the same. Similarly, when we say, 'I am in pain', we are 'committed by the generality requirement to recognize that in a similar situation you would be in pain'. That is the simple, unproblematic first step of Searle's argument.

The second step is to see that my pain creates a need. I am in pain so I need help. Accepting the generality requirement means that I therefore have to accept that if anyone else is in pain, their pain too creates a need. I cannot make a special case of myself: if my pain creates a need for me, then the pain of others creates a need for them.

The third and final step is to see that my need for help is a reason for other people to help me. Once more, the generality requirement comes into play and so I have to accept that, to be rational, if my pain creates a reason for other people to help me, then the pain of others creates a reason for me to help them.

This is enough, believes Searle, to establish strong altruism. Independently of what I desire or not, I have to recognise that there exist reasons why I should help others. These reasons are rationally binding in that they exist merely as a consequence of my recognition of what rationally follows from the fact that I myself say things like 'I am in pain'. Therefore, Searle concludes, we have rationally binding desire-independent altruistic reasons for action and the existence of strong altruism has been established.

2. Whose reasons?

Searle's argument contains a flaw that ensures not only that it fails, but that any other similar argument that tries to establish a disinterestedly rational, desire-independent basis for morality must also fail. The problem is not with the generality requirement, which I accept. Nor will I take issue with the second premise: that I see that my pain creates a need, that I need help. Strictly speaking, this does not logically follow. I only need help if my pain ought to be relieved, which obvious though it sounds does not follow as a matter of logic from the fact that I feel it. For instance, there are not only imaginable but actual religious outlooks which see suffering as something to be endured and ought not to be relieved.

I'll say more about this shortly, but first there is a bigger, less contentious flaw that matters more than whether it is possible to establish that humans have objective needs. This error comes in the third and final step. As we have seen, Searle says that 'I believe my need for help is a reason for you to help me.' This belief is generated by the generality requirement, since, on pain of contradiction, if I believe my need for help is a reason for you to help me, I also have to accept that your need for help would be a reason for me to help you.

But Searle has glossed over an important distinction. What we need to do is state *for whom the reason is operative*. Depending on how we interpret this, there can be two possible interpretations:

I believe my need for help is a reason *for me* for you to help me.

I believe my need for help is a reason *for you* for you to help me.

Reasons *for me* for you to help me are not necessarily reasons *for you* for you to help me. A simple example shows why the difference is real and important. I apply for a job, you are the person who decides who gets the job and I would be greatly helped if I got this job. This fact – that the job would help me enormously – provides me with a reason for you to give me the job. My need, in other words, is a reason *for me* for you to help me. But it is not a reason *for you* for you to help me. The reasons which are operative for you are ones concerning the need to give the job to the person best suited to do it well, and so on.

As this is an important point, I will risk labouring it with a second example. I have entered a painting competition and I know that if I win, I will appreciate the prize much more than my rivals. That gives a reason *for me* for the judge to choose me as the winner. But it is not a reason for the judge to pick me: the only reasons operative for him are those concerning artistic merit.

In order for Searle's argument to work, the reason for you to help me must be as good a reason for you as it is for me. Only if I accept that my need for help is a reason *for you* for you to help me must I, meeting the generality requirement, accept that your need for help is a reason *for me* for me to help you. If it does not, then all the generality requirement demands is that I believe your need for help is a reason *for you* for me to help you. That is insufficient to establish that there are rationally binding desire-independent reasons for altruistic action.

But Searle's argument is only enough to establish that my need for help is a reason *for me* for you to help me. In recognising that I am in pain and need help, I am only rationally compelled to accept that this provides a reason *for me* for you to help me. Therefore in accepting that my need for help is a reason *for me* for you to help me I am not rationally compelled to believe that I ought to help other people.

There is a second way of showing Searle's flaw which does not require having to follow the complexities involved in clauses like 'reasons for me for you'. This is a variant on the basic idea that reasons which are operative for one person may not be operative for another. In this argument, let us accept that having a need for help is enough to establish that the need is a reason for others to help me. The problem with this is that at any given time innumerable such needs exist. Just in my neighbourhood there are people who need help to cope with their grieving, do their shopping, get over their addictions, escape their loneliness, get money for medical treatment. Extend the circle wider and there are billions in need of clean water, good food, basic healthcare, education. On Searle's view, I ought to accept that these are reasons for me to help them. That is reasonable enough. But that can't mean those reasons are sufficient to place a moral obligation on me to help them. If it did, we would have the absurdity that at any one time, we would all be morally obliged to help other people meet any need they had.

On the only plausible reading, therefore, 'a reason for others to help me' has to be something which does not necessarily carry with it any moral obligation. This makes sense. It is easy to see that there are almost infinite reasons for us to help others but we cannot be obliged to act on all of them. So even if Searle's argument is essentially valid, it cannot mean that anyone is morally obliged in any way to help me just because there is a reason for them to do so. In other words, the fact that there are rationally binding desire-independent reasons for altruistic action does not in any way place an obligation on me to act on those reasons. What Searle calls 'strong altruism' does not, it turns out, place any obligation on me, of any strength.

Whichever way you look at it, the fact that there exists a reason to help someone is not sufficient to establish that someone ought to act on that reason. We need to go further and say why that reason should be *operative* for any particular individual. Recognising that reasons can be operative for different people and that not all reasons can be equally operative for all people is sufficient to show that Searle's argument doesn't work. Recognising 'the interests of others as a valid reason for acting even in cases where he has no such inclination' in no way compels us to act on that reason. We have valid reasons to help others but also valid reasons to go to the movies or stay at home and open a bottle of wine. Unless reason obliges us to behave morally, the Kantian project fails.

Were these just flaws in Searle's specific argument, they would be of only scholarly interest. But they expose something more fundamental in the Kantian project. The general strategy is to attempt to show that reasons for acting morally can be derived purely from considerations of what is required by disinterested rationality. This project can only work if there are reasons to help others or consider their interests which are operative for everyone.

The problem is that it can never follow as a matter of logic that because there is a reason *for me* for you to help me that there is a reason *for you* for you to help me; nor that because there is a reason *for you* for me to help you that there is a reason *for me* for me to help you. These logical gaps are unbridgeable.

3. From facts to values

Those familiar with the historical debate will recognise my argument as resting on a version of the 'is/ought' gap. This was another of Hume's great insights, and it is worth quoting his original lines on this in full.

> In every system of morality, which I have hitherto met with, I have always remarked, that the author proceeds for some time in the ordinary ways of reasoning, and establishes the being of a God, or makes observations concerning human affairs; when all of a sudden I am surprised to find, that instead of the usual copulations of propositions, *is*, and *is not*, I meet with no proposition that is not connected with an *ought*, or an *ought not*. This change is imperceptible; but is however, of the last consequence. For as this *ought*, or *ought not*, expresses some new relation or affirmation, 'tis necessary that it should be observed and explained; and at the same time that a reason should be given, for what seems altogether inconceivable, how this new relation can be a deduction from others, which are entirely different from it.[9]

The essential point is a logical one. If the premises of an argument contain only statements of fact, then the conclusion must also contain only statements of fact, and must not smuggle in assertions of value, such as 'oughts'. In ordinary discourse, we do this all the time. We say, people are starving, they will die unless we send them food, therefore we ought to send them food. The conclusion does not follow logically. In practice, this is usually because premises are not so much absent as unstated. In this case, we take it for granted that we accept a moral premise of the kind 'we ought to prevent people from dying if we easily can'. For anyone who wants to establish moral obligation on the basis of reason alone, however, this is fatal, since we cannot assert such 'oughts' as brute facts about the world.

The is/ought gap, as it is known, has come under tremendous fire in recent decades. The basic thrust of the objection has been that we cannot so neatly distinguish between the two kinds of statement. Most notably, Philippa Foot argued that it is a kind of fact about the natural world that living things have needs and desires and that therefore it is a matter of fact that certain things are of value to them. Take the proposition: 'children are born helpless and have to be taught to learn language and so on.' That, she explains, 'means already that children have to be looked after'. Crucially, these reasons are 'objective and have nothing to do with preferences: some people love children and some people hate them. That doesn't make any difference.'[10] On the one hand, this is a pure statement of fact. But it would also appear to contain implicit within it a statement of value: it is better that a child is looked after than not. We could call such statements 'normative facts', meaning they are facts that contain elements of value.

This is a crucial point worth emphasising. If to be rational is to provide objective reasons for belief, then there is no reason why in appropriate circumstances those reasons cannot include facts about human desire, motivation and feeling, facts which entail values. This does not contravene the requirement I set out that objective reasons must be interest-neutral. The fact that it is in the interests of an animal to eat, for example, is still interest-neutral in the sense that it is a fact everyone ought to recognise regardless of their own interests. It sounds paradoxical to say that we have interest-neutral reasons to accept the objectivity of interests, but the seeming paradox quickly dissolves when you see that the interest-neutrality of reason only concerns the requirement that we do not allow our interests to cloud our judgement of what is the case. It does not prohibit the recognition of real interests in the world. Given that these interests can be emotional as well as biological, this means that emotions can sometimes number among the reasons of rational argument.

Indeed, borrowing an idea suggested by her late friend and colleague Warren Quinn, Foot argues that you cannot undertake practical rational deliberation at all without some kind of idea of what is good. This often goes unnoticed when it is taken for granted that prudential self-interest is unproblematic as a reason for action. Foot's argument is that practical rationality of all descriptions has to start by taking something as a reason for action and there is no logical reason why prudential self-interest is a more rational reason to act than the needs of a child. 'Practical rationality is taking the right things as reasons,' as she put it.

I can accept Foot's argument here and I think Hume could too. This will strike many as odd, as Foot was a strong critic of Hume. But her acceptance that practical reason needs some kind of conception of what is good is not so far from Hume's idea that practical reasoning needs us to desire something we see as good. The difference between them only appears large if you believe Humeans do not acknowledge desires and sympathy as reasons. But sentimentalists who accept my catholic account of reason can accept that a pain creates a need for help because we are not compelled to confine reason to the domain of disinterested facts. Nor are we compelled to limit a good rational argument to one where each step logically follows from the other according to the principles of deduction. For sentimentalists, the existence of a pain can be an objective reason to believe we ought to help, but it is not one that we are strictly compelled to accept, because we acknowledge the role of judgement in taking us from premise to conclusion in such arguments.

Hume's argument should therefore be seen as directed specifically against Kantians whose aim is to show that *disinterested* reason *alone* gets us to moral imperatives. Hume is holding Kantians to their own excessively strict standards, which means any 'infection' of their arguments with assumptions about values has to be removed. But if our conception of reason is more catholic, and we allow needs to count as reasons, we can accept that needs count as reasons for action. What my discussion of Searle shows is that this is not the same as the claim that we can establish morality on disinterested reason alone. If we reject a neat is/ought distinction, we can easily assert that we have rational grounds for thinking that there are reasons to help others, that it would be better if we behaved morally and so on. But none of this is sufficient to establish moral obligation on a disinterested rational basis.

This point is critical. Reason is often assumed to be by definition disinterested. Disinterested reason has its place, of course, in mathematics and science, but sometimes it can legitimately be very interested indeed. Reason needs to be objective, not disinterested, and this means it can recognise the objective existence of needs and desires, good and bad states.

Hume's fundamental point thus remains as robustly valid as ever, just as long as we see that it applies only to the form of disinterested reason advocated by Kant and rationalists such as Descartes. There is no disinterested rational reason why I should not prefer the worse over the better, or why I should not be motivated to prefer one good over an objectively greater one. Callousness is selfish, but it does not require anyone to contravene the laws of logic. Nor is excessively self-sacrificial altruism any more or less logical than excessive selfishness. As Hume should have put it, adding one italicised word, ' 'tis not contrary to *disinterested* reason to prefer even my own acknowledg'd lesser good to my greater, and have a more ardent affection for the former than for the latter'.

4. Reasons for altruism

Once again, we are drawn to a modest Aristotelian mean between those who would claim too much for reason and those who would claim too little. I have argued that morality is not a requirement of disinterested rationality, but this argument has also shown why the alternative to this is not the view that rationality has nothing to contribute to morality. On the contrary, reason is indispensable to morality. Rejecting the Kantian project simply means giving up the idea that the *ultimate* justification for morality is to be found by the operation of *disinterested* reason *alone*. But get rid of the words in italics and suddenly a much more plausible claim emerges: *some of* the justification for morality is to be found by the operation of reason, but not its ultimate justification.

For instance, it could be argued that, at bottom, morality stands on nothing more than moral sympathy, or some such similar good feeling towards others, and that this cannot be established by disinterested reason. But that would be far from accepting that reason has no role to play in morality. At the very least, reason would still be needed to help us to determine whether or not our moral principles are coherently aligned with the emotion-based impulses that lie at their root. For example, moral sympathy might well be the only ultimate justification for the principle that everyone should be treated with equal respect. But if we have false beliefs about the sex or ethnic differences between people, this might not in practice lead to full equality. Hence in 1868 the fourteenth Amendment was added to the US Constitution, which decreed that no state could 'deny to any person within its jurisdiction the equal protection of the laws', and yet racial segregation persisted well into the twentieth century and women only got the vote in 1920. Reason was vital for ending these inequalities, since it was only when people realised that there was no rational reason to treat people of colour differently from white people, or women differently from men, that moral progress was made. Reason forced people to acknowledge inconsistencies between their deepest values and how they were acting.

To take another, even clearer example, we might be utilitarians and argue that the morally right thing to do is whatever increases the greatest welfare of the greatest number. We might also accept that we cannot establish this as the ultimate principle of morality by the use of disinterested reason alone and the best we can do is propose it as the ultimate good and find that no one is able to suggest a more persuasive alternative. Having accepted the principle, however, a utilitarian is likely to believe with some justification that we need reason to determine what actually best achieves the greatest welfare of the greatest number.

This is the standard defence of sentimentalism against the charge of arationality or irrationality. 'Reason gives us our representation of the salient features of the situation we are in, and it gives us the ability to to make further deductions and inferences about that situation,' as Simon Blackburn puts it. 'Reason's office is to represent the world to us as it is. But then, how we react to that situation, and that includes how we react to it emotionally, is another matter.'[11]

However, I think this concedes too much to those who want to emphasise the importance of the non-rational for sentimentalism. I think we should rather challenge the assumption about what reason comprises that is implicit in the charge. To do this, we need to take a little further the line of thought articulated in the previous section, where I talked of 'normative facts' and Foot's blurring of the fact/value distinction. As I suggested, this means we can recognise the objective existence of human needs and see these as reasons for action. If these reasons are comprehensible, assessable, defeasible, interest-neutral and compelling, then they are objective and so a legitimate currency in rational debate. What's more, this can even provide us with an ultimate reason to be moral.

To show that this is indeed the case, it would be helpful to formalise the basic principle of sentimentalism in such a way as to present it as a reason to be moral. My best attempt would be something like this:

> If a creature has interests – being able to pursue projects and live a life which it finds meaningful, and/or can feel pain and pleasure, physical and psychic – then we have reasons to take those interests into account and not frustrate them without good reason, nor refrain from assisting them when it is easily in our power to do so.

This is a very broad principle which does not specify what exactly we must do when we take such a creature's interests into account. So, for example, three people might agree with this and accept that we therefore have a duty to take a farm animal's interests into account. But one might conclude we ought then not to eat it, another that we simply ought to rear it well, while the other might say as long as we don't torture it, we've done nothing wrong. The very fact that it is hard to imagine who could disagree with such a principle would suggest that in its generality it seems to offer a plausible and compelling reason to be moral.

The standard sentimentalist way to understand such a statement would be to say that although it is indeed reasonable, to use Humean language, 'tis not contrary to reason to reject it. A dissenter would be heartless, not brainless. But not so fast. Of course, we can see that no one would be compelled by disinterested reason alone to accept such a principle. But we have already seen that we have no good grounds to define reason as disinterested reason. If to be rational is to offer objective reasons for belief, then cannot this sentimentalist position be justified rationally?

The question is whether a creature's having interests is an objective reason for us to take them into account, a reason which is comprehensible, assessable, defeasible, interest-neutral and compelling. It is certainly an objective fact that other people and animals do have interests. We should not be distracted here by the fact that there is clearly a subjective element to well-being. There is no problem in thinking there are objective truths about subjective states. Most clearly, it is an objective fact that subjective states exist. If we recognise this, it is a small step to accepting that it is an objective fact that some subjective states are preferable for those who experience them than others, and that this gives them an interest in being in those preferable states rather than distressing ones. So it should be clear enough that it is an objective truth that agents have interests.

This is something we can obviously comprehend. We may struggle to understand what it means for a pig or snail to have interests, but we have little difficulty with fellow humans. With many other animals, we can at least comprehend some of their interests, most obviously to avoid unnecessary pain and suffering.

Next, the interests of others are to a certain degree assessable. Let us imagine that someone claims it is in their interests to enjoy decent health, be fabulously rich and torture small children. The former can be judged to be a clear and legitimate interest, the second a questionable and certainly not core one, and the last unacceptable and not necessary for the effective functioning of a human life. Put simply, claims to have interests are not things we have to simply accept at face value: we can and do assess them.

Third, ideas about what interests people have are defeasible. Normally, for instance, we take it for granted that a person has an interest in continuing to live, but when the quality of life is awful and without hope of improving, most of us accept that this interest may no longer be overriding, or even exist. As another example, historically, people have believed we have an interest in divine salvation, while many reject that idea now.

The idea that these interests are in the relevant sense interest-neutral might appear to be oxymoronic, but, as I have explained, there is a very clear sense in which this is true. In order to make a rational judgement about what an agent's interests are, we need to set aside our own interests. In other words, our judgements about the reasonableness of another's interests should not be affected by our own interests, and in that sense they are interest-neutral.

The final step we need to take is to show that these objective reasons add up to a compelling reason to take the interests of an agent into account. The kind of compulsion we are looking for here is what I termed rational, not psychological. In other words, it is about feeling the force of the reasons, not necessarily feeling forced to act on them. In this case, it seems to me that recognising that others have interests is a compelling reason to believe we ought to take them into account, whether or not we feel the kind of psychological force that leads us to act on their interests. To return to an earlier example, a person can feel the moral force of the argument that they should not eat factory-farmed meat and yet not feel inclined to act on it.

Many are not satisfied by this because it is a kind of compulsion which is not rationally binding. For Christine Korsgaard this is at the heart of what she calls the 'the normative question'. 'Even when we are inclined to believe that something is right,' she says, 'and to some extent feel ourselves moved to do it we can still always ask: "But is this really true?" and "Must I really do this?"'[12] But why should we expect or demand that the only good moral reasons are ones which are beyond all conceivable rational dispute? This is simply too high a demand. Bernard Williams mocked those who made it, asking rhetorically, 'What will the professor's justification do, when they break down the door, smash his spectacles, take him away?'[13] If the professor thinks he can stop his aggressors with an argument, he is a fool. Moral reasons can be extremely compelling but this compulsion need not be absolute. After all, the compulsion to accept $2 + 2 = 4$ is not absolute either. As Descartes argued, we know that we can sometimes in dreams take absurdities to be obviously true and so we might harbour a tiny doubt that we're wrong even about basic maths.

The compelling nature of moral reasons can, however, still be very strong indeed and it looks much more like the compulsion to accept that $2 + 2 = 4$ than might be expected. We can certainly imagine some people who just don't feel the force of the argument at all. In the mathematical argument, this blindness might suggest a rare cognitive impairment that simply doesn't allow them to follow logical steps. In the moral argument, the equivalent would be a cognitive impairment such as psychopathy, which makes people indifferent to the interests of others. In both cases, further argument would be fruitless. We would simply have to insist that there is something fundamental that the dissenters are not seeing. Just as we accept that the ability to do maths depends on having a cognitive capacity not everyone has, so we should accept that the ability to be fully moral requires a cognitive capacity some lack.

Sometimes a failure to appreciate the force of an argument is a failure of understanding that can be corrected. For example, I have had students who sincerely argue that it is not necessarily true that $2 + 2 = 4$, because they are either imagining other possible worlds in which the symbols do not mean the same thing or entertaining the purely hypothetical possibility that there is some reason we can't see why it is not necessarily true after all. The first kind of objection misses the point (since we are thinking about these symbols as they are as a matter of fact defined), while the second is merely the defeasibility clause that must attach to any rational claim. The students have to accept that there is no decisive answer to radical skepticism. The most certainty we can have is that we are unable to articulate how what we take to be true could reasonably be thought to be otherwise.

In the case of those who see no rational force behind the argument that we ought to take the interests of an agent into account, I suspect this usually reflects a hard-to-shake assumption that the only rationally compelling reasons must be disinterested ones. Many want to defend this assumption because they fear that otherwise desires and emotions will be admitted to the domain of reason and then they would be left with no criteria to distinguish the reasonable and unreasonable. Everything goes. But it is not good enough to raise the spectre of the slippery slope: you have to show why we are bound to slide down it. That case is lacking.

On the contrary, the opposite case can be made. The recognition, achieved through the operation of our moral sympathy, that others have interests, provides a truly rational basis for morality, since it provides a set of objective reasons to behave morally. As T.M. Scanlon puts it, 'to see something as good reason for acting in a certain way and being disposed to do it is not a matter of logic' but 'it is a matter of rationality'.[14] This has not been generally recognised because we have operated with a mistaken view of rationality, one which understands reason too narrowly. We have, in effect, been presented with a false choice. Kant offered the option of believing that 'The ground of obligation ... must be sought not in the nature of the human being or in the circumstances of the world in which he is placed, but *a priori* simply in concepts of pure reason', while Hume had us believe that 'Reason is and ought only to be the slave of the passions.' The mistake here is to assume that '*a priori* pure reason' – a subset of what I have called disinterested reason – is the only kind of real reason. Hume, by example, showed this was not true, reasoning beautifully *a posteriori* and inductively. However, when he talked about reason he often did so as though it always and only meant *a priori* pure reason. This was clumsy. As Blackburn suggests, a more accurate description of Hume's moral theory does not restrict reason to the *a priori*. 'When we deploy some concerns in order to query or criticize others,' says Blackburn, 'there is nothing to stop us from describing the process as one of reasoning.'[15] The right way to put things is not that 'Reason is and ought only to be the slave of the passions' but that the passions as well as cold cogitations provide reasons.

5. The claims of consistency

There is of course at least one way in which all but the most determinedly arational moralities are subject to the claims of reason. We almost all recognise the need for moral judgements to be consistent. If I assert that eating meat is wrong and then tuck into a reindeer burger, I am a hypocrite, which is what we call someone whose deeds are not consistent with her words.

In chapter nine I will say more about why consistency always has a particular kind of normative force, even when it does not involve ethics. In the moral domain, we can see the demand of consistency as deriving simply from the nature of 'ought'. To say someone ought to do something is to say that there are reasons for behaving in a certain way, or for refraining from behaving in a certain way, which make some kind of demand, however weak, on us. Without that sense of external demand, there can be no ought. This is not a subtle philosophical point but a simple linguistic one. It makes no sense to say 'You ought to do it, but it doesn't matter at all if you don't.'

Sometimes we do indeed say something like this, but when we do, we don't mean quite what we say. One such type of situation is when the obligation is very weak and to fulfil it relatively onerous, so we don't think it is terrible if we don't. For instance, we might think that we ought to take our rubbish off the mountain when we finish our climb, but because we have to help carry an injured comrade, we can't reasonably do so. Strictly speaking, in such cases we believe that there is something which ordinarily one ought to do but in this particular situation our obligations are lifted.

The other kind of case is when we see an obligation as arising from a convention which we don't really endorse. We might say 'you ought to send a thank-you card', for example, but we don't really think you are obliged to, we are simply acknowledging that there is nothing stronger here than a social expectation.

When we say 'ought' and really mean it, however, we cannot but at the same time say that others in relevantly similar situations ought to do the same. This is the basic principle of universalisability that has been accepted by almost all moral theorists, save subjectivists and other moral skeptics. Not even particularists need reject it completely. Particularism is the claim that there are no universal moral principles, and that behaving morally is therefore not about following such principles. Each situation is too idiosyncratic for principles to be useful. But even on this view, if we were to imagine two people in exactly the same situation, with the same knowledge, facing the same dilemma – and if we were to think that one course of action would be the right one for the first person – even most particularists would accept it would also be right for the second. For particularists, the point is that in the real world no two situations *are* exactly alike in all respects, not that we could justifiably be inconsistent if they were.

So we can see why consistency is important in ethics, and there is a vital role for reason in judging whether or not we are being consistent. But although consistency is a value, it is not the master value. To see why, consider this thought experiment.

I meet a very clever person who presents a rationally compelling argument that I ought to press a button which will destroy all of London and everyone in it. What's more, I ought to do so as soon as possible. He proceeds from premises which seem to me indisputable, by steps which seem to be valid, to a conclusion which I consider repugnant. But try as I may to see what is wrong with the argument, I cannot. This means that if I refuse to press the button, I am behaving in a way which is inconsistent: I cannot deny the soundness of the argument but I am behaving contrary to it. In such a situation, should I push the button or not?

I think the answer is no. I could argue this by appeal to a wider consistency. As I argued in the first chapter, there is a holism of rationality which means that arguments do not just cohere internally, they have to cohere with the wider web of belief too. So I could argue that my reasons for rejecting the argument are that although I cannot see the flaw in it, it is inconsistent with the wider web of beliefs which I have stronger, better established reasons to accept as justified.

But my thought experiment could take this into account. I could try to show what these inconsistencies are and yet find that the evil genius before me was able to resolve them. Should I now push the button?

I still think not. If such a scenario were possible, then one of two things must be true. The first is that there is a flaw in the argument I have not yet identified. Note, however, that this judgement is not based on clear reasoning and argument. I am allowing my intuitive sense of what I feel cannot be correct to overrule what my reasoning mind tells me must be correct. So although I am not undermining my belief that, ultimately, the right way to behave will turn out to be rationally consistent, I am not making that judgement on the basis of a rationally consistent argument.

This is a curious circumstance. In effect, I am upholding the principle of consistency but not obeying it. Why would I do such a thing? Because we have very good grounds to doubt our own abilities to reason consistently and correctly. Knowing we are imperfect reasoners, we should not always automatically follow what reason appears to demand of us. This is analogous to the theological problem of following God's will. A theist might believe that she is obliged to do as God commands, but be reluctant to do some things that present themselves as God's will, since she knows that, being human, she might misinterpret it. This is central to Kierkegaard's retelling of the story of Abraham and Isaac in *Fear and Trembling*. It might appear to us that it is clear that God is commanding Abraham to sacrifice his only son, but if you were Abraham, you would be aware that you cannot know for sure God is really asking for this. Perhaps you are being deceived by the devil taking on the guise of God, or perhaps God is testing you, to see, as Woody Allen put it, whether you are a truly good person or simply one willing to 'follow any order no matter how asinine as long as it comes from a resonant, well-modulated voice'.[16]

Rationality is usually contrasted with faith, and with very good reason. But it often takes a kind of faith to be sure that what we believe is in fact demanded by reason, rather than simply being the result of poor reasoning. There is a difference between what *is* rational and what *seems* rational, and too often people assume the latter is the former. This distinction requires no skepticism about the power of reason, only skepticism about our ability to harness that power. We might then accept that, in principle, the demand for consistency is absolute, yet accept that, because we are not reliable judges of what is truly consistent, all things considered, we are not always obliged to behave in what appears to be a consistent way, or to uphold apparently consistent beliefs.

There is, however, a second reason why we might not accept the apparently consistent case to destroy a whole city: it turns out that consistency is not an inviolable principle of morality after all. Of course, my thought experiment rests on an argument that does not exist, and we would be justified in suspecting that it cannot. But I think it is nonetheless important to acknowledge where our bottom line lies. For me, if the demand for consistency were to clash with the demand to avoid mass slaughter without a very clear greater benefit at the very least, then I have no hesitation in saying that it is consistency which would go.

Making this kind of judgement, however hypothetical, is important in identifying the bedrocks I described in chapter one, the core beliefs which anchor all our others. For example, it is important to know whether Christians who argue that their creationism is consistent with science would, if forced to choose, decide between the Bible or science. Knowing this is a test of the sincerity of any claims to be following science. Similarly, I would hope we would accept that in a competition between consistency and avoiding mass slaughter, much as we desire to make our morality rationally consistent, the litmus test of morality is not consistency but moral sentiment, a desire not to do more harm than is necessary. We seek consistency, but we seek decency more. We hope and expect that we will never have to choose one over the other, but we accept that if we do, it is consistency that we will jettison.

To do this would not be to abandon reason, because reason need not in principle be bound by absolute consistency. In this case, we would have two competing sets of objective reasons: inconsistent ones for not destroying an entire city and consistent ones which demand of us its destruction. Because to date we have (at least almost) always found consistent sets of reasons to be more compelling, this scenario is hard to imagine. But if it were to come to pass, we would have to conclude that consistent beliefs are not always the most rationally compelling. I should stress again that I cannot imagine our having to reach this conclusion, but it is nonetheless important to acknowledge its conceivability.

This point is, in essence, the most important and overlooked one regarding the rationality of ethics. The traditional dispute between Kantians and sentimentalists rests on an assumption that to be rational, morality must be grounded on *a priori* principles of disinterested reason. This is false. If we understand what rationality means in an appropriately catholic way, we see that it it is a matter of providing reasons for belief and that the sources of these reasons are not confined to *a priori* principles of logical or scientific facts. Once we accept that, we can see that although the Kantian project of founding ethics on pure reason is doomed, reason is still at the very heart of morality.

CHAPTER EIGHT

Scientific morality

Champions of the rational are often their own worst enemies, especially when they happen also to be scientists. Not only do they over-claim for what reason can achieve, they also often do so on the basis of an excessively narrow understanding of what reason involves, which is essentially evidence-based empiricism, no more and no less. The result is an iniquitous intellectual land grab, in which all meaningful discourse is claimed for science and anything else is razed to the ground as useless. This is scientism: the belief that the only legitimate forms of understanding are scientific ones and anything which is not amenable to scientific methods of inquiry is baseless or meaningless.

One well-known recent example of this kind of intellectual imperialism is Sam Harris's book *The Moral Landscape*, in which he argues that, as the subtitle puts it, 'science can determine human values'. Harris claims that morality can be given a rigorously rational basis, not *a priori*, as Kant believed, but *a posteriori*, on the basis of scientific knowledge. The chief value of *The Moral Landscape* is that it is one of the clearest articulations of the scientistic approach to ethics, which is often less brazenly expressed.

I had the opportunity to meet Harris near his Californian home to put my objections to him directly. Having heard his responses, I remain convinced that his project fails, and understanding why it does is important for understanding the limits of science more generally.

1. *The Moral Landscape*

Harris summed up the central argument of his book to me. 'We know that morality has something to do with human well-being and we know that human well-being must be arising from the physiology of the brain and therefore is constrained by whatever psychophysical laws are in in fact true of the brain, and therefore we know it falls potentially within the framework of science.' This is a very helpful synopsis because it captures the essence of all that is right in Harris's argument and also points to where it goes wrong.

Start with the claim: 'We know that morality has something to do with human well-being.' This is not entirely uncontroversial, but I think it fair to say that most ethicists would say that morality concerns the well-being of sentient creatures, directly or indirectly. There would be no right or wrong in a universe that consisted of only rocks. The key phrase here though is 'something to do with'. There is a lot of disagreement about what that 'something' is. Is it about maximising well-being or merely taking account of it in some other way? Is well-being about happiness, our ability to follow our preferences or something else? There is nothing like universal agreement on these matters, and science certainly can't settle the dispute. Science cannot tell us whether we should pursue happiness or excellence, for example, and it is, frankly, hard to even imagine how it might do so.

The second key claim is: 'We know that human well-being must be arising from the physiology of the brain and therefore is constrained by whatever psychophysical laws are in in fact true of the brain, and therefore we know it falls potentially within the framework of science.' The last phrase is important here. Of course science has a lot to say about much of what human welfare involves. Science, for instance, can tell us a lot about the causes of pain, stress, pleasure and so on. That means science can contribute to our understanding of how to improve human and animal welfare. Take Harris's example of 'a truly fraught, moral, value-laden question like "How should parents raise children?"' To answer this requires knowledge of 'child development, healthy emotional lives, healthy cognition and what is going to equip children to become high-functioning adults', and 'there are scientific truths there waiting to be discovered'. But again, this only implies that scientific knowledge can *inform* ethics, not that it can *determine* it. Similarly, we can learn from a neuroscientific point of view why it is that heartbreak feels so bad, but neuroscience can't tell us if it is worth taking the risk of paying that price by opening ourselves up to love.

Harris went on to say, 'We know enough about human flourishing now to know that certain ways of being in the world are just bad from a scientific point of view, just to talk in terms of mental health, sociological health, the health of societies.' Here again is a truth that is rather more limited than Harris takes it to be. Although it is not entirely uncontroversial, I think it is fair to say that the vast majority of reasonable people agree that it is simply bad to be in pain, to be stressed or to be severely depressed when there is no greater need being served. These things are bad from a 'scientific point of view' because they hinder the organism's capacity to flourish. We can see this by direct analogy with animals. A dog that is traumatised or beaten will suffer stress and anxiety and be less able to take care of itself as a result. This is 'bad' from a biological point of view, and hence a scientific one.

But it simply does not follow from the fact that some things are objectively bad from a scientific point of view that science can determine all that is right or wrong. Take, for example, the old dispute between Mill and Bentham as to whether the pleasure of playing a simple game like pushpin has as much value as the pleasure derived from playing Chopin. Science cannot resolve this dispute. Even if it turned out that, from a neurological perspective, the degree and kind of pleasure each gives is indistinguishable (though I doubt this is the case) that would only settle the issue if you had decided that the ultimate arbiter of value is the brain state. That would be a moral judgement, not a scientific one. No one has been able to explain to me how even in principle looking at brain states would tell us how to prioritise our values.

Harris's way around this lacuna is to claim that it does not matter

because we have to distinguish between answers in practice and answers in principle. There are literally an infinite number of scientifically well-posed questions, for which we know there are right or wrong answers, which we will never answer. If I were to ask you how many birds are in flight over the surface of the earth at the moment, we know there's a clear numerical answer to that, we know we don't know it, we know we'll never know it, and we know the number 15 is wrong. There are surely many questions about human well-being which are every bit as intractable as that, but if we could do the math and could get the data we would discover the right answers. But doing that is helpless. A scientific understanding of well-being is about as complicated as it gets, given how complicated the brain is and the number of influences on our subjectivity.

This strikes me as optimistic hand-waving, an expression of faith that there is an in-principle but unattainable scientific way of measuring well-being that takes account of the qualitative as well as quantitative differences between its different components, as well as the inevitable trade-offs that would be necessary to increase some forms of it. To say that this is in principle calculable but in practice way too complicated looks like bold assertion. Even if true, it would be useless. The claim that science can 'determine human values' is hollow if this determination requires an 'in-principle' measure which is in practice unmeasurable.

The fundamental problem with trying to reduce a well-being-centred morality to science is that what we think of as 'well-being' is not a straightforward biological category. People have chosen pain, misery and self-sacrifice to achieve certain goals in history. Many would prefer death to an ignominious life. This makes no sense from a purely biological point of view, but it makes perfect sense from a human one.

The idea that brain scans could reveal to us what form of life is morally better is absurd because brain scans are value-neutral. They can tell you that a certain experience is more intense, that it has longer-lasting effects and so on, but they can't say whether it is good or bad, except in the narrow sense of whether it promotes the physical health of the organism or not.

Harris's kind of scientistic morality seems to me woefully inadequate; and yet I can see what might motivate people to adopt positions like it. Ethics seems to many to be frustratingly subjective. People are dissatisfied by the apparent absence of an objective basis for it. Hence Harris says, 'What does it mean to say it's really true that something is wrong? If you push there, you either have to come down to some truth that falls within the purview of science – that there's something about our world, human nature or the prospects of human happiness that admits of truth claims – or you're just left with preferences: wrong just because we don't like it or a majority of people don't like it.'

This is, however, a false dichotomy that fundamentally misunderstands the nature of reason and ethics. As I have been arguing, we do not have to choose between objective, indisputable fact and mere opinion. Outlooks, values and beliefs can be *more or less* reasonable, *more or less* objective. As we saw in the previous chapter, this is also true in ethics. The fact that moral principles do not have the same status as scientific ones does not mean they are no more subject to rational scrutiny than a preference for strawberries over peaches.

Harris chooses science as the basis for morality, as for him the alternative is too flimsy. But that is because for him everything is too flimsy compared to science. Like John Stuart Mill, he thinks the way to improve ethics is to make it more like science. 'The backward state of the Moral Sciences,' wrote Mill in 1872, 'can only be remedied by applying to them the methods of Physical Science, duly extended and generalized.'[1] That's why when I asked Harris if he thought moral philosophy would go the way of alchemy and be superseded by science, he replied,

Yes and no. I view philosophy as essentially the womb of the sciences. Whenever a question is not experimentally tractable, not quantifiable, something we can really only theorise about in an armchair way, then it's squarely in the domain of philosophy. But the moment you can run experiments and get data, now you're playing the game of science. But the frontier between philosophy and science never is clear. There are always philosophical assumptions tacitly supposed in any science, and scientific disagreement can often be a matter purely of philosophical conviction, because everyone has access to the same data. So I don't think there's a clear cut distinction between philosophy and science, so there wouldn't be a clear cut distinction between moral philosophy and a science of morality. But the moment you start actually talking about data and neurophysiology it would seem you're playing more the language game of neuroscience than philosophy.

The concession to philosophy is welcome, but it is not enough. Reason and rationality are not the sole preserve of sciences where data rule. And that is a good thing, since there is no algorithm for moral judgement.

2. Science contra morality

Harris is not necessarily representative of mainstream scientific thinking about morality. It is telling, however, that the more common alternative view is equally simplistic and extreme. This is the view that science *debunks* ethics. Science does not determine human values, it reveals them to be a kind of fiction.

Perhaps the most strident and unapologetic advocate of this view in recent years is the philosopher Alex Rosenberg, who lists a number of 'persistent' questions humans ask themselves, along with their scientific answers. Three of these are:

What is the difference between right and wrong, good and bad?
There is no moral difference between them.
Why should I be moral? Because it makes you feel better than
being immoral.
*Is abortion, euthanasia, suicide, paying taxes, foreign aid or
anything else you don't like forbidden, permissible, or sometimes obligatory?* Anything goes.[2]

Rosenberg says that these answers are 'pretty obvious' and 'totally
unavoidable . . . provided you place your confidence in science to
provide the answers'. I find it hard to believe people like Rosenberg
are being entirely sincere when they make such bold claims. In the
third question I quote above, for example, it is interesting that he
does not add to his list child sexual abuse, rape, torture of the inno-
cents and so on. To say 'anything goes' after a list like that would be
extremely hard to take seriously.

Perhaps it is because Rosenberg believes his scientistic answers to
moral questions are so obvious that he doesn't really provide any
arguments for his moral nihilism. It simply flows from his scientism,
a pejorative term that he has reclaimed. The key feature of scientism
as far as morality is concerned is the 'conviction that the methods of
science are the only reliable way to secure knowledge of anything'.[3] If
this is so, since moral judgements are not scientific, they cannot
contain any knowledge.

The roots of this misguided way of thinking are found deep in
assumptions about the very nature of reason and knowledge,
assumptions we have been challenging throughout this book.
These assumptions create a simplistic dichotomy between facts
which can be firmly established, either empirically or through pure
reason, and everything else, which is mere opinion or prejudice. If
this were correct, then morality would stand outside of the rational
sphere. But as I argued in the last chapter, it doesn't. Morality is
not science, but that does not mean we cannot bring reason to
bear on it.

Scientists who reject morality or who claim to have a scientific basis for it are making two versions of the same mistake. The mistake is to believe that the methods of science have a monopoly on the practice of reason. From this it follows that morality must either be taken under the wing of science or cast out as irrational. To avoid this false choice, we have to reject the assumptions on which it rests, chief among them the dogma that scientists have exclusive ownership of reason.

3. Science and morality

It would be just an egregious mistake, however, to pull morality away from science and not to allow science to get its hands on morality at all. Science can contribute to our understanding of morality in numerous ways.

Most obviously, many moral issues hinge upon matters of fact, which science can help illuminate. This is most evident in the case of abortion. Moral concerns about abortion rest on the worry that the foetus is a human being, and it is wrong to kill an innocent human being. Biology helps us to think through what this means in ways which clarify the key terms of the debate. At the most fundamental level, it tells us that the development of a human being is a gradual process and so it is simply not tenable to believe that there is a magic moment which demarcates the arrival of a human individual into the world. The cluster of cells that form immediately after conception, for instance, is not by any normal understanding of the word a 'person'. As Mary Warnock's 1984 report on human fertilisation and embryology concluded, before 14 days not even 'the precursor to what will eventually develop into the nervous system' has been formed. At this stage, it is not yet determined whether the foetus will divide into twins, triplets or other multiples. The central nervous system does not begin even to control basic bodily functions until the foetus is at least five months old, before which time it has no consciousness.[4]

None of these facts settles the issue of the morality of abortion. But they are clearly highly pertinent to it. It should be uncontroversial that in debates about human welfare, facts about what constitutes this welfare should be taken into account, and science can provide many such facts. This is the truth that Harris identifies, but he fails to see the limits of its significance. He jumps from the truth that *certain facts important to morality* fall within the purview of science to the falsehood that *morality* lies entirely within the domain of science.

The other way in which science can help us to understand ethics is by explaining how morality becomes possible in the first place. This can be done in a variety of ways. One is to look at how the brain works. This is what the 'neurophilosopher' Patricia Churchland did in her book *Braintrust*, which describes the 'neural platform' for morality. For Churchland, moral problems are essentially 'constraint satisfaction problems'.[5]

'For many of the social problems that people have to address, problems of scarcity of resources or what have you, they have to come together and negotiate and figure out an amicable solution so that they can carry on,' she has said. 'And sometimes those solutions work out fairly well in the short run and then they have to modify them so they can work out in the longer run, and I conceive of that as problem-solving, aka reasoning.'[6]

Critically, Churchland says, 'I don't think neuroscience has anything to say about those things.' What it does have something to say about is the neural basis which makes such problem-solving possible. This 'neural platform' is

> the circuitry in place that makes us want to be with others, that makes us sometimes sacrifice our own interests because we want to be with others, and feel pain when we're excluded or when we're ostracised, enjoy the company of others, enjoy the feelings of satisfaction when we co-operate. All those things are the platform. And out of the platform then emerge very different social practices and they're influenced by many things.

Churchland's approach to the neural platform avoids the crass kind of reductionism that often spoils efforts to use neuroscience to shed light on morality. What too often happens is that people look at a practice such as deception, look at the brain and see that there's a neural process that underlies that, notice perhaps that this circuitry is universal, and conclude that this kind of behaviour is the inevitable consequence of an evolved, hard-wired rule. Churchland points out that this is wrong, because people all over the world have the same basic brain circuitry and yet moral norms differ enormously. For instance, deception is an especially serious crime in Inuit society, and has sometimes been punishable by death. Churchland says the reason for this is that 'deception really jeopardises the group as a whole, because they're always on the knife-edge of survival. Starvation is always just a seal away. So when someone deceives them about something and the whole group undertakes an activity as a result, they waste precious resources, energy.' This, not neuroscience, explains why deception is worse for Inuits than Polynesians. 'Polynesians probably have much the same circuitry as the Inuit, such as sensitivity to deception, but for them, well, you know, it's kind of a misdemeanour.'

A second way in which science can help us to understand how morality emerged, and to some extent how it still works today, is to look at its evolutionary origins. Those who have pursued this seriously have tended to agree that we can see an evolutionary explanation for the emergence of co-operation, but also of freeloading and cheating in certain circumstances too. Evolutionary psychology also suggests how basic moral emotions such as sympathy and empathy emerged and why they worked to our reproductive advantage.[7]

These findings – or more often theories, since few have been established beyond reasonable doubt – are useful for ethics since they help us to recognise what goes with or against the grain of evolved human nature. As Peter Singer once put it, 'I think the Darwinian is going to alert us to what rules are going to work and what rules are going to meet a lot of resistance, and I think we have to bear that in mind.'[8] If we are interested in an ethics which works in the real world, rather than just in theory, this is essential.

It is vital, however, to distinguish this from a cruder kind of evolutionary ethics that says we can only do what we have evolved to want to do. The reality is more complex than this. As Singer put it, 'there's always a trade off between how important the values are to us and the strength of the evolved tendency in our natures.' If we decide something is really very important morally, then we would be justified in trying to promote it, even if that means challenging deep-rooted instincts.

As with every other area where science informs ethics, it is very easy to get the relation between the two wrong. One such mistake arises when people look at evolution, see it as a battle red in tooth and claw, and then use that to justify cut-throat competitive capitalism. Not only is this a misreading of evolution, which actually explains a lot of co-operation at the level of individual animals, it also fails to distinguish between 'is' and 'ought'. As we saw in the last chapter, the so-called fact/value distinction is not an absolute divide, but it remains clear that nothing follows straightforwardly from how things are to how they ought to be.

There is no clearer example of what goes wrong when you ignore this principle than the case of the biologist Randy Thornhill and anthropologist Craig T. Palmer, who proposed the idea that rape was an adaptive strategy that evolved to increase the chances of the rapist's genes being passed on. When they published their research they were denounced by many who misunderstood them to be justifying rape. But the authors themselves were always clear that they were *explaining* why rape was a rational strategy from an evolutionary point of view, not *justifying* it. In their view rape was morally abhorrent. They introduced themselves in the first sentence of the book 'as scientists who would like to see rape eradicated from human life'.[9]

The second mistake evolutionary thinkers often make is to conclude that evolutionary psychology debunks ethics by showing that it is 'nothing more than' reciprocal altruism or enlightened self-interest. The idea here is that what we call morality is simply a set of evolved behaviours to help us further our own interests (or that of the gene, group or whatever the unit of selection is taken to be). Mathematician and economist Ken Binmore is especially forthright in denying that morality could be anything else. Moral rules are evolved social rules and so 'asking how we ought to live makes as much sense as asking what animals ought to exist'. So 'if one wishes to study such rules, it doesn't help to ask how they advance the Good or preserve the Right. One must ask instead how they evolved and why they survive. That is to say, we need to treat morality as a science.'[10]

But this does not follow at all. Binmore is committing the genetic fallacy: confusing an account of something's origins with its justification. Evolutionary psychology might well explain what gave rise to ethics but this is not the same as fully accounting for all that it has now become. What started out as a mere adaptation has become something more. The law of unintended consequences plays out here (in two senses of 'unintended', because there is no initial intention in evolution anyway). What evolved because it helped our selfish interests enabled us to see beyond those, to empathise with others and sometimes to put our own interests second.

We therefore see with evolutionary psychology the same basic pattern that we find wherever science and ethics meet. You find those who claim ethics for science as well as those who claim science debunks ethics. Fortunately, however, you also find more sensible souls who realise that ethics has plenty to learn from science, but not everything. A scientifically informed ethics is to be welcomed, but a purely scientific ethics is an impossibility.

CHAPTER NINE

The claims of reason

There have been two key recurring themes in my argument so far. The first is that reason requires judgement, that it is not a pure algorithm that can be set up and left to run by itself to produce true conclusions. The second is that reason, by itself or in the service of science, can neither provide us with all we need for ethics nor debunk it. Both these claims are in a sense deflationary: they take reason off a pedestal and show it to be less omnipotent than some of its more zealous advocates believe.

Nonetheless, this is not to belittle reason. It is less powerful than some have supposed but it is certainly not a mere veneer for irrational beliefs and prejudices, a smokescreen for the use of power. Reason has force. In this chapter I want to say more about the most important aspect of this force: its normative nature. The normative concerns what we *ought* to do, think or believe. The normative nature of reason is usually taken to be obvious. When we complain that someone is 'not being rational' we are as good as saying that they ought not to be behaving that way. If someone replies, 'Why?' to the demand, 'be reasonable' we often find we have nothing more to say: if people can't see why they should be reasonable then they are beyond help.

But perhaps there is a better answer to this 'why'. We are wrong to take the normative force of reason for granted. If we look carefully to see where it comes from we can understand much better what reason is and why we ought to respect it.[1]

1. Reason's own 'ought'

Let's go back to the defining characteristics of rational argument. A reason (which may or may not be an argument) is rational when it provides objective grounds for belief. Making such a judgement of rationality implies that such a reason has a claim on us: it is a reason which, just as long as we understand it, should make us believe what we think it is a reason to believe. To say 'this is a compelling, assessable, comprehensible, defeasible and interest-neutral reason for believing X' is to say that you should believe X on the grounds of the reason offered. This is not necessarily a moral 'ought'. It is rather rationality's own 'ought', the 'ought' we recognise in statements such as 'given the evidence, you ought to be able to see that smoking is unhealthy'.

This example is an apt one, because it allows us to see the clear distinction between the rational and the ethical ought. Reason demands that we accept that smoking is unhealthy, but it does not demand that we don't smoke. Someone who says, 'I know smoking is bad for me, but I like it so I do it', is not defying the normativity of reason. She is defying reason if she says she wants to do what is most healthy for her, she sees that smoking is unhealthy, but she does it anyway. In that case, the person in question would almost invariably accept that she was being irrational. She would not deny that given the facts and her desires she ought to do differently; she would simply be admitting that for one reason or another she is unable or unwilling to do so.

Reason's own ought flows simply from the nature of reason itself. Start with the fact that rationality is in the business of providing objective reasons for belief. The very notion of objectivity contains within it the idea that the reason in question does not depend on the particular perspective of the individual but has a more universal validity. If we accept that an objective reason is equally sound for all, then we are accepting that it ought to be sound for us. This is precisely what distinguishes it from a subjective reason, which we can happily reject on the grounds that it rests on too particular a perspective to lay claim to us.

The normativity of reason is reflected in the sense in which rational arguments and reasons are compelling. A good argument is one we feel we must accept. But the grounds upon which the argument is based are in principle assessable and comprehensible by others. So if you feel *you* must accept the argument, you must also feel others should too. Since the grounds are also interest-neutral, it does not matter that others have different desires or preferences to you. This is irrelevant to the soundness of a rational argument.

So rational arguments are compelling – they make us feel we ought to accept them – and they are compelling for reasons which are, in principle, equally compelling for other rational agents. Therefore, to accept that an argument is rational and objective is to accept that oneself and others ought to believe what it is an argument for.

The idea that there is a normative element to reason is not new. Indeed, in some sense it has surely been accepted historically by all who believe reason has some kind of objective validity. There is, however, one important way in which this standard conception of the normativity of reason is a little misleading. When it is said that rationality has a normative component, that is usually interpreted to mean:

If *X* is rational, then one ought to believe it.

Here, the normative follows from the factual.[2] Whether or not *X* is rational is a factual matter. Having established that, in fact, *X* is rational, it is argued that we therefore ought to believe it. But there is something very misleading about this way of putting it. As we have already seen, although the fact/value distinction is not as clear-cut as sometimes supposed, Hume's basic logical point is robust: you cannot get a normative conclusion from entirely non-normative premises.

By the same general principle, it would be magical if reason generated any normative conclusions unless normativity were somehow already embedded in it. For the normativity of rationality to flow from the nature of reason, the source of that normativity must be contained within the nature of reason itself. Rationality, objectivity and normativity cannot be separated. To accept that there are objective reasons for preferring one belief over another just is to accept that one ought to believe it. Judging that an argument is a sound, objective, rational one is at the same time saying that one ought to accept it.

The normativity of reason implies what I call the Normative Principle of Rationality:

We should believe what it is most rational to believe.

To deny this would seem perverse. Who would believe that, given more than one option, we should believe what it is *least* rational to believe? I can only assume that those tempted to say that misunderstand what reason is and so believe it is only by rejecting it that we can preserve all that is good in intuition or emotion.

What needs to be stressed here is that, because there is an essential element of judgement in reason, this normativity does not flow from some kind of impersonal authority. In judging something to be objective, we judge that it has a claim on us. But we cannot escape the fact that we are *judging* it to be objective, not simply *recognising* or *acknowledging* it to be so. This is the inescapable precariousness of reason. It makes claims of universal validity while all the time resting on judgements that only we can make for ourselves. There is no contradiction here, only a kind of fundamental insecurity.

This insecurity seems to me to be very close to, if not identical to, the inescapable responsibility described in existentialism. For existentialists, we cannot escape the fact that we are always responsible for what we do and what we believe. No matter how much we might strive to find external authorities to justify ourselves, at the end of the day we have to choose whether to accept their authority or not. In that sense, every claim of reason is personal. And yet at the same time, when it comes to what is reasonable or rational, our choice is never entirely personal since our judgement by implication holds for others as well as ourselves.

Sartre expressed something very much like this in his famous lecture, *Existentialism is a Humanism*:

> The first effect of existentialism is that it puts every man in possession of himself as he is, and places the entire responsibility for his existence squarely upon his own shoulders. And, when we say that man is responsible for himself, we do not mean that he is responsible only for his own individuality, but that he is responsible for all men. [. . .] To choose between this or that is at the same time to affirm the value of that which is chosen; for we are unable ever to choose the worse. What we choose is always the better; and nothing can be better for us unless it is better for all.[3]

In Sartre's formulation, the emphasis is on choice. But it seems to me the same basic truth holds if we think instead of judgement. Indeed, one might describe the account of reason I advocate as a more sober existentialism. While denying the extravagance of claiming that we are free to choose whatever we want, it nonetheless acknowledges that our judgements of what is rational are in some sense choices because there is nothing in the nature of reason or the world that strictly compels us to make them. We *feel* compelled to accept what we judge to be objective, but we always judge and never dispassionately assess.

2. The rationality of the moral ought

I have argued that morality cannot be grounded in reason alone. At the same time, I have also argued that reason has an important role to play in morality. I think the normativity of reason helps explain why reason is in this intermediate position, neither the grounds of all ethics nor irrelevant to it.

Take a straightforward example of where an ethical claim is clearly related to a factual one. One of the most irresistible reasons why racism is morally unjustified is the empirical fact that there is no evidence whatsoever that any racial group (in itself a dubious category) is on balance superior to another. Some people with certain genetic histories may have some advantages over others. The huge success of runners from mountainous districts beside the Rift Valley in East Africa, for instance, might be at least in part to do with how thousands of years of living at high altitude have given then a higher red blood count than is the norm. But any such specific advantages are rare, marginal and in no way justify the claim that any particular ethnic group is overall superior or inferior.

The facts therefore suggest that you ought to believe that no racial group is superior to any other. But that doesn't decisively settle the moral issue of racism. There might be any number of reasons (none persuasive to me) why someone might accept this factual claim and yet still feel entitled to discriminate on the grounds of ethnicity or skin colour. One might, for instance, cite the evidence that almost everyone has some kind of implicit prejudice against people they perceive to be different, and that this suggests discrimination is natural. Combine that with an idea that we have the right to follow our natural instincts and you get an attempted justification of racism that does not deny that we ought to accept that all races are equal.

This is an instance of what we discussed previously: the inability of reason to determine absolutely what is right and what is wrong. Nonetheless, I would suggest that the normative force of many factual claims does and should have an impact on our moral thinking. The fact that we ought to believe all races are equal adds weight to the judgement that we ought to treat them equally, even if it does not strictly demand that conclusion. At the very least, it shifts the burden of argument (proof being too strong a word here). If there is no empirical basis for a belief in the superior rights of one ethnic group, then in the absence of a good justification for discrimination, the default is equal rights.

One reason why there is a link between what we ought to believe and what we ought to do is that belief is rarely entirely theoretical. Take, for instance, the belief that nuts are wholesome. The very concept of 'wholesome' is a practical one: it means that something is good for you to eat, that it contributes to a healthy diet. There is therefore a practical dimension tied up in the word's very meaning.

Let us refer to such words as *praxic*: they are concepts that if understood properly already contain within them some kind of practical implication. I would suggest that a great many of our superficially merely factual beliefs are praxic because we hold them within the context of a lived life where their truth or falsity makes a practical difference. Merely to accept them as true is to accept that they should influence decisions about how we behave. Tea being hot is reason to drink it if we are cold. That a car is cheap is a reason to consider buying it if money is short.

Traditionally, I think most philosophers would distinguish sharply between the factual content of a belief and any practical import it might have. So 'tea is hot' and 'the car is cheap' are simply statements about things which might be used in a practical context but they are not inherently praxic, as I have defined it. But I don't think this neat division is tenable. The very concepts used only make sense in a context where practice is central. Tea is hot only in the context of a human drinker, a car cheap only in the context of a typical consumer. There is nothing merely factual about either truth: we would not even state either unless we understood that they had a practical significance.

In the same way, terms like 'different' and 'superior' have a praxic quality, depending on the context of their use. In creative work, for example, 'different' suggests (all other things being equal) that there is something worth attending to. Even if the work fails, to point out that it does something different is to point out that there is something about it that merits attention. (This is perhaps why people who struggle to find something good to say about a work of art but want to be nice will often volunteer that it is 'different'.) 'Superior' is always praxic, since things are never better or worse in an absolute sense but always and only with regard to certain purposes. To say a person is a better musician than another is a reason to choose her performance over another but not a reason to give her greater rights in a court of law.

This idea that many terms have a praxic element fills out the notion of 'normative facts' that I introduced in chapter seven. Facts are normative when they contain within them some idea of what is good or right, of what we ought to do. This normativity often – perhaps always – arises when the praxic element relates to some imperative that is not merely hypothetical, to borrow Kant's terminology. To take the car example, to say that it is cheap might be a reason to buy it, but only if you want to buy a car and have limited funds. To say that people of different nationalities are equal, however, is a reason to treat them equally, irrespective of your goals and circumstances, all other things being equal.

Although I would commend the idea that many beliefs and concepts have a praxic quality, my essential point can be made even if you want to distinguish clearly between a mere fact and its practical application. This can be done simply by observing how close the connection often is between the fact and its practical import. Even if a fact is nothing more than a fact, put it into the world and its practical implications are immediately evident. And as soon as that happens, the normative has been introduced. To repeat, I am not saying that what we ought to do automatically follows from simple facts. Rather, it is that simple facts often have an important effect on what we judge we ought to do. 'Is' does not imply 'ought', but within many an 'is' an 'ought' is already lurking.

3. The passion of the philosopher

That judgement and belief are drenched in normativity helps in part to explain what might otherwise appear to be a puzzling feature of philosophical life: why philosophers get so worked up about their arguments and ideas. Philosophy has a reputation as a dry discipline but we know from experience that people care passionately about their arguments and ideas. Wittgenstein hurling a poker at Bertrand Russell might be the exception, but passions often rise when the soundness of arguments is at stake.[4] The restrained conventions of the seminar room and the formal language of journal papers conceal this, but anyone who has spent time around philosophers knows that they generate some heat as well as light. Occasionally, this will erupt in public. In one notorious recent dispute, Colin McGinn described one of Ted Honderich's books as 'shoddy, inept, and disastrous'. When McGinn denied that this harsh language was personal, Honderich replied, 'For McGinn to say that is for him to be a philosopher on the moon. Nobody on Earth believes that his review is not motivated by animus.'[5]

Public outbursts like these are unusual but the desire at least to thump the table is much more common than academic decorum suggests. There may be many reasons for this, but, I want to suggest, one is that when we think we have a rational argument we inescapably think that others should accept it. This might be mitigated by our acceptance that all beliefs are defeasible and all philosophers fallible, but psychologically this probably changes very little. Believing that in principle we might be wrong does little to temper our conviction when we cannot see how on earth we could be. It is only when we harbour serious doubts that our argument is sound that we sincerely accept that others should not feel rationally compelled to agree with us.

I think intellectual honesty demands that philosophers accept this all-pervading normativity more openly. Apart from anything else, this helps explain why philosophy matters. We are not just disputing what is true or false, we are arguing about what we ought to think. Persuasion is not the same as rational argument but every rational argument is and ought to be an exercise in persuasion. Ideas only matter because we ought to believe the right ones. Reason in philosophy is therefore in a sense never disinterested.

PART IV: THE KING

'Unless communities have philosophers as kings . . . There can be no end to political troubles, my dear Glaucon, or even to human troubles in general.' This bold assertion by Socrates in Plato's *Republic* was greeted with incredulity by his interlocutors. 'What a thing to say!' said Glaucon, warning Socrates to expect 'hordes of people – and not second-rate people either . . . to pick up the nearest weapon, and rush naked at you with enough energy to achieve heroic feats'.[1]

There has never been a 'sophocracy' in human history, where philosophers have ruled. Nonetheless, Plato's philosopher ruler has given rise to an idea which has been very influential: that reason is powerful enough, and we are good enough at using it, for us to build society on rational principles, excluding all other supposed sources of wisdom.

The idea is a seductive one. After all, who could be in favour of building society on *irrational* principles? But we have to be very careful. Experience should have taught us that the idea that we can know what reason demands of us is closer to the idea that we can know what God demands of us than we might think. In both cases, humans have tended to have too much confidence in their own ability to access certain, objective truth about how human beings should live. The result is too often tyranny in the guise of enlightened liberation.

The call to reason is a powerful one. It is easy to applaud such sentiments as 'Ignorance will come to an end when everything is presented as it really is; it will end when knowledge about everything is made available to every human being in a suitable way.' But when we see that these were the words of Muammar Al Gathafi, erstwhile military dictator of Libya, we are given pause for thought.[2] Before advocating a more rational state, we need to think very carefully indeed about what this really means.

CHAPTER TEN

The rational state

It doesn't take a close reading of Voltaire's *Candide* to persuade most people that '*Tout est pour le mieux dans le meilleur des mondes possibles*' – everything is for the best in this, the best of all possible worlds' – is one of the most tragicomic falsehoods ever uttered. It's not just that nature is fickle and often cruel. We human beings can hardly claim to have organised our affairs with optimal justice and efficiency. When Prince sung about people unable to feed their children while we're sending people to the moon, he echoed a sentiment that must have been expressed millions of times in homes, cafés, markets and bars around the world.[1] The way we run society is plainly irrational, and so it surely follows that if we were only to apply a bit more rationality, everything could be at least better in one possible world.

There is a very real sense in which this has to be true. However, as a matter of historical fact, many attempts to establish society on a more rational basis have been disastrous failures. Understanding why helps us to understand better what reason really is and how it can be best used in the service of building a better world.

1. Socrates' mistake

One of the first attempts to rethink politics along more rational lines was one of the worst, but also one of the most instructive. Plato's *Republic* is one of the most unworkable, unattractive utopias ever conceived. Plato advocated a society in which a separate Guardian class is raised from childhood and 'women and children are to be held in common among the Guardians'. Rulers 'will have to employ a great deal of fiction and deceit for the benefit of their subjects', 'mate the best of our men with the best of our women' and 'bring up only the offspring of the best'.[2]

Fortunately no one has ever got far in attempting to create such a dystopia. It is possible that not even Plato believed anyone should try. The ultimate aim of the dialogue is to illuminate the nature of justice in the individual by analogy with justice in the state and so it is more than possible that it was never conceived as a workable blueprint. Even if Plato was entirely sincere, the *Republic* has to be read in the context of the decline of Athens and Plato's disillusion with a democratic system that decreed the execution of Socrates.

However we are to read the *Republic*, we can see within it the root of an error which has hampered political thinking before and since. This is revealed in a short exchange between Socrates and Glaucon just before Plato reveals that in his Republic the philosophers would be kings. Socrates begins by asking Glaucon whether he agrees with the principles that lie behind his exposition. 'Does practice ever square with theory?' he demands. 'Is it not in the nature of things that, whatever people think, practice should come less close to truth than theory?'[3]

This is an extremely revealing pair of questions. It puts me in mind of the fictional chat show host Alan Partridge, who claims to have a foolproof gambling system that he has tried out many times – in his head.[4] The modern audience laughed straight away, of course. We have become skeptical of ideas that have been worked out only on paper or in our heads, recognising that the litmus test of any practical proposal is whether it works. Today, if someone says, 'That's all very well in theory', the implication is almost always that it won't work in practice. Socrates' questions suggest a way of thinking which is the exact opposite. Theory gets at what is true, and if practice is imperfect, that is the fault of practice, not theory.

These lines in Plato express explicitly what is often an unstated assumption: that we should place our confidence in the truth of our

theories about how society should be run and then approach practical politics simply as a matter of changing society to approximate as
closely to this theory as possible. This becomes clear a few moments
later, when Socrates says that the problem they need to solve is 'to
show what fault it is in the constitutions of existing states that
prevents them from being run like ours'.

Indeed, such is the primacy of theory for Plato that we don't even
need to worry too much about how practical it is, but simply trust
that, being true, it can be relied on as a guide to social organisation.
'Don't insist on my showing that every detail of our description can
be realised in practice,' says Socrates, 'but grant that we shall have
met your demand that its realisation should be possible if we are able
to meet the conditions under which a society can most closely
approximate to it.'

This is a fatal mistake that was destined to be repeated throughout
history. Amartya Sen attacked it in *The Idea of Justice*. Sen criticises
what he calls the 'transcendental' approach to justice. This works by
identifying a single clear ideal of what perfect justice looks like and
then trying to arrange society to approximate this as closely as
possible. Sen has two objections to this.

First, justice, like many goods, may be and probably is plural.
There are several things which can be meant by saying that something is just, and trying to reduce them to one ideal will result in
distortion or loss. Sen illustrates this with a story of three children
and a flute, all of the children having some claim to the instrument.
One says she is the only one able to play it, another that he is the only
one with no other toys and the third that she made it. Sen argues that
'we may not be able to identify, without some arbitrariness, any of the
alternative arguments as being the one that must invariably prevail'.
So it is with justice in general, which can be a matter of giving each
according to need, effort or ability to make the best use of a resource.
Sen argues we must take seriously the 'possible sustainability of plural
and competing reasons for justice, all of which have claims to impartiality and which nevertheless differ from – and rival – each other.'[5]

Second, the transcendental approach simply isn't the best way to create a more just world. We do not need any kind of perfect ideal of justice to identify the worst injustices and see how to reduce them. Where women do not have equal rights with men, we ought to fight so that they have them and there is no need to appeal to any philosophically contentious concept of justice to do this. 'We can have a strong sense of injustice on many different grounds,' writes Sen, 'and yet not agree on one particular ground as being the dominant reason for the diagnosis of injustice.'[6]

I think Sen is right, but there is another problem with Plato's approach which also merits examination. Plato sets up a dichotomy between theory and practice in which reason belongs on the theoretical side. In Plato's rationalist mindset, ideas are always more closer to perfection in the pure, intellectual realm and they lose their crystalline clarity and perfection when they are applied to the messy world of appearances. Plato is extreme in his idealisation of ideas, but I think his basic prejudice lies behind many the ideas of later political thinkers. Their common mistake has been to think that we can be confident in our intellectual understanding of what is good and just and then it is simply a matter of trying to mould reality so as to get as close to that as possible. Principles come first and practice is just detail.

That is perhaps one reason why 'pragmatic' is considered a dirty word in politics, one which is always being cast as opposed to principle. Pragmatism here means compromising your ideals in order to accommodate them to the real world. This is a serious error. Politics must be about changing the world for the better and that means it is inherently pragmatic. A principle that can't be implemented is just a bad principle. Political thinking must be much more rigorously empirical than Socrates suggests in his discussion with Glaucon. It is not just that we can in practice apply our theories incorrectly, but that practice can show theory to be wrong. The way Socrates talks, if would seem that if things aren't working out in his Republic, this can only mean that there is an error of implementation. He shows no sign of being open to the idea that practical failure might reveal a problem with the theory.

Political reasoning cannot be *a priori*. Experience has to have a more engaged and ongoing role to play. Every time we make any kind of inference about what would be best we need to go back to experience to check whether it is sound. This empirical validation is even more important than any logical one, which merely looks to see whether the inference follows on paper. For example, we might easily reason that since economic equality is good, and we can achieve greater equality by redistributing wealth, then this entails that a redistribution of wealth is good. But we have to know a lot about how such a redistribution would actually work to know whether this inference is sound. It might turn out that redistribution has unintended consequences, for example, ones which are so bad that they more than outweigh the good of equality. At the very least we need to be aware that being in favour of redistribution in principle doesn't tell you which of the innumerable ways of achieving it is effective. All the hard work is done with reference to experience, not the theoretical validity of inferences from premises to conclusions.

In this way we can see that political reason is as much – if not more – bottom-up than top-down. Rationality requires attending to objective reasons for belief and many of the most important such reasons are provided by what we observe in the world. Indeed, what we observe is of primary importance: there is no hope of understanding justice, for example, if we attempt to do so purely by examining the concept without any reference at all to what we perceive to be just or unjust in the world. That way lies the absurdity uttered by Ferdinand I, the Holy Roman Emperor: 'Let justice be done, though the world perish.'

Understood in this way, experience does not just provide the *content* of reasoning, it shapes its form. Experience does not just give us premises for argument to work on, it tells us a lot about what we should reasonably believe about how a good society should be. Take, for example, the importance of family ties for human life. Only in some parody of political philosophy do we take this as a premise, conjoin it with others and create a deductive argument. Rather, we simply see that the importance of family ties for almost all human beings is a reason to value and respect them. Plato did not see this because he did not pay enough attention to what actually works and was too spellbound by what reason alone told him would be optimal. Practical reason doesn't work well when it dwells too long in the confines of the thinker's head.

2. The truth in conservatism

The need to pay due attention to the reality on the ground points to the essential truth in Burkean conservative philosophy, eloquently articulated by Roger Scruton. For Scruton, society is like a living organism, and individuals are not distinct 'atoms' of autonomous self-determination, as characterised by liberalism, but parts of a whole which only flourish when that whole is itself flourishing. This means that human life only makes sense, values only have currency and projects only have meaning when understood as part of a social history that extends both before and after our own lives.

The political upshot of this, for conservatives, is that we need to preserve the institutions, customs and practices of our society in order for us to flourish in that society. Conservatism is therefore 'an exercise in social ecology' whose goal is 'to pass on to future generations – and if possible enhance – the order and equilibrium of which we are the temporary trustees.'[7] What we must not do is start with a blank slate, determining what the ideal society will look like and then attempting to reorder society to meet this utopian vision, irrespective of how society is now. That way lies ruin.

Connected with this point is the observation of the nineteenth-century English cleric Charles Caleb Colton, that 'It is far more easy to pull down, than to build up, and to destroy, than to preserve.'[8] Society is a product of a long process of gradual evolution. From an objective viewpoint, it may seem hard to see why any particular part of it is necessary. But what might seem like anachronisms – in Britain, the House of Lords, the monarchy, the lack of a written constitution, for example – are the products of centuries of gradual adaptation. When we destroy these institutions and replace them with something designed by theoreticians, we risk dismissing the wisdom of history, of our ancestors, and replacing it with something with much shallower roots. But what is more, we are destroying what took years to develop and replacing it with something untried and untested. For conservatives, this is folly and hubris.

The basic truth in conservatism is then that society is a delicate 'ecosystem', and one should always be careful about how one reforms it. The more violent the change, the greater the risk of causing harm. The more the reform goes with the grain of society as it is, the greater the chances of its success. Therefore, before undertaking any reform, we need to ask if it is really necessary and whether it fits in with or jars with society as it is.

One does not need to be a conservative to accept the basic truth being articulated here. Nothing in these arguments justifies any particular political policy. After all, only the most inveterate conservatives would say that their philosophy requires that society is never changed and never reformed. No respectable conservative would argue, for example, that we should have preserved slavery or continued to deny women's suffrage. So the fact that any custom or institution is a product of history, a history that is part of what gives citizens their sense of identity, is not an argument against reform. Conservatism does not provide a rule that tells us when reform is necessary or dangerous; it merely warns us to proceed with extreme caution.

I think that liberals and leftists need also to accept this conservative insight. This requires us to expand our notion of what it means to order society rationally. Reason requires that we attend very carefully to how things are now, how they work and how they evolved. The process of designing a better society has to start by looking at the society we have, since we cannot build a new one from scratch to replace it. This is using our reason in the fullest, most complete way. Giving due weight to the contingencies of the present world is not to dilute rationality but to fortify it with precisely the kind of data that allows it to draw on more and better reasons for coming to the right conclusions.

This approach was first exemplified by Plato's successor, Aristotle. Aristotle's way of approaching politics had two features that Plato's lacked. First, he began by examining the political systems currently in existence, seeing their relative strengths and weaknesses. He never made the mistake of thinking about the relative merits of oligarchy, democracy or monarchy in purely abstract terms. Second, he had a realistic expectation that political philosophy can never be clear-cut and that a certain amount of unclarity and imprecision is inevitable. 'Our account will be adequate if its clarity is in line with the subject matter, because the same degree of precision is not to be sought in all discussions,' he wrote. Hence in politics, 'we should be content . . . to demonstrate the truth sketchily and in outline, and because we are making generalisations on the basis of generalisations, to draw conclusions along the same lines'.[9]

Aristotle was not relying on reason less than Plato. In acknowledging that the kinds of reason which inform rational debate about politics are by their nature inconclusive he was actually being more properly rational. To be as rational as possible means not trying to get more from rationality than is possible. In no domain is this true more than in politics.

3. Anarchism and communism

Arguably the most disastrous result of trying to wipe the slate clean and impose a rational political system was the communist experiment of the twentieth century. The failure was in part the result of an excessive confidence in the power of reason to design a better world.

This was not, as with Plato's Republic, a matter of putting too much faith in *a priori* reasoning. Communists of various stripes saw their project as rooted in an understanding of the material world. Mao, for instance, instructed: 'Discover the truth through practice, and again through practice verify and develop the truth. Start from perceptual knowledge and actively develop it into rational knowledge; then start from rational knowledge and actively guide revolutionary practice to change both the subjective and the objective world. Practice, knowledge, again practice, again knowledge. This form repeats itself in endless cycles . . .'[10]

Communists have always sought to pay due attention to the real world, but they have tended to have too much confidence that the theories they derive from observation have the status of a sure, exact science. In *The Communist Manifesto*, for example, Marx and Engels claimed that 'The theoretical conclusions of the Communists are in no way based on ideas or principles that have been invented, or discovered, by this or that would-be universal reformer. They merely express, in general terms, actual relations springing from an existing class struggle, from a historical movement going on under our very eyes.'[11]

What is lacking here is an Aristotelian realism and hence modesty about the imprecision of political science. When people depart from this it is, I suspect, often because they are too impressed by what they understand and not sufficiently aware of what they don't. I can illustrate this most clearly with Marx's idea of surplus value. Lenin summed up the basic idea in his 1914 essay 'Karl Marx'. For a capitalist to make money he must sell things for more than it costs him to buy or make them. One of the main ways he does this is by paying for labour at less than its true value. So, for example, if a worker puts in 12 hours, 'in the course of six hours ("necessary" labour time) the worker creates product sufficient to cover the cost of his own maintenance; in the course of the next six hours ("surplus" labour time), he creates "surplus" product, or surplus value, for which the capitalist does not pay.'[12] To put it another way, in order for an employer to earn money, the employee must work enough to pay his own wages but also some more for which the employer keeps the reward. Wage labour is therefore always a kind of exploitation.

The theory of surplus value has proved to be one of the most powerful and persuasive economic and moral justifications for communism. Its force lies in the fact that the essential core of the idea is rationally irrefutable. Although it is possible to have individual employees who do not generate enough profit for the capitalist to pay them, over a whole profitable business it must be the case that the workers produce more wealth than their own wages. Capitalists only employ people because they can profit from them.

Surplus value is therefore real. The question is what follows from its discovery. For Marx, it seemed self-evident that it was irrational and unjust for workers to go along with a system that led them to receive less than their 100% share of the wealth they generated. But this conclusion is not as indisputable as the premise from which it was reached. Communists have tended to be seduced by the rational and moral clarity of the idea of surplus labour when what was actually needed was a more rigorous questioning of why, if it was so manifestly unjust, people had indeed been going along with it.

Once you ask this question with an open mind, the answers become obvious. One factor is that capitalists profit only because they take the risk of investing in the business and taking any losses that might come along if there is a slump or some other unforeseen problem. Greater reward is linked with greater risk. (At least it should be: when governments shield big businesses, such as banks, from risks, this no longer applies.) A related mistake the communist analysis makes is to assume that the counterfactual to the status quo is essentially the same, but with the workers keeping all their share rather than letting the capitalist take it. That is indeed all that would change if, at a stroke, you took an existing business and handed it over to its workers. But in the real world, you have to think about how businesses emerge in the first place, and what leads them to develop and grow. All that involves enterprise, entrepreneurship, innovation, competition – the very things that all communist economies to date have undermined in the long run. So if we reason more carefully, starting with observation of how the economy actually works, we can see that there are good reasons why we have capitalists.

The question now becomes, is it actually better for the worker to live in an economy where there is no surplus value? There is no *a priori* answer to this. The answer requires us to look at how the real world actually works. With the benefit of hindsight, we can conclude that the answer is most certainly no. Even if the actual communist states that emerged had been full realisations of Marx's ideals rather than imperfect, oppressive bastard offspring, they would have almost certainly lacked the economic dynamism of regulated market economies. All other things being equal, it is much better for a worker to generate £200 of wealth and keep £150 of it than it is to generate £100 and keep it all.

Of course, there is plenty more here that needs arguing before we conclude what the optimal system is. Could we perhaps have a market economy in which all the actors were co-operatives, combining the benefits of economic competition with the fairness of zero surplus value? Should there be limits on how much surplus value business owners should be able to extract from their workers? My purpose here is not to suggest that having seen communism's error we now know precisely what we should do instead. Indeed, it is the exact opposite. If the mistake is to read too much into a rationally unarguable conclusion, we would be making the same mistake if we thought we could easily read off what follows from a rationally unarguable rejection of that mistake. The whole point is that politics is incredibly complicated and we must always resist the lure of what appears to be a theoretically clear diagnosis of a problem or a prescription for its solution.

Communists are of course not alone in being overconfident in the rationality of their alternatives to the status quo. Take the anarchist response of Mikhail Bakunin to the communists. Bakunin completely rejected Plato's ideal that philosophers should be kings. 'Let him govern,' he said of the scholar, 'and he will become the most unbearable tyrant, for scholarly pride is repulsive, offensive and more oppressive than any other. To be the slaves of pedants – what a fate for mankind!'[13] He decried the 'perfect logic (in their own terms)' of 'idealists of every stripe', including 'doctrinaire revolutionaries' who worked from the 'utterly false' premise 'that thought precedes life, that abstract theory precedes social practice'.

Bakunin is clearly advocating something close to what I have been arguing for here. 'Natural and social life always precedes thought (which is merely one of its functions) but is never its result', while 'abstract reflections' are 'always produced by life but never producing it'. However, his inverted Platonism is as simplistic as the view it replaces. Rather than seeing the need for any interplay between experience and reflection, Bakunin writes as though the truth simply flows from the facts in some unmediated way. Let 'natural and social life' be your guide and you can never go wrong. But of course the world needs interpreting and unless you recognise that this is an enterprise filled with the possibility of error and distortion, you risk a hubris equal and opposite to that of the rationalists.

Hence in the part of Bakunin's *Statism and Anarchy* I have been quoting from, he says, 'The living, concretely rational method of science is to proceed from the real fact to the idea that encompasses it, expresses it, and thereby explains it. In the practical world it is the movement from social life to the most rational possible organization of it.' Bakunin is no less in awe of reason than Plato, only for Bakunin, reason proceeds from the social world to the mind, not the other way around. Having made this critical change from Plato, he nonetheless appears to have no doubt that simply by following reason we can know for sure what the most rational way to order society is.

But of course, anarchism proved to be an even less tenable system than communism, albeit a more humane one. You can count on the fingers of one hand the number of anarchist cities or communes that have been established long enough to leave a mark on the world, and each lasted for months rather than years.

Both the communists and the anarchists vastly overestimated their ability to understand how the world should work, in the former case by elevating their theories to the level of a precise science and in the latter by believing that the most rational order was somehow already evident behind the veneer of so-called civilised society. The key lesson we should draw from both is the same. The attempt to create a more rational society requires that we have good, objectively grounded reasons for making the changes that we do. And these reasons have to be placed in the context of one extremely important reason to be cautious: human society is complicated and if anyone proposes a radical new model of how we should organise society then we have good grounds to suspect that the model is grossly and dangerously simplified. Radical reform should be possible, but it should usually be piecemeal. It is sheer hubris to imagine that we understand what we are messing with enough to justify anything more wholesale.

This might sound depressingly conservative, but to believe anything else is to grant reason – or at least our own reason – much more power than is justified. To be truly rational we need to acknowledge the limits of our rationality: nothing is more irrational than an unwarranted faith in reason.

4. *Homo economicus*

Poor political reasoning is not confined to the left, of course. Faith in the rationality of human action reached its peak – or perhaps its nadir – in the free market economics that was mainstream through most of the twentieth century and into the twenty-first. It is neatly described by the Nobel Prize-winning economist Daniel McFadden in his presidential address to the American Economic Association in 2006. 'Economic theories and ideologies are founded on the

principle that consumers have well-defined preferences, and consistently behave to advance their self-interest,' he told his audience. 'Most
economists accept this concept of the consumer' and along with it an
economic theory that maintains the efficiency of decentralised,
competitive markets.[14]

This image of humankind has been called *Homo economicus*,
whom McFadden describes as 'sovereign in tastes, steely-eyed and
point-on in perception of risk, and relentless in maximization of
happiness'. What economists have come to realise alarmingly late,
however, is that this kind of human being is what McFadden calls a
'rare species', far from representative of the norm. Rather, *Homo
actualis* is often uncertain or ambiguous in preferences, blurry-eyed,
poor at risk assessment and inconsistent in the maximisation of
happiness.

The standard critique of *Homo economicus* is that human beings
are simply not as rational as the model assumes. To be fair to those
who used the model, I am not sure that *Homo economicus* was ever
supposed to be a fully formed theory of human nature. Economists
always knew that not everyone all of the time behaved as a perfect
rational self-maximiser. But they did assume that this was how
people tended to act, and so economic models that aggregated across
populations could work on the assumption that *Homo economicus*
provided a decent model of human agency. One reason they could
do this was that it could be assumed – or so it was thought – that
people would generally behave rationally. Hence there is a normative
component to *Homo economicus*: this is how humans ought to
behave, if their behaviour is to be understood as rational.

I think this is wrong. It is not simply that human beings are not as
rational as the model of *Homo economicus* assumes, it is that *Homo
economicus* assumes a false model of what being rational means.
First of all, take the idea that the rational actor has 'well-defined preferences' and is 'sovereign in tastes'. Life would certainly be easier if
our desires were so constant and clear, but would that make us more
rational? I can't see why. It is irrational for desires and preferences to

flip-flop for no reason, but it is not at all irrational for them to change in line with short-term variations in circumstances and evolve in line with long-term ones. Life is a dynamic process and the same options have very different meanings at different times. To take a trivial example, it is not irrational to choose the pulled pork sandwich one day and a hummus wrap the next. We tire of some things, while the sheer novelty of others gives us a reason to prefer them temporarily over more enduring favourites. In more serious matters, whom we would like to share our lives with might change over time. It is sad, but not irrational, when people who once loved each other deeply decide they ought to separate.

The model of the human being as having stable, settled preferences is best exemplified in people who most of us find rather inhuman, such as those who eat the same things every day because that allows them to refuel with the minimum of effort and thought. But on what definition of rationality, for instance, it is rational to live on Soylent, a complete food made by mixing a pre-prepared powder with water? This would only be rational if you simply had no interest in the aesthetics of food or believed that the only purpose of eating was to fuel the engine of the body. Those of us who fall into neither category are not irrational, we simply have an idea of how to live well that gives some weight to the pleasures of food and eating.

Human beings are often ambivalent, and this may not be due to any irrational confusion. For example, there are goods associated with remaining childless and so being able to pursue a vocation wholeheartedly, and there are goods associated with raising a family. We can rarely, if ever, maximise both goods. Compromise is inevitable. Someone who finds it difficult to decide which way to go or which compromises to make is not necessarily just failing to think straight. It is irrational to try to fulfil two conflicting desires, but it is not irrational to have desires that conflict. Having clear, settled and well-defined preferences is therefore not in any way a definition of being rational. Consistency in one's desires is not the same as being rationally consistent in one's deliberations about one's desires.

The second feature of *Homo economicus* is being 'point-on in perception of risk'. It certainly does seem to be true that human beings are often very irrational in their responses to risk. The most notorious example of this is the shift away from aeroplanes to roads in the wake of the 9/11 attacks in New York. Because driving is much more dangerous than flying, this led to more deaths, not fewer. In the year following the attacks, there were an estimated 1,595 excess road fatalities as a result of the switch.[15]

Nonetheless, it is not at all clear what a truly rational response to risk would look like. Take the question of buying a national lottery ticket. Economists tend to treat this as deeply irrational, since only around 50% of the stakes placed are returned as prizes, which means that over the long run the average player can expect to lose half the money gambled. This assumes that the rational way to think about a lottery ticket is as a financial investment. But that's not how many, probably most, lottery players think about it. They see it as a bit of fun, with the bonus that much of the stake goes to charities. Is it irrational to spend a small amount of spare cash on something that benefits good causes, prompts you to fantasise a little and carries a tiny chance of winning a large sum of money? There is no clear answer to this question, but it is far from obviously negative.

The same problem arises with other perceptions of risk. Economists assume that the rational thing to do is to treat every potential choice in terms purely of the statistical relationship between the probability of a good or bad outcome and the costs of either acting or doing something else. But this assumes that the costs and benefits can be sensibly quantified when in real life they form part of such a complex network of preferences and desires that this often becomes impossible.

Take as an example a major purchasing decision, such as whether to buy a house. The economist would look for a way to make the choice that maximised profit over the long run, trying to buy at a time and place that maximised the potential for the value of the asset to grow. But, of course, we live in our houses and we need to like them. Furthermore, we might find that thinking too much about the long-term returns on our choice might not be conducive to living the kind of life we value: we don't want to turn into one of those people who become obsessed by house prices and values. So we might rationally decide not to think too much about what is in our longer-term financial interests.

The orthodox economist could accept this, saying it fits into the model. This is because the model assumes that we place a monetary value on everything, and that includes not having to think about money. It is therefore rational in orthodox economic terms to choose anything if we would prefer to have its benefits more than the money we would lose by taking this choice. In the extreme case of ascetics and mendicants, no amount of money would be sufficient to compensate them for the loss of their simple, materially unencumbered lifestyle. For everyone else, everything has its price. I might be rational to forgo a £50k profit on a property over ten years by living somewhere I prefer, but not, perhaps, to be left half a million pounds worse off. Whether my choice is rational therefore comes down to whether the economic price I pay is worth it.

But this analysis misses the point. It might well be true that if we make a decision that is grossly against our long-term financial interests we might regret it, but that is not because we can always place a financial price on the non-financial goods we value. The economist will insist that this is implicitly exactly what everyone does, but the insistence is nothing more than that. The plausibility of this insistence rests on the fact that you can almost always get someone to answer a hypothetical question about how much money they would accept in place of something they truly value. That is taken as proof that everything – with the exception of some people and perhaps a handful of treasured goods – has a price. But of course in the real world we rarely face such clear choices with determined outcomes. Everything is about risk, and there are some risks we just don't want to take. We might not want to risk living in a home we don't like because we think we might be richer in the long run, or we might not want to risk the small pension we have for a bigger one, even if the risk of losing our money is small. Is this irrational? No, because these decisions do not boil down solely to risk–benefit analyses but also depend on our desire to avoid spending time on making such analyses in the first place.

The third characteristic of members of *Homo economicus* is that they are 'relentless in maximization of happiness' and 'consistently behave to advance their self-interest'. But why is it most rational to pursue self-interest? If being rational means adopting an objective viewpoint then it would seem that greater rationality would involve less concern for self, not more. For instance, the utilitarianism advocated by Peter Singer starts from the premise that, from a rational point of view, the welfare of everyone is equal. If then the morally right thing to do is to increase human welfare, we should do whatever it takes to do so, even if it means that we are not as well off as we could be. Singer's most striking example of what this means in practice is Zell Kravinsky, a man who had already given away most of his $45 million fortune to charity when he donated a kidney to a stranger. His calculation was simple: his risk of dying if he went ahead with the donation was one in 4,000, and so he believed that if he did not donate he was valuing his own life at 4,000 times that of a stranger.[16] There may be good reason to dispute this conclusion but it certainly involves taking a more objectively rational view than simply looking after yourself.

Overall, then, the attempt to construct a rational economics based on *Homo economicus* was riddled with basic mistakes. The problem was not with the desire to be rational per se, but with the assumption that the 'rational' was simple and self-evident. Human beings do not become more rational if they deny the complexity and plurality of their desires and values, they merely become simpler. Nor is it rational to govern your life by algorithms of risk, if that means living in such a way as to treat yourself as a wealth-maximisation machine. And putting your own happiness first is not rational, it's just selfish.

5. Fatal traction

If the model of *Homo economicus* is so evidently wrong, why did it ever catch on in the first place? Similarly, why were the mirages of communist and anarchist utopias mistaken for realities? There are obviously several reasons, some of which I have already mentioned. One worth paying particular attention to is how adopting simplified models of reality makes the real world seem more tractable, and that is very seductive.

In in the case of *Homo economicus*, its attraction was that it allowed economists to develop simple models which enabled them to build their discipline on 'rigorous' calculations. In short, the assumption of *Homo economicus* made economics more tractable. This would appear to be an endemic weakness in the discipline. Epidemiologist Michael Marmot, for instance, reports being told by a senior economist that his peers 'are taught that health is a contribution to wealth, rather than the other way around, because it is easier to model in their equations'.[17] That may be true, but it is clearly not rational to prefer hard data over messy facts if those data fail to capture what they are supposed to capture.

Communism fell under the same spell. The idea that central planning on a simple principle of 'from each according to his needs, to each according to his abilities' could solve all societies' ills is much more appealing than the grim alternative, which involves piecemeal changes here and there, none guaranteed to succeed. Likewise, anarchism was based on the simplistic premise that, freed from the chains of government, people's common decency would suffice to enable them to live together co-operatively and fairly.

There is an irony here. On the one hand, all of these mistakes point to hubris, a belief that human reason is more powerful than it really is. But on the other, all these mistakes implicitly acknowledge how limited the power of reason is, because they require us to simplify our conception of the world in order to make it tractable to reason. It is as though in order to preserve the illusion that human reason is mighty, we have to rig its challenges to make them easier to overcome.

It is much more difficult to accept that the world is too complex and reason too weak for us to be able to devise political solutions or economic models that can at a stroke explain all that matters and prescribe what we ought to do. But this is precisely what we must do. Reason must know its limits, especially in politics and economics, since the failure to respect these always leads to disaster.

CHAPTER ELEVEN

Political reason

An inflated sense both of the power of reason and of the power of human beings to use it lies behind the flawed idea that philosopher kings and other intellectual elites should guide the masses. Nonetheless, a realistic conception of reason has to be at the heart of the political process. To abandon reason in the public square would not just be absurd, it would be catastrophic.

The need to articulate both the need for reason and its role in politics is as urgent as ever. It might seem reassuring that democracy and freedom have been on the rise over the recent medium to long term. Freedom House, one of the leading organisations that attempts to measure such things, ranked only 40 countries as free in 1975, comprising 25% of the world's independent states. By 2014 this had risen to 88 countries, 45% of states. However, we have good reason to suppose that these advances are fragile and reversible.

My argument is that the case for democracy cannot be separated from the case for reason. The only fair and tenable political systems are ones that put deliberative reason at their hearts, since reason is the only justifiable tool for negotiating political differences. The problem is that it is a tool that many want to set aside. All over Europe, there is increasing disillusion with the secular democratic process and a turn to populism, accompanied by demands to bring religion back to the heart of civic life. We need to understand why both these moves are dangerous and how they can be tackled.

1. Political pluralism

When Western leaders proclaim their values on the world stage they tend to talk about democracy and freedom as though they were self-evidently good things. If we ask why we should value both so much, one part of the answer is rarely properly appreciated: pluralism.[1]

In its most general sense, pluralism is the belief that there is no one, single, complete and unified true perspective. There is more than one legitimate way of seeing and no one perspective can maximally accommodate all that is good or true. This is not to say that there are no wrong perspectives or that there are never good reasons for preferring one perspective over another. It does mean, however, that we will expect there to be times when we cannot objectively decide which perspective is superior and there are losses as well as gains in adopting one perspective rather than another.

Pluralism need not be universal. One can be a pluralist in some domains but not others. One might be a moral pluralist, for instance, but a scientific 'monist', believing that where two scientific theories are in contradiction, only one is correct.

Political pluralism accepts that there is no one way of ordering society so as to satisfy completely all legitimate aspirations for the good life. Different citizens have different needs, some of which might be related to their different histories, cultures and circumstances. But even within cultures, not all legitimate desires can be met. Some do not want their deeply held religious beliefs to be offended while others demand the right to ridicule; businesses want to keep their costs down but the disabled want them to adapt their premises or vehicles to accommodate them; many consumers want cheap meat while others want higher animal welfare. The role of a pluralist politics is to balance and negotiate between competing claims and demands so as to enable as many compatible goods from different incompatible positions as is possible.

Political pluralism is not the same as democracy, and democracy is far from sufficient to create a fair and decent pluralist society. In a democracy, a majority could promote only its own interests and ignore those of minorities, abandoning pluralism. Political theorists have for a long time distinguished this kind of 'mere majoritarianism' from democracy proper, but this distinction cannot be made purely by appeal to the nature of democracy itself without begging the question. In order to avoid slipping into majoritarianism, democracy needs to be combined with some kind of embrace of pluralism, so that it becomes a means of negotiating between different interests and visions of the good life and not merely a way of deciding collectively which one path to follow.

In some ways pluralism is therefore a higher value than democracy. However, in practice it depends on democracy. History tells us it would be foolish to entrust judgements of how to govern society to a small unelected elite, even if that elite started out fully committed to pluralism. Without pluralism, democracy is the tyranny of the majority; but without democracy, pluralism is benign dictatorship, which always risks descending into something more malign.

Political pluralism is attractive to many who are liberally minded, but what justifies it? The obvious answer is ethical pluralism: the view that there is more than one legitimate conception of the good life for human beings. Because one of the main functions of politics is to enable people to live good lives, ethical pluralism entails political pluralism.

We can call political pluralism underpinned by ethical pluralism *ethico-political pluralism*. However, if the only justifiable form of political pluralism is ethico-political, it is in trouble, for the simple reason that many people are not ethical pluralists. Indeed, although ethico-political pluralism is a liberal position, it is not even the case that all liberals are ethical pluralists. One could, for example, have a liberal policy of toleration on the basis that people have the fundamental freedom to pursue misguided visions of the good life, just as long as they do not impinge on the ability of others to live according to the correct one. Something like this has underpinned the liberalism of various nations which have nonetheless been deeply rooted in a religious tradition. The relative openness of the Islamic golden age, for example, was not premised on the belief that Islam did not represent the one true path, merely on a tolerance for those who for reasons of conscience or culture refused to follow it. Liberal political pluralism without ethical pluralism is therefore a real possibility, but it doesn't involve the same kind of embrace of difference as ethico-political pluralism.

However, this still leaves many people who are neither liberals nor ethical pluralists, and many of these cannot be expected to change their minds. That means there are many people with competing values who do not believe that it is right simply to accept the existence of these differences and negotiate their coexistence. In order to run a society on pluralist lines, it would therefore seem necessary first to create a society of liberals and ethical pluralists, and this is not realistic.

Fortunately, a case for political pluralism can be made which does not require ethical pluralism or liberalism. The justification for a pluralist polis is normative, but it is epistemological, not ethical. In other words, the case rests on what follows from the demands of reason.

As I argued in chapter nine, rationality is essentially normative, in that it entails that there are things we ought to believe or assent to. The most general statement of this is what I called the Normative Principle of Rationality:

We should believe what it is most rational to believe.

This principle of rationality is of political as well as philosophical importance. To reject the idea that we ought to have reasons for what we believe would be to say that we can believe what we like without reason. That takes away any requirement to justify our own beliefs or criticise those of others. Dialogue is impossible and conflicts become matters of will.

Although the Normative Principle of Rationality should be reasonably uncontroversial, in practice there is a major problem with it, namely that it is not the same as:

We should believe what *it seems to us* is most rational to believe.

There is clearly a difference between what *is* most rational and what might *seem to us to be* most rational. But this appears to place us in a bind: it would be sheer arrogance to equate the rational with *what seems rational to me* and hubris to believe any individual can transcend the way things seem and see how they really are. How then can one distinguish between what is most rational and what merely seems to be so? What is needed here is a way of deciding when we ought not to take something as seeming to be rational as sufficient evidence that it is rational. Fortunately, such a method is suggested by the very nature of rationality itself.

As I have argued, rationality requires objective reasons and these need to be interest-neutral. That is to say, what is most rational to believe should not depend on who the reasoner is and what her interests are. (Of course, that does not mean that what is rational for one person *to do* in one situation must also rational for another person to do in a similar situation. What it is rational to do is of course often situation-specific.) This implies that, all other things being equal, different reasoners should tend to converge on the same beliefs about what is rational.

But, of course, as we have seen in discussions of religion and science in particular, even rational agents who reason very well often do not converge on the same belief. Either they come close together but don't agree on important details, such as is currently the case in physics, or they come to quite widely different conclusions, as is the case with religion. How then do we square the fact that rational argument ought to lead to convergence of belief with the fact that it often does not?

It's not hard to meet this challenge if we have fully appreciated the limits of reason and our need for modesty as reasoners. If rationality entails convergence, but convergence does not occur, then that provides *prima facie* evidence of an absence of rational justification sufficient to make us refrain from making a definitive judgement on the matter. Although we may be justified in making a judgement, and for practical purposes might have to do so, we ought to be appropriately tentative about it and not assume it is certain enough to be decreed as the truth for all.

This is not to say that mere disagreement by itself is enough for you to give up the belief that what seems rational to you really is rational. You may, for instance, have a convincing error theory: an explanation as to why apparently rational people disagree. They may lack vital evidence you have, for instance, or not have had the opportunity to test your argument. Or they might be deeply wedded to a belief that makes them resistant to counter-evidence or counter-argument. However, one needs to be careful to adopt a principle of sufficient charity. It is too easy to dismiss those we disagree with as having their judgements distorted by prejudice, as though we ourselves were immune from such things.

In any case, the main upshot of seeing that rational judges dissent is not to suspend judgement. It is simply to accept a greater defeasibility for our beliefs than we otherwise would, and so to insist on them less forcefully. So, one can accept that there is a sufficiently strong case to believe something, but that it is not strong enough to insist that anyone who does not agree must be irrational. This distinction should seem both familiar and straightforward. Without ever having formalised it, people routinely find themselves 'agreeing to disagree' because they can see there is no way of settling the issue to everyone's satisfaction.

This can be summed up in what I will call the Principle of Epistemological Pluralism:

In the absence of an overwhelmingly strong error theory, the impartiality of rationality entails that where competent rational judges disagree, we should accept that we have insufficient grounds to insist on the truth of one conclusion and so do what we can to accommodate reasonable different ones, even if we believe only one of them to be the sole truth.

Of course, in this broad form, certain key notions are left under-specified, most notably the idea of competent rational judges. Nonetheless, it is sufficient to identify what is important for the purposes of my argument here.

This Principle of Epistemological Pluralism grounds political pluralism. No matter how convinced we as individuals might be that certain conceptions of the good life are misguided, or that certain principles for ordering society are wrong, we cannot but accept the fact that competent rational agents disagree, sometimes considerably, as to what the good is, for individuals and for society. If, as we should, we accept the political corollary of the Normative Principle of Rationality – namely that society ought to do what it is most rational to do – we are led to the political corollary of the Principle of Epistemological Pluralism, formed by the addition of one phrase which identifies its specific political application (which I have italicised):

> In the absence of an overwhelmingly strong error theory, the impartiality of rationality entails that where competent rational judges disagree *about how society should be run*, we should accept that we have insufficient grounds to insist on the truth of one conclusion and so do what we can to accommodate reasonable different ones, even if we believe only one of them to be the sole truth.

This principle is not infinitely accommodating and does not imply an anything-goes, laissez-faire relativism. First of all, not every political claim is underpinned by a sufficient quantity or quality of competent, rational judges. Second, we may at times have an error theory that we judge strong enough to dismiss dissent, even the dissent of a large number. For instance, where we can see that a position is held on the basis of an ideology, zealously upheld by appeal to authority, we have good reason to dismiss the claims to rationality of that position.

In such cases, that does not necessarily mean intolerance. As we have seen, there are reasons for being tolerant that do not require any acceptance of uncertainty as to the falsity of that which we tolerate. What it does mean is that tolerance is not automatically demanded. This is important, because it provides a justification for the kind of robust liberalism that does not allow pernicious ideologies to thrive in its midst, under the protection of just that which it threatens.

By this route, it should now be clear that we have arrived at political pluralism, along with its justification:

> There can be no one way of ordering society so as to satisfy completely all aspirations for the good life because competent rational judges disagree about how society should be run, and the impartiality of rationality entails that in such cases we should accept that we have insufficient grounds to insist on the truth of one conclusion and accommodate different ones, even if we believe only one of them to be the sole truth. Therefore the role of politics is to balance and negotiate between competing claims and demands so as to enable as many compatible goods from different incompatible positions as is possible.

We could call this kind of political pluralism *de facto* pluralism. What makes this so powerful is that it does not require commitment to any particular ethical principle. The normative power comes purely from the normative nature of rationality itself. Nor, as we have seen in the ethical case, does it entail permitting everything and preventing nothing.

Of course, there is no such thing as a normative principle which everyone will or must assent to. It is always possible for someone merely to assert: 'I will not be bound by reason.' This is, however, harder to do with honest conviction than it sounds. Since the fundamental nature of rationality is that it is reason-driven, the person who really rejects reason must offer no good reason for that rejection, and few are so hard-headed in their anti-rationality.

2. Threats to pluralism

When considering the threats to political pluralism, it is easy to think only of authoritarian regimes, be they secular dictatorships or theocracies. But pluralism can also be threatened by majoritarian democracy. That is why one of the most serious threats to established democratic pluralist states is populism, which is one of the most dangerous threats to a reason-led polis in the West today.

This is not populism as defined in the United States, which is rooted in a particular historical grass-roots political movement. This is the populism as understood everywhere else in the world. In social science, populism is almost always understood as entailing a malign kind of simplification in which the virtuous and the wicked are neatly divided between 'us' and 'them'. Hence the editors of a recent academic book on populism define it as pitting 'a virtuous and homogeneous people against a set of elites and dangerous "others" who were together depicted as depriving (or attempting to deprive) the sovereign people of their rights, values, prosperity, identity, and voice'. Here, it is the phrase 'virtuous and homogeneous' which invites us to assume that populism inevitably results in simplistic fallacies.[2]

Populist discourse undermines all the key underpinnings of political pluralism. Take, first of all the Normative Principle of Rationality. Populists would agree that 'We should believe what it is most rational to believe' but they do not appreciate the difference between this and 'We should believe what it *seems to us* is most rational to believe'. The reason for this is that populism rejects the idea that what appears as plain truth to the ordinary person in the street can be anything other than what it is. What seems true *is* true, and only obfuscating, dissembling elites could pretend otherwise.

In a similar way, populism distorts the idea that rationality ought to lead to convergence of belief. When conjoined with the fact that some do not agree about what is rational, they take that not as evidence that certainty is impossible, but that the dissenters are not rational. When it is believed that what is most rational is just self-evident, there is no cause for self-doubt when others take a different view. What follows from this is that in place of the Principle of Epistemological Pluralism we have a principle that where apparently competent rational judges disagree, we should accept the verdict of ordinary people.

The logic of populism is therefore toxic to political pluralism, because it simply denies the possibility of meaningful disagreement about issues of major political significance. Populism is diametrically opposed to pluralism: it promotes a single set of values instead of a plurality, offers simplistic solutions instead of complex compromises, and represents the people as a uniform whole rather than a community of diverse communities and individuals. In place of reason, it puts conviction; in place of evidence, the seeming self-evidence of common sense.

Given its often nationalistic character, the only concession made to difference by populism is generally a culturally relative one: people of different cultures may disagree, but people within one culture will all share the same basic values. Cultural relativism is usually thought of as a driver for tolerance and diversity. In this case we can see it as a driver for division. In the absence of any absolute standard to judge between different value systems, the solution is simply to keep them separate.

There has been no shortage of warnings about the rise of populism in Europe from think tanks and political commentators.[3] How much of a threat it appears to pose, however, ebbs and flows. Many take comfort from the fact that since the 1980s no populist party outside Switzerland has managed to sustain more than around 15% of the vote, and few have entered government and exercised any real power. Those that do end up sharing power, such as Progress in Norway and Syriza in Greece, have become softer and more benign as they do so.

However, the severest threat of populism does not come directly from populist parties. The threat comes from the way in which mainstream politics is increasingly being conducted in the populist mode. The rise of populist parties has exacerbated this problem, by encouraging mainstream parties to adopt their rhetoric. But the roots of the problem lie deeper than this.

The root is a shift from real politics – which involves messy compromises between competing interests – to what I call political consumerism. Consumerism is about giving people what they want, without the mediation of politicians or experts. Political parties have adapted to this accordingly. Rather than reflecting the settled will of the party membership, from whose ranks they are drawn, today's career politicians are a like executive managers. In true consumerist style, the manager's job is to deliver to the public what it wants, or to make it want what the party is able to deliver. The mathematics of elections means it seems obvious that it is more important to listen to public opinion than that of the party membership. From this it follows that parties must appeal to the centre, and that their policies must be driven by opinion polls.

What this erodes is any real sense of representation. The politician represents neither the electorate nor her party. No matter how hard she strives to give people what they want, she belongs to the 'them' whose job it is to serve 'us', and inevitably she does not fully succeed. The irony is that precisely by trying to pander to the will of the majority, the mainstream political parties have caused a dislocation between political elites and the public, creating the conditions for populism.

This means we are living in a dangerous time for genuine democracy. The populist mode of politics – which is in essence an anti-politics – has become part of ordinary politics. This insidiously undermines the very foundations of a democratic, pluralist state, replacing any sense of the need for reasoned dialogue, compromise and accommodation with a simplistic idea that the government's role is to reflect the clear, unified will of the people.

One major problem with this is that if you are elected on the basis of a myth – that all 'ills originate from outside "the people", who are united in their interest' and that '[t]here are no major contradictions or issues to be resolved within this homogeneous entity', as Aristos Doxiadis and Manos Matsaganis put it – there is simply no way you can govern.[4] At best, you have a short-term disaster and a return to traditional parties to clean up the mess. At worst, you create an ongoing situation in which governance becomes impossible, since the only electable parties are irresponsible. This is arguably already the position in Italy, a country that has not really managed to create widespread faith in the legitimacy and efficacy of real politics for any sustained period in the post-war era. Cynicism about politicians is endemic. The only reason why so many were prepared to elect and re-elect Silvio Berlusconi is that they simply did not believe that principled politics was possible. If you think all criminals are crooks, you vote for the most effective crook.

Disenchantment with politics is therefore toxic, and populism can only increase such disenchantment, since it leads to the promise of simple solutions that cannot be delivered, while removing from the public square the more nuanced kind of discourse that is needed to explain why it can't work.

3. Secularism

Pluralism also faces another threat. It is very hard for a political culture to be truly pluralist if it is not also secular.[5] Any polis which privileges a particular religion will struggle fully to accept the claims of others with different substantive world-views. And yet, like pluralism, secularism is under threat, more overtly, as an explicit target of criticism. It is therefore important to defend secularism and in particular to distinguish it from more aggressive anti-religious political structures.

Secularism is not a doctrine of religious unbelief, but of state neutrality on matters of religious belief. Secularism allows freedom of religious belief, but does not privilege any one form of belief or non-belief. A secular state is therefore not necessarily a godless one. France's *laïcité*, for example, is so strict that the government is not allowed to collect data on people's religious affiliations. Still, even the most liberal estimates put the proportion of atheists at around a quarter of the population, while more sober assessments leave them at around one in ten, in line with the UK.

In a secular state, religion becomes invisible at the political level, even when still prevalent at the personal level. Secular governments and politicians do not invoke scripture or religious authorities to defend their policies. Instead they speak to principles and concerns that all the population can share irrespective of their belief or non-belief.

Secularism certainly appeals to atheists. A secular state is obviously preferable to a theocratic one, but it is also superior to one in which atheism is imposed on the population. The modern, Western atheist tradition respects the ability and right of people to determine matters of belief for themselves, and so the proper role for the state in matters of religion is to stand back, not to ban.

Secularism did not take off primarily because it suited atheists. Rather it suited believers, because it allowed the state to be neutral with regard to the merits of competing religious views and so allowed many varieties of faith to flourish. Originally, these were mostly denominational and did not even involve more than one religion. This is what explains the apparent paradox of resolutely religious America's strictly secular division of religion and state. The principle was established, not on the assumption that religion was unimportant to Americans, but on the exact opposite idea that Christianity in particular was utterly fundamental to them. The US Declaration of Independence, for instance, is infused with theism. In its first sentence it talks of the powers 'which the Laws of Nature and of Nature's God entitle' us, and the second lists the rights of human beings 'endowed by their Creator'. The division of Church and state was established because there were many different Christian denominations and so for the state to have privileged one would have been unacceptable. That is why Article 3 of the Bill of Rights decrees that 'Congress shall make no law respecting an establishment of religion, or prohibiting the free exercise thereof.' The wording of this suggests that the freedom to practise your own religion is of paramount importance. The state therefore stayed neutral to protect faith, not to weaken it.

Secularism's flourishing therefore may have suited atheists, but was not in any way a triumph for them. Secular neutrality applies as much to atheists as to believers. Just as it is not acceptable to premise a political policy argument on the teachings of the Bible or the Koran, so it is unacceptable to argue for a public policy on the basis of God's non-existence. Nevertheless, there is one way in which secularism suits atheists more than believers. In a secular state religious vocabulary is absent from public discourse in a way in which the natural lexicon of atheism is not. A secular discussion of human rights, for example, is couched in terms which both the religious and non-religious can accept. However, there are few distinctly atheist beliefs or concepts this discourse must omit, while there are rather more religious ones it cannot include. So although secular discourse is not the same thing as atheist discourse, it is closer to the natural mode of expression of atheism than to that of religion.

This in part explains why, over the last decade or so, the complaint has increasingly been heard that secular societies, by demoting matters of religious belief to the purely personal realm, have denied the importance of religion in society. Because it was not acceptable to couch political debate in religious terms, religious viewpoints were expressed less and less and became almost inaudible. Hence the increasing demand for the traditionally secular West to find more room for religion in public life and not to leave it entirely in the private sphere.

How would we do this? One influential line of argument is perhaps most fully and rigorously articulated by Bhikhu Parekh, who advocates bringing religion back into the public square.[6] Excluding religion from it fails fully to respect religious beliefs and their importance in people's lives. Furthermore, it privileges a certain atheistic, liberal world-view that is not widely shared. Secularism is not, as it is claimed to be, neutral with regard to belief. Rather, it robs the genuinely religious of the right to assert their belief publicly and it therefore privileges godless liberalism over other belief systems. It is not ideologically neutral but is just another ideology being imposed.

Traditional secularism, it is therefore argued, has to go. In its place must be a public domain in which religion is allowed back in. The idea is not to create conflicts of belief, but to allow disagreements to be resolved openly, without people feeling the need to deny the differences in the fundamental convictions that shape their views. The secret of a harmonious society in which different religious and non-religious beliefs are held is not for everyone to remain silent on the things that divide them, but to discuss differences openly and in a spirit of mutual respect and understanding.

In many ways this sounds appealing. It is explicitly a kind of pluralism, and, as I have argued, pluralism is the bedrock of liberal society. But the kind of pluralism that puts religion at the heart of the public square is not the only option. There is a kind of secular pluralism which is more suited to the tasks of granting the respect and recognition believers are demanding, and negotiating our differences. This is not quite the secularism of the status quo, which often exhibits a certain kind of theophobia. The desire to preserve secular neutrality has sometimes led to an over-zealous purge of religious symbols, language and practice from the public square. The result is that people feel their beliefs are not being granted the respect that they deserve. This is counter to secularism's own tenets, since the whole purpose of secularism is to allow each their own beliefs, not to erase them. Secularism is not therefore fundamentally flawed, but it has taken a wrong turn.

Such is the diagnosis, but what is the cure? Not, I would argue, the kind of pluralism advocated by Parekh, even though his account of secularism's failings hits many of its targets. There is a line Parekh wants to cross that I think we should not. We need to allow more expression of religious beliefs, but the civic space of politics and government has to be kept religiously neutral.

To see why, we need to remind ourselves of secularism's greatest strength. The late Stuart Hampshire captured an important truth about politics in the title of his last book: *Justice is Conflict*.[7] Politics exists because the interests, needs and desires of people and groups within societies conflict. Politics is thus essentially a matter of conflict resolution and a just society is one which does this fairly and, hopefully, peacefully.

This sounds like a somewhat adversarial view of politics, but it is no more than realistic, as it acknowledges the divisive dimension of the fact of pluralism. We don't think of the political square as being all about conflict, precisely because in Western democracies we have found civilised and peaceful ways of dealing with these conflicts. Overt or violent conflict rarely breaks out in public although we can see examples on a small scale all the time in protests, strikes and occasional campaigns of civil disobedience.

Dealing with these conflicts fairly and peacefully is a tremendous achievement, and our secular tradition deserves most of the credit. Secularism is the most powerful bulwark against sectarianism we have. Central to secularism is a conception of political reason as a shared enterprise. Secularism demands that in the civic sphere we only use a language we share, and leave out the substantive world-views that divide us, and so it forces us to the common ground. Crucially for the current debate about religion, it does not require us just to leave behind our personal convictions to do so: everyone brings their personal beliefs to the secular table. The trick is that we find a way of expressing them in universalist and not particularist terms. Take debates about abortion. A devout Catholic is obviously going to be strongly influenced by her religious beliefs on the subject, and when speaking in a civic forum, such as Parliament, these beliefs will come through. But, vitally, she must find some way of expressing them in terms that everyone can understand and appreciate. If she says, 'we should not allow abortion because it is against the teachings of the Roman Catholic Church', she has failed to make an argument that has any purchase beyond her own faith. If she argues for the sanctity of human life in terms which are for her grounded in the tenets of Roman Catholicism, but are not the sole preserve of it, then she is making a contribution to the secular debate, *even though at root her basic commitments are grounded in religion.*

Secularism does not deny people the right to be motivated by and to live by their religious beliefs. Nor does it even prohibit them from bringing these commitments to the secular polis. All it prohibits is that the debate itself be couched in sectarian terms. As the political philosopher John Rawls put it: 'Reasonable comprehensive doctrines, religious or non-religious, may be introduced in public political discussion at any time, provided that in due course proper political reasons – and not reasons given solely by comprehensive doctrines – are presented that are sufficient to support whatever the comprehensive doctrines are said to support.'[8] Remove the 'in due course' clause from this formulation and it's about right.

Now consider Parekh's alternative. On this view, traditional secularism forces us to disguise our religious beliefs, or pretend they don't exist, and that devalues them in some way. What we should allow is for people to speak in their own authentic voices. If Catholicism does indeed lie at the root of someone's opposition to abortion, let her say so. As long as we can all speak freely, we can still resolve conflicts, but in an honest and respectful way.

This looks like an appealing way forward. But the danger is clear: instead of a somewhat artificially neutral secular discourse, we have one in which arguments are made in sectarian terms, not shared ones. To put it another way, it takes away the demand to present our arguments as objectively as possible and encourages us to put them in the more subjective terms of our specific, comprehensive worldviews. The idea that in such a discourse we would nonetheless all be mature and open-minded enough to come to agreement seems to me far too optimistic. Rather, we are likely to end up more divided than ever. The extent to which agreement is possible will become much less obvious as we focus on what divides rather than what unites. Politicians will be speaking no longer as citizens but as

Christians, Jews, Muslims, atheists, Buddhists and whatever else. People will also be more likely to vote on sectarian lines: if people speak from specific ideological viewpoints, we will want our own to be represented.

This would be a disaster for civic life. The intention to respect fully the diversity of beliefs and not to impose a homogeneous, blurred-out secularism is a noble one. But the way to do this is not to scrap secularism and let a cacophony of different belief systems fight it out instead. The way forward is to reform existing secularism much more modestly and to rid it of its theophobia. There is no need for a secular society to pretend religion doesn't matter to people. Nor should it prohibit anyone from expressing their religious view publicly.

As one example of how this approach is duly respectful to different beliefs, consider the debate over religious schools. I was the co-author of a pamphlet written by a group of humanist philosophers making the case against religious schools.[9] We did not disguise our own non-religious views, which obviously influenced how we argued. But we did attempt to make our case in terms everyone could accept. Most obviously, we never used the alleged falsity of religion as a reason not to have religious schools. Rather, we argued on the basis of factors such as the autonomy of the child and social cohesion, in terms which included rather than excluded the religious. The principle behind this was classically secular: we needed to make a case that the religious could agree with too. Indeed, several years later, the Accord Coalition was formed to oppose the spread of religious schools, and its members include religious groups, humanists, trade unions and human rights campaigners.

The case *for* religious schools needs to be made in the same way, and indeed it usually is. There may be theological reasons for having religious schools, but they are irrelevant to the political debate. Rather, we need to debate issues of parental freedom, equity of treatment of people of different faiths and so on. None of this involves a ruthless purging of all mention of religion, because true secularism never involves this.

4. Secular pluralism renewed

What in practice does this all mean? In terms of the secular part of the equation, it would mean a tighter, smaller civic core where secular neutrality is required, and a loosening of restrictions on religious expression outside of this.

First, the tighter core. No religious group should have a privileged status in any democratic country. In the UK this means disestablishing the Church of England and abolishing with it the automatic right of senior bishops to sit in Parliament's second chamber, the House of Lords. This is an obvious first step: we cannot hope to persuade people of other faiths and none that all are equal in the eyes of the state when one denomination has a privileged place. All democratic institutions should be similarly fully neutralised with regard to belief.

But apart from this, we need to be more relaxed about letting the religious express themselves. There is no reason why civil weddings, for example, should not include religious songs or words at the request of couples. There is no reason why someone should never be allowed to wear symbols of their religious faith at work. There is no reason why there should not be God slots on public television, as long as there are also specifically non-God slots in which atheists can be allowed the same opportunities to utter unedited propaganda of their own and irritate believers as much as the believers' thoughts and prayers for the day irritate them. There is not even any reason why senior politicians shouldn't acknowledge the importance of their religious faith, although they would need to be very careful not to invoke these beliefs as justifications for where they stand on policy.

Some secularists are beginning to accept that there needs to be an opening up of civil society to allow more religious expression. The French philosopher Alain Badiou, for example, talks of Europe needing to choose between an open or a closed ideal, and a need to create a new space in which immigrants and minorities can be accepted.[10] Connected with this is a recognition that the 'official' secular line is not always the most defensible one. For example, Badiou has written scathingly of French attempts to ban the hijab, attacking arguments that claim such a law is needed to protect *laïcité* or indeed women.[11]

Jürgen Habermas is another secular liberal who has acknowledged the need to be less dismissive of religion. He has said 'the liberal state has an interest of its own in unleashing religious voices in the political public sphere, for it cannot know whether secular society would not otherwise cut itself off from key resources for the creation of meaning and identity'.[12] Habermas also insists on the requirement for such contributions from the religious to be made in a 'generally accessible language', preserving something, if not all, of secularism's traditional neutral mode of public discourse. However, he also places some responsibility on the non-religious to make this translation.

Of course there are difficulties in 'unleashing religious voices'. The right to free religious expression does not entail the right to do anything you believe your religion requires of you. Halal slaughter that fails to meet animal welfare standards is unacceptable, for example. The right to believe does not necessarily entail the right to educate your children in sectarian institutions. The right to wear religious dress does not entail the right to wear a burkha in places where it is necessary to see a full face for security reasons. But these difficult cases are not typical. Most of the time, people can live fully observant religious lives without threatening secular principles.

If religion is allowed to reassert itself in those domains where secularism should properly allow it to assert itself, I hope that the impetus to bring religion into the properly secular political sphere will disappear. And that would be a very good thing. For secular neutrality with regard to belief is what stands between us and a society which is divided even more than it already is by religious beliefs. That is why secularism is in the interests of everyone, believers and non-believers. If you believe in a compassionate God who values humanity's ability to choose beliefs for itself, then the conclusion should be obvious: God would be a secularist too.

As to the pluralist part of the problem, although the case for political pluralism can be clearly made, democracies do not secure the consent of their electorates by appeal to philosophical arguments, no matter how (relatively) straightforward. Furthermore, since populism is not rooted in rational arguments but appeals to common sense, it seems unrealistic to suppose argument can uproot it. What's worse, once populism takes hold, it becomes increasingly difficult to make the case for pluralism, since to do so would appear to be offering precisely the kind of elitist over-complication that populism rails against.

In order to defend pluralist politics, we need therefore to set aside the philosophical argument and think in more political terms about what will be effective.

First, there may be some rhetorical bridges between the complex arguments for *de facto* pluralism and clear, simple political messages. Making the complex clear is difficult but rarely impossible. People need to be regularly made aware of the trade-offs and accommodations that society depends on. These should not be presented as problematic compromises but as achievements to be celebrated. For instance, people do not like the compulsory surrendering of personal wealth through taxation but they do like roads, schools and hospitals, and they should be grown-up enough to see that one requires the other.

Although many of these issues are not directly ones which concern pluralism, it is important that the whole tone of politics is one which acknowledges complexity and compromise. The more solutions are presented as cost-free and obvious, the less tolerant people become of the costs when they finally become clear, or of complexity when things do not turn out to be all that straightforward after all.

A further resetting of the everyday discourse of politics is one which rejects the simplistic rhetoric of 'the people' and other meaningless, bogusly homogeneous groups like 'hard-working families'. The rhetoric should be: We are all different, we have different needs. The job of government is to meet as many of these needs as possible. Everyone is equally important, and equally unique.

A final strategy must be a willingness to face down simplistic pseudo-solutions directly and to explain clearly why they are not possible and what their costs would be. Politicians must not be afraid to appear to be telling the population it is wrong if it is indeed wrong. Defying the popular will, when done with good reasons, is a sign of strength in a leader which will ultimately be rewarded. Consider how the most successful British politician of recent decades – in electoral terms at least – was Margaret Thatcher. Loathed by many, her perceived resolve often won her grudging respect.

What then is really needed to counter populism and protect pluralism is nothing less than a renewal of politics as an arena of difference, debate and diversity, where everyone's interests and concerns are included. In other words, politics must become centred around reasoned discussion. This requires rebuilding trust in the political system.

These tentative solutions seem in some ways modest, in others utopian. They are modest in that they appear to amount to little more than a change in the way we talk. But in some sense politics is simply a matter of how we talk: the ways in which we structure dialogue to reach compromise with minimal conflict.

They are utopian, however, in that they require politicians to refuse to tell people what they most want to hear. It's a bitter pill but it can be sugared by celebrating the ability of already existing pluralist nations to accommodate different values, without losing those core values which allow for the rule of law and respect for the rights of all.

Even if we are pessimistic about the chances of changing our political culture to make it more reasoned, we have little choice but to try. In politics, the waters beneath the thin ice of reason are especially rough and icy. The predators that swim in them are opportunistic populists and divisive nationalists, destined to devour the few naïve idealists who are equally blind to the complexities of real politics. Reason might seem to be a meagre defence against such dangers, but it is the only one we've got.

Conclusion: using reason

Some may be surprised to have found that my defence of reason has been so eager to point out its limitations. With friends like me, you might wonder if reason needs enemies. But reason needs this kind of tough love. It cannot be treated like a child that needs unconditional support. Rather, it needs to be treated like an elite athlete that always needs to be pushed to work harder and improve, because otherwise nothing can be achieved. The most difficult issues we face often require us to go to the edge of reason, stretching its capacities to breaking point. To extend the training analogy, it would be a mistake only to praise it for what it does well almost effortlessly, such as analysing the formal logical validity of arguments or spotting contradictions. It needs also to pay attention to where it is naturally weaker, such as when it has to deal with ambiguity or premises that cannot be proven, and when it requires the careful use of judgement.

1. The uses of skepticism

The idea of reason I have defended is therefore a skeptical one. For readers who have detected the fingerprints of this book's main historical inspiration, that will come as no surprise. That inspiration is the eighteenth-century genius, David Hume. Hume was more skeptical about the power of reason than many other philosophers, but his skepticism was extremely focused and measured and it is simply mistaken to characterise him as a debunker of reason. As Michael P. Lynch argues, 'In the broadest sense of the term, reason is the ability to explain and justify our beliefs and commitments.' But people often use 'reason' in a narrower sense, 'using certain methods, appealing to certain sources, and engaging in certain practices', including 'logical inference' and 'observation'. Lynch says that 'Skeptical worries about reason concern this narrower sense.'[1] Careless skeptics mistake this for skepticism about reason in general. Careful skeptics, such as Hume, see that this leaves plenty of room for reason to do important work.

Hume's modest skepticism implores us 'to begin with clear and self-evident principles, to advance by timorous and sure steps, to review frequently our conclusions, and examine accurately all their consequences; though by these means we shall make both a slow and a short progress in our systems; are the only methods, by which we can ever hope to reach truth, and attain a proper stability and certainty in our determinations.'

There is no clearer summary of what it means to use our reason. We have to remember, however, that for Hume each step in this process is always less than perfect. We aim for a 'proper impartiality' but can never be completely impartial or free from prejudice. We can try to 'begin with clear and self-evident principles' but none of these are entirely transparent or beyond doubt. We look to advance by 'sure steps' but we can never be completely sure. All the more reason, then, to 'review frequently our conclusions, and examine accurately all their consequences'.

Hume say that skepticism cannot be pushed too far. We have simply to accept that our ways of thinking rest on fundamental principles that we cannot prove by pure reason or scientific observation. We either do this and accept the limits of reason, or we follow skepticism into a cul-de-sac. Hume argues that no one can follow the latter course in good faith. An ultra-skeptic 'cannot expect, that his philosophy will have any constant influence on the mind: or if it had, that its influence would be beneficial to society. [. . .] All discourse, all action would immediately cease; and men remain in a total lethargy, till the necessities of nature, unsatisfied, put an end to their miserable existence.' Such extreme skepticism is not intellectually serious because it becomes a kind of game that no one can keep playing.

Hume therefore advocates a more moderate form of *mitigated* skepticism, which acts to correct the tendency of 'the greater part of mankind' to be 'affirmative and dogmatical in their opinions', seeing only one side, with 'no idea of any counterpoising argument'. This kind of mitigated skepticism teaches that 'there is a degree of doubt, and caution, and modesty, which, in all kinds of scrutiny and decision, ought for ever to accompany a just reasoner'. The mitigated skepticism of Hume is the model for my account of a form of rationality that is modest yet essential.

2. What is at stake

Some might believe that such a skeptical defence of reason leaves it thin and emaciated. But I think any thinness in the account is necessary and desirable. The true spirit of the Enlightenment can be found in diverse thinkers who have very different specific beliefs about the power and scope of rationality. All they share is a commitment to a very thin notion of rationality, the idea that disagreements can be discussed and argued, in a common, intellectual space in which everything is open to everyone and no appeals to authority are allowed to trump others. Lynch calls this shared currency of reason 'the one really inspired idea of the enlightenment'.[2] The problem is that, to listen to many Western intellectuals, you would think that it doesn't exist, even though many earn their living at universities that are concrete manifestations of institutions committed to this thin rationality.

We also seem to forget that there are people outside this domain. To use another word with unfortunate connotations, fundamentalists of all descriptions have opted out of the domain of rational inquiry. What they hold to be true is certain, not defeasible. It is assessable only by God, not man. There is no attempt to understand the interests of others who take a different view, and the compulsion they advocate comes not from the ideas themselves but the force of violence.

But religious fundamentalists have no monopoly on these distorted values. For instance, the manner in which the US government conducted itself in the lead-up to the second Gulf War seems to me to indicate a disturbing disdain for the values of rationality I have defended. I am not convinced that the administration had any interest in making its true reasons for action comprehensible. Its main claims about Saddam Hussein were not genuinely assessable but had to be taken on trust. There was a certainty of purpose which seemed to me to ignore the demand that we accept the defeasibility of our beliefs. Nor was enough attention paid to the interests and perspectives of others who took contrary views. And finally, it did not matter that the reasons given were not compelling; compulsion was achieved militarily.

And yet many of the academics and intellectuals who were among the strongest critics of the war need to accept some responsibility for eroding the rational domain and helping to make this disregard for it possible. Think of how the senior advisor to President George W. Bush told journalists how his people had no time for 'what we call the reality-based community' in which people 'believe that solutions emerge from your judicious study of discernible reality'. Rather, 'We're an empire now, and when we act, we create our own reality. And while you're studying that reality – judiciously, as you will – we'll act again, creating other new realities, which you can study too, and that's how things will sort out.'[3] I do not think such a statement could have been conceivable if it weren't for the steady, reality-eroding drip of relativist and anti-rationality discourse leaking from academe into the public square.

Our obsession with our differences has created the impression that there is no common domain of rationality within which disagreements can be thrashed out. We just have a multiplicity of discourses and rationalisations to legitimise different interest groups. This is not just a criticism of those currents of thought broadly and loosely labelled postmodern. The enemies of postmodernism have set themselves up as the sole champions of reason – something made easier by their opponents' willingness to relinquish the labels of rationality and reason. In so doing they too have contributed to the sense in which the intellectual sphere is too fragmented and divided along factional lines for any general dialogue to be possible. By dismissing large sections of the intellectual community as anti-rational, the anti-postmodernists have also contributed to the sense that it is pointless to seek to argue one's case in the widest possible forum.

We need to accept more willingly that there are still shared values of rationality, a thin conception to be sure, but it is precisely the thin-ness of the notion which allows it to be shared by so many who have otherwise very different views. This we need to do to re-legitimise the domain of intellectual discourse as the right place to discuss differences and settle disagreements. It is time Western intellectuals took a wider view and realised that unless they stress what they have in common, the whole enterprise of rational inquiry will only come to seem more and more irrelevant to those who seek solutions to the problems of today. Those who think that they reason on firm ground are as deluded as those who believe thinking can float free from the oppressive constraints of rationality. Both are skating on the same thin ice, and the less they understand this, the more likely they are to crack it.

3. A user's guide

This book is not a 'How To . . .' guide, but the account of reason it defends is one that has practical implications. By understanding reason better we should be able to reason better. This is a very different kind of help to that offered by most books on how to reason, which tend to focus on the nuts and bolts of formal logic and argument, or on cataloguing fallacies. The user's guide with which I conclude sums up the main claims of this book in such a way as to point towards the better use of reason. It is more concerned with fostering the right attitude towards reason than to provide hints and tips or techniques.

The guide is a mixture of the thick and thin. Much of what it includes I believe should be accepted by the entire community of reason; some might be more contentious. The spirit of the whole is one of inclusion. I hope it reflects the way in which our shared reason is not so 'thick' as fundamentally to divide us, nor so 'thin' as to be platitudinous. Like any strong community, the community of reason needs to be held together by values that are both strong and that command wide assent. Thankfully, I think these values exist, and I commend them to you.

A user's guide to reason

1. Honest and sincere reasoners need to accept the *catholicism of rational discourse*. Despite the fact that there is wide disagreement about what rationality is and what it demands, we would not even be able rationally to discuss these differences unless we shared some thin conception of rationality. Differences within this broad 'community of reason' are largely due to placing emphasis on different elements of the rational toolkit.

2. Arguments should generally be criticised as flawed or weak, not irrational. To dismiss others as irrational is to attempt a kind of excommunication from the community of reason when what we should do is keep as many as possible within it.

3. Subtle reasoning has its place but when it comes to the big issues, it's the big arguments that carry weight. Since it is rational to proportion belief to the evidence and arguments, it is entirely proper to give more weight to arguments that rest on general observations and points of logic where the truth is clear, rather than on smaller observations and arcane logical technicalities.

4. Reason is not a purely objective, impersonal judge but something used by reasoners to help them to form good judgements.

It is bad faith to think that reason can decide for us, when only reasoners can make decisions.

5. Reason requires the use of personal judgement. We cannot reach conclusions or form theories by an appeal to facts and/or logic alone. Reason therefore has to be autonomous, not heteronomous. It has to be something we use for ourselves and fully own, taking responsibility for how we use it.

6. Reason works holistically. We believe what we do because of a number of overlapping and mutually reinforcing reasons and arguments, rarely because one settles the issue either way. This means it is irrational to 'follow *the* argument wherever it leads' rather than to follow the *arguments* wherever *they* lead, recognising that they do not individually all lead the same way.

7. Although our beliefs support each other in a 'web' that we strive to keep coherent, some 'critical nodes' are more important than others in keeping the network of justified beliefs intact. As Wittgenstein put it, we 'might almost say that these foundation-walls are carried by the whole house'.

8. Among these critical nodes are some 'basic' beliefs that we have to accept in order to believe anything at all.

9. Some basic beliefs have to be taken as incorrigible or self-evident, or else the justification of belief would never come to an end. But there is no strict test to distinguish what *is* from what merely *seems* incorrigible or self-evident. Hence it is always possible that different people, equally committed to reason, might take different beliefs as basic and reach significantly different conclusions on other substantive matters as a result.

10. Not just any belief can be justifiably claimed as a basic belief. Properly basic beliefs have to be either genuinely necessary or reliable.

11. A rational argument is one which *gives objective reasons for belief*.

12. No reasons are perfectly objective. Rather, our understanding becomes more objective the less it depends on idiosyncratic

features of our viewpoint, reasoning, conceptual framework and senses.

13. Objective reasons must be *comprehensible*. All other things being equal, the more comprehensible any description or explanation is in principle, the more objective it is.

14. Objective reasons must be *assessable*. Unless others can judge the truth of what is claimed, it remains in the domain of the subjective.

15. Objective reasons must be *defeasible*. A rational argument is always in principle open to revision or rejection by public criteria of argument and evidence.

16. Objective reasons must be *interest-neutral*, making no reference to the particular interests, values and desires of living creatures.

17. *Practical rationality* concerns what we ought to believe, given our goals and values, and is not interest-neutral. Nonetheless, this practical rationality should base its judgements on what can be justified by value-neutral reason.

18. Objective reasons must be *compelling*. This 'rational force' is not the same as 'psychological force'. Rational force concerns only the sense that a conclusion ought to be accepted, not that we feel motivated to act on it or to accept it.

19. Honest and sincere reasoners should accept that though they strive for objectivity, how we reason is in part determined by our personalities. This means arguments and evidence alone are often not enough to convince all clear-thinking minds to come to the same conclusion, even in science. Reason can never completely escape the personal and the human.

20. Honest and sincere reasoners should accept that although they strive for objectivity, psychology tells us that to think of oneself as an objective judge actually tends to increase the role of subjective bias in thinking. One should aspire to objectivity without claiming that one has succeeded in achieving it.

21. Honest and sincere reasoners should avoid being too impressed by what they understand and should be mindful of what they don't.

22. Adopting simplified models of reality makes the real world seem more tractable, but honest and sincere reasoners do not simplify the challenges reason faces in order to preserve the illusion of its might.

23. To pay attention to feminist, minority and marginalised perspectives is not to give up objectivity for a plurality of subjectivities, but to help achieve greater objectivity by getting a clearer, more expansive and fuller view of our shared reality.

24. In order for reason to flourish, it needs to be practised in the right environment. What goes on in the head can't be optimal if what surrounds the head is not conducive to good reasoning.

25. Honest and sincere reasoners should reject *scientism,* the belief that the only legitimate forms of understanding are scientific ones and anything which is not amenable to scientific methods of inquiry is baseless or meaningless. Since this claim is not itself scientific, it is self-refuting. Science is one of the greatest achievements of reason, but it does not follow that if we want to know how to think, we should always try to emulate how scientists think.

26. There are many scientific methods, but no single scientific method, just as there are many methods of reasoning but no algorithm for reason.

27. Logic is one of the most powerful tools of reason, but it is not the essence of rationality itself. The deductive mode of argument, formalised in logic, is neither how we do or should reason about much of life and the world.

28. Because reason goes beyond science and logic it often has to rely on forms of judgement that can only deliver their verdicts in frustratingly vague terms such as 'reasonable' or 'credible'.

29. Reason has aspects which are systematic and conscious but also aspects which are unknown and unconscious. Good reasoners, including scientists, rely on judgement, intuition and moments of insight. Conscious, systematic reason can license the use of some unconscious, automatic mechanisms, since there can

be rational justifications for what is usually thought of as non-rational because it involves no conscious reasoning.

30. To use our reason well, careful attending is often more useful than argument.

31. Good reasoning requires that we attend to the role of *intonation* in discourse. Very often, important disagreements do not hinge on the facts, but on attitudes towards the facts, often expressed simply by a tone of despair, dismissal, horror or incredulity, as well as belittling words like 'mere', 'only' and 'just'.

32. We can give more or less truthful accounts, but 'The Truth' – the one true, complete account of anything – is impossible. To give any account we have to select what we judge to be most pertinent at the time, and this is bound to reflect our values and attitudes as well as our raw reasoning power. Judgement is required to decide which parts of the picture we pick out to 'praise'.

33. Needs and desires, good and bad states have an objective existence. These are sources of 'normative facts', facts that contain elements of value.

34. Normative facts are often *praxic*: containing within them some kind of practical implication.

35. Because normative and praxic facts are objective, they are part of the proper subject of reason. Hence reason is not only disinterested reason, acting independently of anything other than value-free facts and logic.

36. We cannot look to disinterested reason to provide the basis of morality.

37. Reason also has an important role in ethics, helping us to determine whether or not our moral principles are coherently aligned with the empathetic impulses that lie at their root.

38. Moral reasons and arguments can be as rationally compelling as purely factual ones, even though not everyone feels compelled by them. Just as we accept that the ability to do maths depends on having a cognitive capacity which not everyone has, so we

should accept that the ability to reason morally requires a kind of empathetic cognitive capacity that some lack.

39. Consistency is not an inviolable principle of morality. If the demand for consistency were to result in the demand to do something truly terrible, consistency should go.

40. Morality is not science, but since many moral issues hinge upon matters of fact, science can help illuminate moral discourse.

41. Science can help us to understand the origins of ethics and the neural platform upon which it rests, but neither of these should be confused with the justification of ethics, which science cannot provide.

42. Reason has its own 'ought', captured in the Normative Principle of Rationality: we ought to believe what it is most rational to believe. This ought flows from the nature of reason itself and is not an additional judgement made upon it.

43. Reason justifies *de facto* political pluralism in politics. There can be no one way of ordering society so as to completely satisfy all aspirations for the good life, because competent rational judges disagree about how society should be run. Therefore the role of politics is to balance and negotiate between competing claims and demands so as to enable as many compatible goods to be gained from different incompatible positions as is possible.

44. In politics, the community of reason needs to discuss and debate in secular terms, in a language we share, leaving out the substantive world-views that divide us.

45. Political reasoning cannot be *a priori*. We should not start with abstract ideals and then approach practical politics simply as a matter of changing society to approximate as closely to this theory as possible.

46. Nor are politics or economics precise *a posteriori* sciences. As Aristotle advises, in politics, 'we must be content, then, in speaking of such subjects and with such premisses to indicate the truth roughly and in outline, and in speaking about things

which are only for the most part true and with premisses of the same kind to reach conclusions that are no better'.

47. Giving due weight to the contingencies of our present society and its history is not to become slaves to tradition or to dilute rationality, but to fortify it with precisely the kind of data that allows it to draw on more and better reasons for coming to the right policies.

48. Rational behaviour is not the same as self-interested behaviour.

49. Skeptical doubts can never be entirely eradicated. The key to their resolution is to understand why it is that they arise, learn from this the limitations of philosophy and then work within these limitations.

50. Honest and sincere reasoners must strive to avoid reason merely as a form of *apologetics:* rationally justifying what we have already decided we want to believe.

51. Honest and sincere reasoners should be mindful of the difference between what *is* rational and what *seems* rational. This distinction requires no skepticism about the power of reason, only about our ability to harness that power.

52. An appropriate skepticism should make philosophers and others accept that what they do is indeed inherently somewhat speculative and always in danger of collapsing into bullshit. Reason is thin ice on which we have no choice but to skate.

Notes

Introduction

1. Ballard (2014: 89).
2. Letter 120.3. Augustine (2004: 131).
3. Plato (1994: 150–1).
4. Aristotle (2000: 21–2).
5. Remarks by President Obama in Address to the United Nations General Assembly, The White House, Office of the Press Secretary, 24 September 2014, www.whitehouse.gov/the-press-office/2014/09/24/remarks-president-obama-address-united-nations-general-assembly.
6. Mill (1962: 160).
7. Plato (1994: 90).
8. Plato (2000: 17).
9. Baggini and Stangroom (2007: 113).
10. Williams (2015: 330).
11. Lynch (2012: 9).

Chapter 1: The Eternal God argument

1. Paragraph 1 of this chapter draws on material in Baggini, 2009b.
2. 'Homer the Heretic', Episode 4, Season 4, *The Simpsons*. First broadcast 8 October 1992.
3. Baggini and Stangroom (2003: 78).
4. Plantinga (1981).
5. Plantinga (1981: 42).
6. Plantinga (1981: 49).
7. Plantinga (2011: 16, 309).
8. Descartes (1986: 12), §17.
9. Knapton (2014).
10. Chowdhury *et al.* (2014).
11. Rescher (2001: 173).
12. See Haack (2009).
13. Wittgenstein (1969: 33), §248.
14. Russell (1967: 71).
15. Descartes (1986).
16. Locke (1976: 274), Book 4, Chapter 2, §6.
17. Wittgenstein (1969: 21e), §142.
18. Lynch (2012: 17).

19. Baggini and Stangroom (2003: 227–8).
20. This and what follows draws on material in Baggini, 2012b.

Chapter 2: Science for humans

1. Kumar (2014: 358).
2. Schlosshauer *et al.* (2013).
3. Kumar (2014: 211). Kumar's book on the Einstein–Bohr debate is highly recommended and is my source for many of the quotes from scientists cited in this chapter.
4. Kumar (2014: 336).
5. Mill (1843: 22), Book 3, Chapter 14, §6.
6. Bostrom (2003).
7. Kumar (2014: 287).
8. Debate on 4 February 2014, video at https://youtube/z6kgvhG3AkI. Transcript archived at www.youngearth.org/index.php/archives/rmcf-articles/item/21-transcript-of-ken-ham-vs-bill-nye-debate.
9. Wolpert (1992: 101).
10. Baggini (2008).
11. Wolpert (1992: 108).
12. Lewens (2015: 40–1).
13. Medawar (1996: 33–9).
14. Kumar (2014: 61).
15. Kumar (2014: 56).
16. Wolpert (1992: 92).
17. Poincaré (1913: 388).
18. Wolpert (1992: 62–3).
19. Medawar (1996: 35–6).
20. Wolpert (1992: 95).
21. Wolpert (1992: 95).
22. Wolpert (1992: 99).
23. Wolpert (1992: 97).
24. Wolpert (1992: 100).
25. Kumar (2014: 18).
26. Kumar (2014: 226–7).
27. Kumar (2014: 302).
28. Aspect (2007).
29. Kumar (2014: 163).
30. Kumar (2014: 229).
31. Kumar (2014: 209).
32. Kumar (2014: 220).
33. Kumar (2014: 142).
34. Kumar (2014: 155).
35. Kumar (2014: 224).
36. Kumar (2014: 125).
37. Poincaré (1913: 367).
38. Kumar (2014: 134).
39. Kumar (2014: 123).
40. Attributed to Einstein in Wigner (1979: 230).
41. Jogalekar (2014).
42. Dirac (1963: 47).

43. Dirac (1938–9).
44. Ellis and Silk (2014).
45. Ball (2014).
46. Cartwright (1999: 24, 31).
47. Wolpert (1992: 92).
48. Baggini (2008).
49. Kumar (2014: 17).
50. Kumar (2014: 20).
51. Kumar (2014: 262).
52. Kumar (2014: 320).

Chapter 3: Rationality and judgement

1. This chapter draws on material in Baggini (2004a).
2. Singer (1972).
3. Chalmers (2015: 359).
4. Baggini and Stangroom (2003: 167–8).
5. Baggini and Stangroom (2002: 134–5).
6. Baggini and Stangroom (2002: 16).
7. Baggini and Stangroom (2003: 230).
8. Zhuangzi, Chapter 26, in Ivanhoe and Van Norden (2005: 20).
9. Baggini (2012a).
10. Hume (1988: 71) §4.1.
11. Descartes (1986: 17) §25.
12. Hume (1962: 301–2) Book 1, Part 4, §6.
13. Nozick (1974: 42–5).
14. Wittgenstein (1969: 2e) §3.
15. http://philpapers.org/surveys/results.pl.

Chapter 4: Lives of the mind

1. This chapter draws on material in Baggini (2002b).
2. Mill (1989: 111–44).
3. Rousseau (1996: 17).
4. Quine (1985: 76–7).
5. Quine (1985: 9).
6. Feyerabend (1995: 20).
7. van Inwagen (2004: 334).
8. Chalmers (2015: 352).
9. Bourget and Chalmers (2014).
10. Chalmers (2015: 348).
11. Wittgenstein (1980: 24).
12. Honderich (2001: 141).
13. Honderich (2015: 3).
14. Baggini (2015a: 195).
15. Baggini and Stangroom (2002: 207).
16. Honderich (2001: 87).
17. Russell (2000: 149).
18. Honderich (2001: 403).
19. Honderich (2001: 405).
20. Honderich (2001: 390).

21. See Goldman (1999).
22. I am unable to recall the source of this distinction, though I do not believe it is one I can claim to have invented myself.
23. Quine (1985: 1).
24. Ayer (1977) and Ayer (1984).

Chapter 5: The challenge of psychology

1. Auden (1940).
2. Foot (1978: 19–32).
3. Kahneman (2011: 20–1).
4. *All in The Mind*, BBC Radio 4, presented by Claudia Hammond, 16 November 2011.
5. Macdonald (2014).
6. *Start the Week*, BBC Radio 4, 17 March 2014.
7. Bartels and Pizarro (2011).
8. Pascal (1995: 127), §423 (277).
9. Macdonald (2014).
10. Baggini (2009a).
11. Baron-Cohen (2004: 8).
12. Irigaray (2004: 38).
13. Beebee and Saul (2011).
14. Baggini (2011).
15. https://beingawomaninphilosophy.wordpress.com/2010/12/11/show-me-a-grad-student-i-can-fck/.
16. https://beingawomaninphilosophy.wordpress.com/2015/08/04/that-might-impede-your-promotion/.
17. Kahneman (2011: 29).

Chapter 6: Guided by reason

1. This chapter draws on material in Baggini, 2004a.
2. See Nagel (1986).
3. Williams (2015: 331).
4. Lynch (2012: 95).
5. Hume (1988: 71–2), §IV.
6. Ayer (1946: 41).
7. Putnam (1991: 126–7).
8. Foucault (1984): 74–5).
9. Irigaray (1987: 110).
10. Sokal and Bricmont (1998: 100).
11. Lewens (2015: 154–8).
12. See www.badscience.net/2007/11/a-kind-of-magic/.
13. The following section draws on material in Baggini, 2004b.
14. Freud (1955: 116).
15. Horkheimer and Adorno (2002: 18, 159).

Part III

1. Plato (1996: 62), §358D.
2. Mackie (1977: 23).

Chapter 7: Rational morality

1. Kant (1998: 45), § 4: 389.
2. Hume (1972: 156), Book 2, Part 3, §3.
3. See Plato (2000).
4. This chapter draws on material in Baggini, 2002a.
5. Searle (2001: 158, 161).
6. Searle (2001: 158).
7. Searle (2001: 158).
8. Searle (2001: 159–61).
9. Hume (1972: 203), Book 2, Part 1, §1.
10. Baggini and Stangroom (2007: 104).
11. Blackburn (1998: 240).
12. Korsgaard (1996: 47).
13. Williams (1985: 23).
14. Scanlon (2015: 169).
15. Blackburn (1998: 240).
16. Allen (2002: 26).

Chapter 8: Scientific morality

1. From Book 6 of *A System of Logic*, published as Mill (1988: 19).
2. Rosenberg (2011: 3).
3. Rosenberg (2011: 6).
4. Warnock (1984).
5. Churchland (2011: 12–26).
6. Baggini (2012a).
7. Ridley (1996: 127–47).
8. Baggini and Stangroom (2003: 18).
9. Thornhill and Palmer (2002: xi).
10. Binmore (2005: 1).

Chapter 9: The claims of reason

1. This chapter draws on material in Baggini, 2004a.
2. See, for example, the contributions to Dancey (2000).
3. Sartre (2001: 29).
4. See Edmonds and Eidenow (2001).
5. Jeffries (2007).

Part IV

1. Plato (1994: 193), §473d–474a.
2. Al Gathafi (2005: 77).

Chapter 10: The rational state

1. Prince (1987).
2. Plato (1955: 177, 240, 246), §412b, 459de, §461e.
3. Plato (1955: 262), §473a–c.

4. *Knowing Me, Knowing You with Alan Partridge*, Episode 5, BBC Radio 4, 29 December 1992.
5. Sen (2009: 12–13).
6. Sen (2009: 2).
7. Scruton (2006: 34).
8. Colton (1849: 477).
9. Aristotle (2000: 4), §1094b.
10. Tse-Tung (1968: 20).
11. Marx and Engels (2015: 11), §2 'Proletarians and Communists'.
12. Lenin (1975: 23).
13. Bakunin (1999: 74).
14. McFadden (2006).
15. Gardner (2008: 4).
16. Singer (2015: 14).
17. Marmot (2015: 110).

Chapter 11: Political reason

1. This section draws on material in Baggini, 2015b.
2. See Baggini (2013a).
3. Counterpoint produced a whole series of reports from across Europe (one of which I wrote), while Policy Network has been reading 'the populist signal' for several years.
4. Doxiadis and Matsaganis (2012: 12).
5. This section draws on material in Baggini, 2006.
6. Parekh (2000a) and Parekh (2000b).
7. Hampshire (1999).
8. Rawls (1997: 783).
9. Humanist Philosophers Group (2001).
10. See interview with Badiou at www.rebelion.org/cultura/040426ln.htm, 26 April 2004.
11. Badiou (2004).
12. Habermas (2005).

Conclusion

1. Lynch (2012: 3).
2. Lynch (2012: 138).
3. Suskind (2004).

Bibliography

Al Gathafi, M. (2005). *The Green Book*. Reading: Ithaca Press.

Allen, Woody (2002). The Scrolls. In: *The Complete Prose*. London: Picador. pp. 31–8.

Alston, William P. (1992). Foundationalism. In: Dancy, Jonathan and Sosa, Ernest (eds). *A Companion to Epistemology*. Oxford: Blackwell. pp. 144–7.

Aristotle (2000). *Nicomachean Ethics*. Trans. Crisp, Roger. Cambridge: Cambridge University Press.

Aspect. Alain (2007). To Be or Not To Be Local. *Nature*. Vol. 446, 866–7.

Auden, W.H. (1940). In Memory of Sigmund Freud. In: *Another Time*. London: Random House.

Augustine (2004) [410]. *Letters 100–155 (The Works of Saint Augustine, a Translation for the 21st Century: Part 2 – Letters)*, ed. Boniface Ramsey. New York: New York City Press.

Ayer, A.J. (1946). *Language, Truth and Logic*. Harmondsworth: Pelican Books.

Ayer, A.J. (1977). *Part of My Life*. London: Collins.

Ayer, A.J. (1984). *More of My Life*. London: Collins.

Badiou, Alain (2004). Behind the Scarfed Law, There is Fear. *Le Monde*. Translated for IslamOnLine by Norman Madarasz. (www.islamonline.net/English/in_depth/hijab/2004-03/article_04.shtml), 22 February.

Baggini, Julian (2002a). Morality as a Rational Requirement. *Philosophy*. Vol. 77, no. 301, 447–53.

Baggini, Julian (2002b). Philosophical Autobiography. *Inquiry*. Vol. 45, no. 2, 1–8.

Baggini, Julian (2004a). Philosophy as Judgement. In: Carel, H. and Gamez, D. (eds), *What Philosophy Is*. London: Continuum. pp. 141–55.

Baggini, Julian (2004b). Reason To End The Truth Wars: Rationality Reconsidered. Paper presented at Humanism East and West Conference. Oslo, 4–5 June.

Baggini, Julian (2006). The Rise, Fall and Rise Again of Secularism. *Public Policy Research*. Vol. 12, no. 4, 202–10.

Baggini, Julian (2008). Interview with Lewis Wolpert. *The Philosophers' Magazine*. 42, 120–6.

Baggini, Julian (2009a). Interview with Luce Irigaray. *The Philosophers' Magazine*. 44, 18–26.

Baggini, Julian (2009b). Atheist, Obviously. In: Blackford, Russell and Shüklenk, Udo (eds), *50 Voices of Disbelief*. Oxford: Wiley-Blackwell. pp. 139–44.

Baggini, Julian (2011). The Long Road to Equality. *The Philosophers' Magazine*. 53, 14–19.

Baggini, Julian (2012a). Interview with Patricia Churchland. *The Philosophers' Magazine.* 57, 60–70.

Baggini, Julian (2012b). How Science Lost its Soul, and Religion Handed it Back. In: Stump, J.B. and Pedgett, Alan G. (eds), *The Blackwell Companion to Science and Christianity.* Oxford: Blackwell. pp. 510–19.

Baggini, Julian (2013a). *A Very British Populism.* London: Counterpoint.

Baggini, Julian (2013b). Science is at Odds with Christianity. In Moreland, J.P., Meister, Chad and Sweis, A. (eds), *Debating Christian Theism.* Oxford: Oxford University Press. pp. 313–22.

Baggini, Julian (2015a). *Freedom Regained.* London: Granta.

Baggini, Julian (2015b). The Populist Threat to Pluralism. *Philosophy & Social Criticism.* Vol. 41, nos 4–5, 403–12.

Baggini, J. and Stangroom, J. (2002). *New British Philosophy: The Interviews.* London: Routledge.

Baggini, J. and Stangroom, J. (2003). *What Philosophers Think.* London: Continuum.

Baggini, Julian and Stangroom, Jeremy (2007). *What More Philosophers Think.* London: Continuum.

Bakunin, Mikhail (1999) [1873]. Statism and Anarchy. In: Rosen, Michael and Wolf, Jonathan (eds), *Political Thought.* Oxford: Oxford University Press. pp. 73–6.

Ball, Philip (2014). The Mechanical Interface of the Tardis. *Aeon.* 19 May, http://aeon.co/magazine/philosophy/beauty-is-truth-theres-a-false-equation/.

Ballard, J.G. (2014). *The Atrocity Exhibition.* London: Fourth Estate.

Baron-Cohen, Simon (2004). *The Essential Difference.* London: Penguin.

Bartels, Daniel M. and Pizarro, David A. (2011). The Mismeasure of Morals: Antisocial Personality Traits Predict Utilitarian Responses to Moral Dilemmas. *Cognition.* Vol. 121, no. 1, 154–61.

Beebee, Helen and Saul, Jennifer (2011). Women in Philosophy in the UK. SWIP-UK and the British Philosophical Association Committee for Women in Philosophy. www.swipuk.org/notices/2011-09-08/Women%20in%20Philosophy%20in%20the%20UK%20(BPA-SWIPUK%20Report).pdf.

Binmore, Ken (2005). *Natural Justice.* Oxford: Oxford University Press.

Blackburn, Simon (1998). *Ruling Passions.* Oxford: Oxford University Press.

Blackburn, Simon (2015). The Majesty of Reason. In: Honderich, Ted (ed.), *Philosophers of Our Time.* Oxford: Oxford University Press. pp. 173–91.

Bostrom, Nick (2003). Are You Living In a Computer Simulation? *Philosophical Quarterly.* Vol. 53, no. 211, 243–55.

Bourget, David and Chalmers, David J. (2014). What Do Philosophers Believe? *Philosophical Studies,* Vol. 170, no. 3, 465–500.

Cartwright, Nancy (1999). *The Dappled World.* Cambridge: Cambridge University Press.

Chalmers, David J. (2015). Why Isn't There More Progress in Philosophy? In: Honderich, Ted (ed.), *Philosophers of Our Time.* Oxford: Oxford University Press. pp. 347–70.

Chowdhury, R., Warnakula, S., Kunutsor, S., Crowe, F., Ward, H.A., Johnson, L., *et al.* (2014). Association of Dietary, Circulating, and Supplement Fatty Acids with Coronary Risk: A Systematic Review and Meta-analysis. *Annals of Internal Medicine,* 160, 398–406. doi:10.7326/M13–1788.

Churchland, Patricia (2011). *Braintrust.* Princeton: Princeton University Press.

Colton, Charles Caleb (1849). *Lacon: Or, Many Things in Few Words: Address - to Those Who Think*. New York: William Gowans.

Dancey, J. (ed.) (2000). *Normativity*. Oxford: Blackwell.

Descartes, René (1986) [1641]. *Meditations on First Philosophy*. Trans.: Cottingham, John. Cambridge: Cambridge University Press.

Dirac, Paul Adrien Maurice (1938-9). The Relation between Mathematics and Physics. *Proceedings of the Royal Society (Edinburgh)*. Vol. 59, Part II, 122-9.

Dirac, Paul (1963). The Evolution of the Physicist's Picture of Nature. *Scientific American*. Vol. 208, no. 5, 45-53.

Doxiadis, Aristos and Matsaganis, Manos (2012). *National Populism and Xenophobia in Greece*. London: Counterpoint.

Edmonds, David and Eidenow, John (2001). *Wittgenstein's Poker*. London: Faber and Faber.

Ellis, George and Silk, Joe (2014). Scientific Method: Defend the Integrity of Physics. *Nature*. Vol. 516, no. 7531, 321-3.

Feyerabend, Paul (1995). *Killing Time*. Chicago: University of Chicago Press.

Foot, Philippa (1978). The Problem of Abortion and the Doctrine of the Double Effect. In: *Virtues and Vices*. Oxford: Basil Blackwell. pp. 19-32.

Foot, Philippa (2001). *Natural Goodness*. Oxford: Oxford University Press.

Foucault, Michel (1984). Truth and Power. In: Rabinow, Paul (ed.), *The Foucault Reader*. London: Penguin. pp. 51-75.

Freud, Sigmund (1955). *Moses and Monotheism*. Trans. Jones, Katherine. New York: Vintage Books.

Gardner, Dan (2008). *Risk: The Science and Politics of Fear*. London: Virgin Books.

Goldman, Alvin I. (1999). *Knowledge in a Social World*. Oxford: Oxford University Press.

Haack, Susan (2009). *Evidence and Inquiry* (2nd edition). Amherst, NY: Prometheus.

Habermas, Jürgen (2005). Religion in the Public Sphere. Speech at the University of San Diego, 4 March. www.sandiego.edu/pdf/pdf_library/habermaslecture031105_c939cceb2ab087bdfc6df291ec0fc3fa.pdf.

Hampshire, Stuart (1999). *Justice is Conflict*. London: Duckworth.

Honderich, Ted (2001). *Philosopher: A Kind of Life*. London: Routledge.

Honderich, Ted (2015). *Philosophers of Our Time*. Oxford: Oxford University Press.

Horkheimer, Max and Adorno, Theodor W. (2002). *Dialectic of Enlightenment: Philosophical Fragments*. Trans. Jephcott, Edmund. Stanford: Stanford University Press.

Humanist Philosophers Group (2001). *Religious Schools: The Case Against*. London: British Humanist Association.

Hume, David (1962) [1739]. *A Treatise of Human Nature (Book One)*. London: Fontana/Collins.

Hume, David (1972) [1739-40]. *A Treatise on Human Nature (Books Two and Three)*. London: Fontana/W.C. Collins.

Hume, David (1988) [1748]. *An Enquiry Concerning Human Understanding*. La Salle, IL: Open Court.

Irigaray, Luce (1987). Sujet de la science, suject sexué? In: *Sens et place des connaissances dans la société*. Paris: Centre National de Recherche Scientifique. pp. 95-121.

Irigaray, Luce (2004). *Luce Irigaray: Key Writings*. London: Continuum.

Ivanhoe, Philip J. and Van Norden, Bryan W. (2005). *Readings in Classical Chinese Philosophy*. Indianapolis/Cambridge: Hackett Publishing.

Jeffries, Stuart (2007). Enemies of Thought. *Guardian*, 21 December.

Jogalekar, Ashutosh (2014). Truth and Beauty in Science, *Scientific American* blog, 21 May 2014, http://blogs.scientificamerican.com/the-curious-wavefunction/truth-and-beauty-in-science/

Kahneman, Daniel (2011). *Thinking Fast and Slow*. London: Penguin.

Kant, Immanuel (1998) [1797]. *Groundwork of the Metaphysics of Morals*. Trans. Gregor, Mary J. Cambridge: Cambridge University Press.

Knapton, Sarah. (2014). No Link Found between Saturated Fat and Heart Disease, *Daily Telegraph*, 18 March.

Korsgaard, Christine (1996). *The Sources of Normativity*. Cambridge: Cambridge University Press.

Kumar, Manjit (2014). *Quantum: Einstein, Bohr and the Great Debate about the Nature of Reality*. London: Icon Books.

Lenin, V.I. (1975). Karl Marx. In: *On Marx and Engels*. Peking: Foreign Language Press.

Lewens, Tim (2015). *The Meaning of Science*. London: Penguin.

Locke, John (1976) [1690]. *An Essay Concerning Human Understanding*. London: Everyman.

Lynch, Michael P. (2012). *In Praise of Reason*. Cambridge, MA: MIT Press.

Macdonald, Toby (2014). How Do We Really Make Decisions? BBC News website. 24 February. www.bbc.co.uk/news/science-environment-26258662 www.bbc.co.uk/news/science-environment-26258662.

McFadden, Daniel (2006). Free Markets and Fettered Consumers. AEA Presidential Address, 7 January. https://eml.berkeley.edu/~mcfadden/aea/presidentialaddress.pdf.

Mackie, J.L. (1977). *Ethics: Inventing Right and Wrong*. Harmondsworth: Penguin.

Marmot, Michael (2015). *The Health Gap*. London: Bloomsbury.

Marx, Karl and Engels, Friedrich (2015) [1848]. *The Communist Manifesto*. London: Penguin.

Medawar, Peter (1996). Is the Scientific Paper a Fraud? In: *The Strange Case of the Spotted Mice and Other Classic Essays on Science*. Oxford: Oxford University Press. pp. 33–9.

Mill, John Stuart (1843). *A System of Logic: Volume 2*. London: John W. Parker.

Mill, John Stuart (1962) [1859]. *On Liberty*. In *Utilitarianism*. London: Fontana Press.

Mill, John Stuart (1988) [1867]. *The Logic of the Moral Sciences*. Chicago and La Salle, IL: Open Court.

Mill, John Stuart (1989) [1873]. *Autobiography*. London: Penguin.

Nagel, T. (1986). *The View from Nowhere*. Oxford: Oxford University Press.

Nozick, Robert (1974). *Anarchy, State, and Utopia*. New York: Basic Books.

Parekh, B. (2000a). *Rethinking Multiculturalism: Cultural Diversity and Political Theory*. Basingstoke: Palgrave Macmillan.

Parekh, B. (2000b). *The Future of Multi-Ethnic Britain*. London: Profile.

Pascal, Blaise (1995) [1670]. *Pensées*. Trans. Krailsheimer, A. J. London: Penguin.

Plantinga, Alvin (1981). Is Belief in God Properly Basic? *Noûs*. Vol. 15, no. 1, 41–51.

Plantinga, Alvin (2011). *Where the Conflict Really Lies: Science, Religion and Naturalism*. Oxford: Oxford University Press.

Plato (1955). *The Republic*. Trans. Lee, Desmond. Harmondsworth: Penguin.

Plato (1994). *The Republic*. Trans. Waterfield, Robin. Oxford: Oxford University Press.

Plato (1996). *Protagoras*. Trans. Taylor, C.C.W. Oxford: Oxford University Press.

Plato (2000). *Euthyphro*. In: *The Trial and Death of Socrates* (3rd edition). Trans. Grube, G.M.A. and Cooper, John M. Indianapolis/Cambridge: Hackett.

Poincaré, Henri (1913) [1904]. *The Foundations of Science: Science and Hypothesis, the Value of Science, Science and Method*. Trans. Halsted, G.B. New York and Garrison, NY: The Science Press.

Putnam, Hilary (1991). The 'Corroboration' of Theories. In: Boyd, Richard, Gasper, Philip and Trout, J.D. (eds), *The Philosophy of Science*. Cambridge, MA: MIT Press. pp. 121–37.

Quine, W.V.O. (1985). *The Time of My Life*. Cambridge, MA: MIT Press.

Rawls, John (1997). The Idea of Public Reason Revisited. *University of Chicago Law Review*. Vol. 64, no. 3, 764–807.

Rescher, N. (2001), *Philosophical Reasoning: A Study in the Methodology of Philosophising*. Oxford: Blackwell.

Ridley, Matt (1996). *The Origins of Virtue*. London: Viking.

Rosenberg, Alex (2011). *The Atheist's Guide to Reality*. New York: W.W. Norton.

Rousseau, Jean-Jacques (1996) [1781]. *The Confessions*. Ware, Herts: Wordsworth.

Russell, Bertrand (1967). *The Problems of Philosophy*. Oxford: Oxford University Press.

Russell, Bertrand (2000). *Autobiography*. London: Routledge.

Sartre, Jean-Paul (2001) [1945]. Existentialism and Humanism. In Priest, Stephen (ed.), *Jean-Paul Sartre: Basic Writings*. London: Routledge.

Scanlon, T.M. (2015). Reasons Fundamentalism. In: Honderich, Ted (ed.), *Philosophers of Our Time*. Oxford: Oxford University Press. pp. 157–70.

Schlosshauer, Maximilian, Kofler, Johannes and Zeilinger, Anton (2013). A Snapshot of Foundational Attitudes toward Quantum Mechanics. *Studies in History and Philosophy of Science Part B Studies In History and Philosophy of Modern Physics*. 44, 222–230. doi: 10.1016/j.shpsb.2013.04.004.

Scruton, Roger (2001). *The Meaning of Conservatism* (3rd edition). Basingstoke: Palgrave.

Scruton, Roger (2006). *A Political Philosophy*. London: Continuum.

Searle, John (2001). *Rationality in Action*. Cambridge, MA: MIT Press.

Sen, Amartya (2009). *The Idea of Justice*. London: Allen Lane.

Singer, Peter (1972). Famine, Affluence, and Morality. *Philosophy and Public Affairs*. Vol. 1, no. 1, 229–43.

Singer, Peter (2015). *The Most Good You Can Do*. New Haven: Yale University Press.

Sokal, Alan and Bricmont, Jean (1998). *Intellectual Impostures*. London: Profile.

Spinoza, B. (1982) [1677], *The Ethics and Selected Letters*. Trans. Shirley, S. Indiana: Hackett.

Suskind, Ron (2004). Faith, Certainty and the Presidency of George W. Bush. *New York Times Magazine*, 17 October. www.nytimes.com/2004/10/17/magazine/faith-certainty-and-the-presidency-of-george-w-bush.html?_r=0.

Thornhill, Randy and Palmer, Craig T. (2002). *A Natural History of Rape: Biological Bases of Sexual Coercion*. Cambridge, MA: MIT Press.

Tse-Tung, Mao (1968). On Practice. In: *Four Essays on Philosophy*. Peking. Foreign Language Press.

van Inwagen, Peter (2004). Freedom to Break the Laws. *Midwest Studies in Philosophy*. 28, 334–50.

Warnock, Mary (1984). *Report of The Committee of Inquiry into Human Fertilisation and Embryology*. London: Department of Health & Social Security, www.hfea.gov.uk/docs/Warnock_Report_of_the_Committee_of_ Inquiry_into_Human_Fertilisation_and_Embryology_1984.pdf.

Wigner, Eugene Paul (1979). *Symmetries and Reflections: Scientific Essays*. Woodbridge, CT: Ox Bow Press.

Williams, Bernard (1985). *Ethics and the Limits of Philosophy*. London: Fontana Press/Collins.

Williams, Bernard (2015). Philosophy as a Humanistic Discipline. In: Honderich, Ted (ed.), *Philosophers of Our Time*. Oxford: Oxford University Press. pp. 327–42.

Wittgenstein, Ludwig (1969). *On Certainty*. Trans. Paul, Dennis and Anscombe, G.E.M. Oxford: Basil Blackwell.

Wittgenstein, Ludwig (1980). *Culture and Value*. Trans. Von Wright, Georg Henrik. Oxford: Blackwell.

Wolpert, Lewis (1992). *The Unnatural Nature of Science*. London: Faber and Faber.

Index

NOV -- 2016

TWO WEEKS

DISCARD
MT. PLEASANT